A
First
Hymn a Day

By

G. E. Stevens.

Mathetes Publishing,
34, North Hill Rd., Ipswich, Suffolk, IP4 2PN.

A First Hymn a Day

By
G. E. Stevens.

ISBN 978-0-9557881-7-8

First Published in England (in 2012) by:
Mathetes Publishing, 34, North Hill Rd., Ipswich, Suffolk, IP4 2PN.
Telephone: 01473 216811. Email: georgestevens@tiscali.co.uk

Printed in Great Britain for Mathetes Publishing by Printondemand-worldwide, 9, Culley Court, Bakewell Rd., Orton Southgate, PE2 5BJ

Acknowledgements.

The scriptures quoted in this book are taken from the "Authorised Version" (otherwise known as the "King James Version") of the Bible which was originally completed in 1611. It remains under Crown Copyright.

Thanks are also due to John Pollard of Ipswich who kindly proof-read the book. My wife, though suffering an terminal illness during the writing of these hymns, is to be gratefully acknowledged as she still found time to give advice on the structure of some of them.

I am also thankful to the many hymn writers of the past whose meditations prompted some of the thoughts expressed in these hymns.

The "Cyber Hymnal" website of Christian hymns is also to be commended as it has helped me to match tunes to the hymns I've written.

It was about five years ago that I asked my Lord and Saviour if we could write a hymn-a-day together. Despite my own weaknesses, He has been faithful in this. The lyrics to more than 1800 hymns/poems have been composed since that time. Praise His name!

Dedication.

To the Lord my helper

Psalm 46.1:
To the chief Musician for the sons of Korah,
A Song upon Alamoth.
God is our refuge and strength, a very present help in trouble.

1Samuel 7.12:
Then Samuel took a stone, and set it between Mizpeh and Shen, and called the name of it Ebenezer, saying, Hitherto hath the LORD helped us.

Preface.

As noted in the acknowledgements, it was about five years ago during a Christian conference that I asked the Lord to help me write a hymn a day. I'm afraid that I can't remember the circumstances that prompted this request; but I do know that the Lord has not let me down. He has been faithful!

Most of the hymns in this particular book were written in the year that led up to the death of Helen, my wife. She passed into the presence of the Lord Jesus Christ in June, 2010 following a four-year battle with cancer.

The verses in the book were prompted by many things. For example, thoughts I picked up from things people said or snippets found in other songs or hymns. Sometimes, I would wake up in the morning with a line for a hymn already in mind. (Hence, the notepad and pen at my bedside). A number picked up and adapted clauses from popular songs, past and present. A few were even written to summarise Christian teaching or preaching that, in the grace of God, I had heard or given. However, most came from regular meditations upon the scriptures themselves.

For the most part the hymns address God, although some that are more like songs or poems relating to Christian experience or teaching may call upon Christians. Others take the form of prayers rather than praise or worship. Overall, there may well be an overlap of more than one of these aspects in a single hymn.

The book is set out as daily readings. In most cases, where space allows, a hymn may be followed with a few verses from the scriptures to complement its theme.

May God be glorified by these hymns and scriptures; may Christians be encouraged and comforted; and may those who, as yet, do not believe be challenged by them.

Colossians 3.16: Let the word of Christ dwell in you richly in all wisdom; teaching and admonishing one another in psalms and hymns and spiritual songs, singing with grace in your hearts to the Lord.

Index of First Lines.

January.

February.

4. Lord, To Thee We Lift Our Voice
5. We're Gathered to Your Name, Dear Lord
6. Please, Grant Us Your Presence, Father
7. Oh, Who Can Make the Sun Rise?
8. The Bible is the Word of God
9. There's History and Geography
10. When Do the Children with Joy Sing?
11. What kind of child were You
12. Lord, I can see the stars
13. Thoroughly faithful! Thoroughly wise!
14. Lord, carry our burdens
15. Lord, friendship is a treasure
16. Oh, have you seen my true love
17. Blest Lord, You see each sparrow fall
18. Our Father, when we're well and strong
19. O come and worship Christ the Lord!
20. The Lord's my Shepherd, shall I want?
21. Father, at the evening of another year
22. Father, keep me day by day
23. You are the mighty God who made
24. I'll always love you as day passes day
25. Father, hear me as I pray
26. I sent My only Son
27. O Lord, we see You weeping
28. Come and help us!
29. O Lord, the torch now flickers

March.

1. Go forth and tell lost souls of Me
2. Father, we miss our brother
3. Lord, please look upon our land
4. I'm saved to serve through Jesus' blood!
5. Lord Jesus, we remember
6. Forgiveness from God above
7. Lord Jesus, unto You we... praise
8. Let All the Saints, Who are by Grace Most Blessed.
9. Father, Please Teach Us How to Pray.
10. All glory, Laud and Honour.
11. Delivered from the law, dear Lord
12. Jesus is the Son of God.

13. The Word of Life art Thou, O Lord.
14. Lord, may the treasures of Thy word.
15. The Scriptures are inspired by Thee.
16. Lift up Your banner, Lord,
17. How wonderful that by faith I can see
18. Lord, when I stand before Thy "throne"
19. We who are weary come to You
20. Patience! Quiet patience
21. We come to Thee, our Father
22. O Father, we'd remember
23. Eternal is Thy purpose
24. O Lord, we would be zealous
25. We seek Thy wisdom from above
26. "I'll live! I shall not die"
27. Help us to give, blest Father
28. Lord Jesus, stand among us
29. You see the word, blest Saviour
30. "Hosanna!" Lord, we cry
31. Lord Jesus, lead the singing

April.

1. I need a Saviour, Lord
2. Let's shout our glad hosannas
3. It is Your power, blest Father
4. I cannot do without Thee
5 God brought me up! He brought me up
6. Thy King is set
7. As a bright light send out Thy truth
8. Father of Lights, our blest God
9. Oh, the riches of wisdom and knowledge of Thee
10. Lord, give us the will to walk in light
11. Dear Lord, Your word is like a fire
12. Come, ye saints, the sight is glorious
13. That time was filled with trouble
14. Marvellous mercies, O my God
15. Banished by Thee, O Lord, I see
16. Sion, the mountain of our God
17. You are my great Shepherd
18. Born to sing of our Creator
19. Lord, by love, my heart You won

20. 'Twas in the womb of Mary mild
21. As Thy redeemed, Lord Jesus
22. When He brings forth His own
23. As members of Thy body, Lord
24. There is one body, Lord,
25. Lord Jesus, precious Corner Stone
26. Believe His words and sing His praise
27. Co-equal with th'eternal God
28. We hear Thy gracious word, blest Lord
29. Born of the virgin in Bethl'em's stable
30. No tears, no zeal, no labour!

May.

1. When I sit sad and alone
2. We're more than conquerors
3. You call us friends, blest Lord
4. Oh, let the words of my mouth
5. Blest Lord, we see Thee as the Lamb
6. Lord Jesus, from Thy blessèd hand
7. Nothing to do!
8. The summer is ending
9. Bless'd be the God!
10 Faith will soon give way to sight
11. Rejoice in prayer for all the saints
12. Our Father God, to Thee
13. Love is the kiss of Calvary
14. Rise up, my soul, and sing with joy
15. Our eyes look up to Thee above
16. Thy love, O Lord, we've tasted
17. You're the First, Lord Jesus
18. Lord, Thou art love, the purest love
19. Love! Love! Wonderful love!
20. Lord, gathered to Thy precious name
21. You did not leave us orphans
22. Closer than a brother, Lord
23. Father, when my friends forsake me
24. You glorified the Father, Lord
25. Rejoice! Rejoice!
26. A little while - we'll see You, Lord

27. Receive the word with gladness
28. Our wickedness was dreadful
29. Jesus, Shepherd of your sheep
30. In Jesus Christ, I will rejoice
31. The death of the cross! Oh, what can it mean?

June.

1. Thou art coming soon, Lord Jesus
2. Father, mockery, we hear
3. You came at first, so long ago
4. How glorious was Thy house, Lord
5. Lord, You went on together
6. We find grace in the Saviour
7. We have a God who's great
8. The half has not been told
9. Lord, You feel all my pain
10. Lord, manifest in flesh, we see
11. There is no-one like You, Lord
12. Lord, I'd see Your kingdom come
13. The Baby in a manger laid
14. Forever with the Lord
15. Rescued through the cross of shame
16. Oh, faithful is the saying, Lord
17. Lord Jesus, my beloved
18. O Lord, we see Thy glory bright
19. My Christian friend, there's work to do
20. I have a little corner, Lord
21. The sweetest sound I've ever heard
22. Eternal was the notion
23. I've often thought of heaven above
24. Lord Jesus, once a Stranger
25. You are the Potentate
26. There is a new world coming
27. There was grief and there was pain,
28. Father, we would not be ashamed
29. When I'm lonely and despised
30. Father of lights, we praise Thy name

July.

1 Just believe and be sin free

2. Soldiers of Christ, arise!
3. Lord, look upon my younger son
4. Father, I thank You for the skills
5. Swish! Clash! Clang! Crash!
6. Lord, You taught us everything
7. Ring, ye bells! Ring out for freedom!
8. Give me the mind to be like You
9. Happiness is the joy in You
10. Thy word is shining, Lord
11. You are the Father's only Son
12. My tears, You'll wipe away
13. Oh, it is finished!" Wondrous thought!
14. Lord, hear my song; please, hear my song of love
15. The power of death is found in sin
16. God, our Father, we adore Thee!
17. Fill us with all Thy wisdom, Lord
18. Greatness and power and glory
19. Thank You, Lord, for all Your goodness
20. We need Thy grace, Lord Jesus
21. Fear not, ye suffering saints of God
22. Lord Jesus, mighty Saviour
23. Ashamed of Thy name, I cannot be
24. There's nothing to do! Nothing to pay!
25. You're my Lord and my Defender
26. Peace! Peace proclaim in Jesus' name!
27. The earth's foundations, You have laid
28. Well, has the rain a father?
29. Beneath the cross of Jesus
30. Draw me, O Lord, by cords of love
31. Waves of blessing surge and swell

August.

1. From every race and every tribe
2. How pleasant is Your praise, blest Lord
3. Unto the cross of Jesus
4. I looked to Jesus set on high
5. You came to this sad earth below
6. Father divine, to Thee we bow
7. Father, we would work on in faith

8. O God, ‘tis grace indeed
9. Saviour, gentle Saviour
10. Lord Jesus, we would copy Thee
11. Saviour, Thy wounds have made me whole!
12. Jesus, never leave me
13. Eternity! Eternity!
14. Only a prayer to Jesus
15. So near to the Saviour
16. Look upon the cross of Jesus
17. Majesty and strength, Lord Jesus
18. We would be like Thee, Lord Jesus
19. Father, we, Thy children, praise Thee
20. Pray for us, Lord Jesus
21. Look to Jesus on the tree
22. Rejoice in prayer for all the saints
23. Tell me of God’s mercy
24. O come, ye people, lost in sin
25. Tell me of Jesus, the story of love
26. “There is no God!” the sinner cries
27. Jesus never leave me
28. The origin of species, Lord
29. ‘Twas unto death You loved us, Lord
30. Cleansed by blood ‘tis Christ I see
31. Jesus calls you from the labour

September.
1. Are you standing?
2. Glory to Thee, blest Father
3. My love, we part, but not for long
4. Behold, what kind of love is this
5. My love, we part, but not for long
6. Come! See the work our God has done
7. Father, we see Thy glory
8. Come, Jesus is waiting, is waiting for you!
9. Lord, You’re our everlasting song
10. Love made Him an Apostle
11. Father, it’s in Your Son we see
12. Grace is free! Christ died for me!
13. Seek out the LORD and you shall live
14. Without the Son, there is no life!

15. Jesus, Lord, made of a woman
16. Lord Jesus, Thou hast glorified
17. Jesus, Almighty Saviour
18. Mighty to Save! Mighty to save!
19. There is a better world, we know
20. How vast and wondrous was the love
21. When the shout of Jesus calls us
22. Grace divine, so full and free
23. Boundless mercy flows from heaven
24. Before the world's foundation
25. Saved without money
26. What a bundle of blessing
27. We see Thy mighty pow'r, O God
28. Hear the voice of love and mercy
29. I'm cast upon You, precious Lord
30. O Lord, the day is over

October.

1. Sound out the song of love divine
2. Through Christ alone, we're saved from sin
3. The trumpet of salvation sounds
4. You must be born again
5. You crown the year with goodness, Lord
6. Lord, in this water, I recall
7. Lord Jesus, we have died with Thee
8. Lord, Thou wast once a Guest divine
9. Father, allow my soul to rise
10. New every morning is the love
11. We have a great High Priest above
12. Immortal God, invisible
13. Another year is rising, Lord
14. Father, we thank Thee for the Gift
15. Every day with God my Saviour
16. Lord, at our table take Thy place
17. Lord Jesus, You have been here
18. The Lamb will be the light
19. Father, 'tis where Thy people meet
20. Lord Jesus, to Thy holy name
21. Thy face we seek, blest Father

22. Lord Jesus, as You faced the foe
23. Eternal God, before Thy face we fall
24. O Father, in Thy courts above
25. For me to live is Christ
26. Father, Your eye is keen to see
27. See the serpent lifted high
28. Father, we're saved by grace alone
29. After Thee, Lord, I would run
30. Your love won't let me go
31. I saw the symbol of Your cross

November.

1. Look, ye saints, the sight is wondrous
2. Lead us, Saviour, in the way
3. Wash my feet, Lord Jesus
4. "Jesus the Christ is Lord!"
5. Would you believe God's word?
6. Rise up, Christian! Onward go!
7. 'Tis in my prayer, Father, I'd see
8. Onward press through rolling billows
9. A Man's enthroned in glory
10. Come with joyful song
11. What kind of love is this
12. Father, lead us through this desert
13. Pilgrims of the Lord above
14. Death on the cross, Lord Jesus
15. Father, how precious are the thoughts
16. Dear Saints, the road is rough and long
17. Blessed with all blessings in the heav'ns above
18. Put on your armour, children of the day
19. Dear Christian, when the way is rough
20. Lord, you are able to keep us from falling
21. Sow the seed in faithful witness
22. Mem'ries prompted by Your blest words upon a page
23. Love is as strong as death
24. Jerusalem! Jerusalem!
25. Lord Jesus, for a little while
26. All things above the skies are bright
27. We'll sing of the mansion on high
28. Show me Thy hands, dear Saviour

29. Hallelujah! See your Saviour
30. We see You clothed in glory

December.

1. O Lord, Your people know Your name
2. Lord Jesus, we Your love recall
3. Washed in blood that's wonder-working
4. O Lord, Your death has won our love
5. Father, we as children bless Thee
6. Lord, once my life was such a bore
7. Rise up, ye saints, before the day
8. You look to those, blest Father
9. You are the God of wisdom
10. O Lord, I know that when I sleep
11. You're mighty in power
12. Acts of kindness, acts of grace
13. There is a time of birth
14. Overcome when sin invades thee
15. From a lowly cattle stall
16. Your love, O Lord, has kept us day by day
17. Baby of the virgin born
18. Extra error
18. Eternally the Father's love
19. You are the light, dear Lord
20. Kingdoms here both rise and fall
21. See the snowflakes falling
22. Awake, my soul, and sing
23. Israel's God is our God
24. Lord, we belong together
25. The Father's light, the Father's love
26. Lord, You are worthy of worship and praise!
27. O solemn hour, when Saviour Thou
28. My soul is Yours, Lord Jesus
29. You gave Yourself for us, dear Lord
30. I don't know why I suffer so
31. "See!" the lust of eyes would say

1st January.

76.76.

We Love You, Blessèd Father.

1.
We love You, blessèd Father;
Shield us from every ill.
Save us from all our troubles;
Keep us in Your blest will.

2.
The shadow of Your wings
Shades us from scorching heat;
Beneath them, we are safe;
Beneath them, we're complete.

3.
We love You, blessèd Father;
Our urgent prayers, You hear.
Your presence shall go with us,
Whom then have we to fear!

4.
You are our great Defender;
In You, we trust this day;
You'll keep us safe from danger
And guide us in the way.

5.
We love You, blessèd Father;
The Shepherd of our soul.
Long life, You gladly promise
And You will keep us whole.

6.
All glory, praise and honour
Be to You, Lord, above.
There we shall bow in worship
With all the joy of love.

Tunes: 76.76: River City, Vulpius, Matrimony, Cara. 76.76D: Ahnfelt, Mountain, Thornbury, Passion Chorale.

Psalm 57.1; 61.4; 63:7

To the chief Musician, Altaschith, Michtam of David, when he fled from Saul in the cave. Be merciful unto me, O God, be merciful unto me: for my soul trusteth in thee: yea, in the shadow of thy wings will I make my refuge, until these calamities be overpast.

I will abide in thy tabernacle for ever: I will trust in the covert of thy wings. Selah.

Because thou hast been my help, therefore in the shadow of thy wings will I rejoice.

2nd January.

88.88.

I Once Was Blind, But Now I See.

1.
I once was blind, but now I see
That You are walking here with me.
I thought my life was all my own
Until You brought me to Your throne.
And there before Your mercy seat
I found my cleansing was complete.
There sprinkled blood revealed Your love
And now my hope's to dwell above.

2.
Now I am Yours! Yes, Yours alone!
And thank You for the grace You've shown.
There's no-one knows me as You do!
Help me be faithful, kind and true.
Fill me with Your blest Spirit, Lord,
And from my heart, let love be poured.
That all may see Yourself in me
And trust in You implicitly.

Tunes: Sweet Hour, Duane St., He Leadeth Me, Nazareth, Stephenson, Sagina, Hayes, Maryland.

Luke 7.22
Then Jesus answering said unto them, Go your way, and tell John what things ye have seen and heard; how that the blind see, the lame walk, the lepers are cleansed, the deaf hear, the dead are raised, to the poor the gospel is preached.

John 10.3
To him the porter openeth; and the sheep hear his voice: and he calleth his own sheep by name, and leadeth them out.

Song 7.10
I am my beloved's, and his desire is toward me.

3rd January.

CMD.

‘Slave of the True and Living God.

1.
‘Slave of the true and living God,
Thou art His lovely Son.
Show us the way to serve Him here
Until His work is done.
We see Thee in the light of dawn
Approaching Him in prayer.
We see Thee list’ning to His word
The day’s work to prepare.

2.
Driven into the desert waste
And weakened day by day,
Thou didst the devil’s darts defy
By keeping to God’s way.
To do His will was Thy delight;
His words and work were Thine.
And by the Spirit of the Lord,
Thy pathway was divine.

3.
Thy heart was shown in suffering,
In mockery and pain;
And in the garden of the press
Thy love was seen again.
‘Twas there Thine agony of soul
Was seen in sweat like blood;
And in that all-submitting prayer,
Thy faithfulness to God.

4.
We see Thee, as the Lamb of God,
Led to Golgotha’s tree.
We see Thee, as God’s offering,
Made sin to set us free.
And from the darkness of the tomb,
We see Thee on God’s throne.
The Servant-Son in majesty.
The living Corner-Stone!

Tunes: No King But Christ, Bethlehem, Ellacombe, Fair Haven, Forest Green, Jesus is God.

Matthew 4.1-4
Then was Jesus led up of the Spirit into the wilderness to be tempted of the devil. And when he had fasted forty days and forty nights, he was afterward an hungred. And when the tempter came to him, he said, If thou be the Son of God, command that these stones be made bread. But he answered and said, It is written, Man shall not live by bread alone, but by every word that proceedeth out of the mouth of God.

4th January.

88.88.

O God of Pardon and of Power.

1. O God of pardon and of power
We bow to Thee this favoured hour
Acknowledging that we are Thine
And all Thine attributes divine.

2. Sin-hardened foes, we were once found;
Our sins pressed us into the ground.
No hope! No joy could fill our heart!
In Hell alone, we had our part.

3. 'Twas then the word of grace came forth
Showing Thy Son in all His worth.
His work upon Golgotha's tree
Announced "Forgiveness!" full and free.

4. Thou couldst not pass the sinner by;
Thy word demanded he should die
But in the death of Christ we see
Thy pardon flowing righteously.

5. We see Him raised and glorified,
The little Lamb once crucified.
We celebrate His victory
And cry, "To Him all glory be!"

6. Soon shall this miracle of love
Take us to be with Him above.
Then, in the joys of Heaven we'll see
There is no pardoning God like Thee.

Tunes: 88.88: Gift of Love, Federal St. 88.88.88.88: Sweet Hour, Duane.

Isa 55.7
Let the wicked forsake his way, and the unrighteous man his thoughts:
and let him return unto the LORD, and he will have mercy upon him;
and to our God, for he will abundantly pardon.

5th January.

77.77D.

Only Once in My Lifetime.

1. Only once in my lifetime
Could I hand myself to You.
Boundless are Your mercies, Lord
So full, so sincere and true!
Take this lowly body now
As a living sacrifice!
Let me serve You faithfully,
Heeding all Your wise advice.

2. By Your grace, renew my mind;
Fill it with humility;
And like Christ may I be found;
My soul transform within me.
Let me shun this evil age
Proving that Your will is best.
Then Your glory, I shall see
And, in Christ, I shall be blessed.

3. Help me run the race of faith!
Keep me in the pilgrim's way!
Take my hand and lead me on,
Till we reach that happy day!
Kiss me with Your precious word;
Hold me tightly in Your love;
And when all my work is done
Call me to Your rest above.

Tunes: St. Edmund Steggall, Hollingside, Mendelssohn, St. George's Windsor, New St. Andrew, Messiah.

Rom 12.1
I beseech you therefore, brethren, by the mercies of God,
that ye present your bodies a living sacrifice,
holy, acceptable unto God,
which is your reasonable service.

6th January.

77.77D.

Come Ye Saints of God Most High.

1. Come ye saints of God most high,
Let men hear your cheerful cry,
"One for all and all for one!
'Tis the cry that God hath won.
One for all, the Saviour died!
One for all, now magnified!
See Him on God's throne above!
Know the wonder of His love!

2. One for all, our Shepherd lives!
Feel the care that He now gives!
One for all, our Advocate
Pleads our cause at heaven's gate!
One for all, the church's Head,
Takes away all fear and dread!
Makes the Jew and Gentile one
Through the work that He has done!

3. Come ye saints of God most high,
Let men hear your cheerful cry,
"One for all and all for one!
'Tis the cry that God hath won.
All for one, we must rejoice
When a heart lifts up its voice!
All for one kneel down to pray
As a soul is tried today!

4. All for one, our tears we shed
As we see deep sorrow spread!
All for one, we gladly give
That the poor may surely live!
All for one, doubt's load we lift
From the soul that's gone adrift!
All for one, we work this way,
God's own glory to display!

Tunes: St. Edmund Steggall, Sabbath, Benevento, Madrid (Carr), New St. Andrew, Hollingside, Mendelssohn.

Romans 12.10-16

Be kindly affectioned one to another with brotherly love; in honour preferring one another; not slothful in business; fervent in spirit; serving the Lord; rejoicing in hope; patient in tribulation; continuing instant in prayer; distributing to the necessity of saints; given to hospitality. Bless them which persecute you: bless, and curse not. Rejoice with them that do rejoice, and weep with them that weep. Be of the same mind one toward another. Mind not high things, but condescend to men of low estate. Be not wise in your own conceits.

7th January.

77.77D.

Come and Worship, Ye Wise Men.

1. Come and worship, ye wise men,
See the Son of God this day.
Find Him with His mother dear,
In the house in which they stay.
Follow His bright star above
From that palace rich and fair.
See it shine upon a place
Filled with love and fervent prayer.

2. Come and worship, ye wise men,
See the Son of God this day.
Humbly bow before Him there,
Own His crown and rightful sway.
Lay your gifts at His blest feet,
Gold and frankincense and myrrh.
Then your way rejoicing go
Telling of our great Saviour.

3. Come and worship, everyone,
Hail the Lord of heaven and earth.
See the King of David's line;
Praise the Son of lowly birth.
Lay your hearts at His blest feet
For they are love's treasure store;
He's your Master and your God
Let your lips His name adore.

Tunes: Madrid (Carr), St. Edmund Steggall, Sabbath, Messiah, Hollingside, Benevento, Aberystwyth (Parry), St. George's Windsor.

Matthew 2.11
And when they were come into the house, they saw the young child with Mary his mother, and fell down, and worshipped him: and when they had opened their treasures, they presented unto him gifts; gold, and frankincense, and myrrh.

8th January.

CMD.

I Have So Many Things To Do.

1. I have so many things to do;
But life is now in doubt;
The cancer that destroys my cells
Just makes me want to shout.
Yet You, I'll trust with all my heart,
With body and with soul;
And knowing all your healing power,
I bid you, make me whole.

2. The treatment that I have to bear,
Makes me so tired and weak;
The tingling in my hands and feet
Just makes me want to shriek.
Yet, grace still strengthens me, O Lord;
And faith pursues Your will;
And even when all things look dark,
Your joy, my heart shall fill.

3. O Lord, the love poured out on me
By those both far and near,
Stirs up emotions deep and rare
And helps remove my fear.
Yet, 'tis Your mercy I require;
'Tis Your touch that I need.
For then Your power, I shall feel
And I'll be blessed indeed.

4. I would not leave my family,
For I do love them so;
Yet, You may want me by Your side;
It may be time to go.
Please, keep my body free from pain,
My faculties sustain.
Yet still, in faith and hope, I pray
I might be well again.

(Upon hearing that there had been a resurgence of my wife's cancer first diagnosed in August, 2007. I tried to write it to express her thoughts at the time).

Tunes: Bethlehem, Fair Haven, I See Thee Standing, Ishpeming.

2Corinthians 12:9

And he said unto me, My grace is sufficient for thee: for my strength is made perfect in weakness. Most gladly therefore will I rather glory in my infirmities, that the power of Christ may rest upon me.

9th January.

76.76D.

When You are Sad and Lonely.

1. When you are sad and lonely
And life is trouble-bent;
When you are tried with sickness,
And life is one lament;
Then, think of all the blessings
Found in God's only Son;
And think of the great vict'ry
That He for you has won!
Refrain:
The love of God our Father,
The love of God our Father,
The love of God our Father,
Works only for the best!

2. When you are poor and needy,
And life seems such a drag!
When all around is ruined,
And hearts begin to sag!
Then, think of your blest Saviour
In sweet Gethsemane,
Under the cross's shadow
And all its agony!
Refrain:

3. When you are pressed and burdened
And ask the question, "Why?"
When plagued by guilt and shame
And joy has passed you by!
Then think of your Redeemer
Forsaken on the tree!
Yet, now, in glory seated,
He lives for you and me!
Refrain:

Tunes: Hankey, Tell Me the Old, Old Story.

10th January.

65.65.

Father, I Would See Thee.

1.
Father, I would see Thee
In my Saviour's face;
There Thy power and glory
Shine out with His grace.

2.
Father, I would love Thee
More and more each day;
Love Thee for Thy mercy;
Trust Thee and obey.

3.
Day by day, my Father,
I would watch and pray!
Day by day, dear Father,
Thy name I'd display.

4.
Father, I would follow
In Thy Son's blest way;
And when work is ended
By His side I'd stay.

Tunes: Quietude, Armentrout, Castle Eden, Ernstein, Eudoxia.

2Corinthians 4.3-6
But if our gospel be hid, it is hid to them that are lost: in whom the god of this world hath blinded the minds of them which believe not, lest the light of the glorious gospel of Christ, who is the image of God, should shine unto them.
For we preach not ourselves, but Christ Jesus the Lord; and ourselves your servants for Jesus' sake.
For God, who commanded the light to shine out of darkness, hath shined in our hearts, to give the light of the knowledge of the glory of God in the face of Jesus Christ.

11th January.

76.76D.

Lord, Tell Me How to Love You.

1. Lord, tell me how to love You
In truth to love You so;
Then show me how to please You
That Your mind, I may know.
Daughter, if you would love me
Then look into God's word;
Commandments there you'll find;
Do them and love's assured!
(*Instrumental arrangement of refrain).*

2. Lord, tell me how to find You
When love has lost its shine;
Then show me how to keep You
And know your power divine.
Daughter, if you would find me
Then meet with saints you know;
My presence there, I've promised,
To those that gather so.

Oh, let's go on together
By grace that God supplied!
Oh, let's go on together
As Bridegroom and as bride!

3. Lord, tell me how to serve You
So I may love impart
To sinner and to saint
That I might move their heart.
Daughter, if you would serve Me,
Love's labour is the key;
And in your work of faith
Keep looking up to Me.
(*Instrumental arrangement of refrain).*

4. Lord, tell me how to praise You,
To bring You honour due;
And teach me how to pray
That I might love pursue.
Daughter, if you would praise Me
Then think on all I do;
And bow in thanks and blessing
Knowing that I love you.

Oh, let's go on together
By grace that God supplied!
Oh, let's go on together
As Bridegroom and as bride!

Tunes: Hankey , O Serve the Lord, Tell Me the Old, Old Story.

Song 8.14
Make haste my beloved, and be thou like to a roe or to a young hart upon the mountains of spices.

12th January.

CMD.

The Lord is Patient, Gentle, Kind.

1.
The Lord is patient, gentle, kind
He pardons all our sin.
His blood poured out upon the tree
Gives us His peace within.
He feels all our infirmities
And bears us up in trial.
He comforts us in sorrow too
And goes the extra mile.

2.
The mercies of the Lord are seen
In all He's said and done.
And even now He pours on us
The blessings He has won.
So lift your voices! Praise His name!
Give thanks to Him above;
And in the knowledge of His work
Bless Him for all His love!

Tunes: No King But Christ, Tyrol,

Hebrews 7.24-28

But this man, because he continueth ever, hath an unchangeable priesthood. Wherefore he is able also to save them to the uttermost that come unto God by him, seeing he ever liveth to make intercession for them. For such an high priest became us, who is holy, harmless, undefiled, separate from sinners, and made higher than the heavens; who needeth not daily, as those high priests, to offer up sacrifice, first for his own sins, and then for the people's: for this he did once, when he offered up himself. For the law maketh men high priests which have infirmity; but the word of the oath, which was since the law, maketh the Son, who is consecrated for evermore.

13th January.

CMD.

Your Promises are Perfect, Lord.

1.
Your promises are perfect, Lord,
True to Your blessèd word;
I know that I can trust in You
Your counsel is assured.

2.
You give in great abundance, Lord!
Your timing is divine!
Your grace and power shall never end!
Better Your love than wine!

3.
You grant me wisdom for the day,
Your will, I know, is best.
Goodness and mercy mark my way
And I am ever blessed.

4.
All praise and glory to you be,
O Son of God most high!
O let me worship and adore
Yourself, beyond the sky.

Tunes: Nativity, Pisgah, St. Agnes, Westminster (Turle)

2Corinthians 1.18-20
But as God is true, our word toward you was not yea and nay.
For the Son of God, Jesus Christ,
who was preached among you by us,
even by me and Silvanus and Timotheus,
was not yea and nay, but in him was yea.
For all the promises of God in him are yea, and in him.
Amen, unto the glory of God by us.

14th January.

76.76D.

I Will Not Fear the Darkness.

1.
I will not fear the darkness;
With You, Lord, by my side.
I will not fear the journey
For You will guard and guide.
Your word's a light, Lord Jesus,
A lamp unto my feet.
You are my Rock – my Refuge,
My Rest and my Retreat.

In You, I find forgiveness!
I'm honoured by Your grace!
In You, I'm blessed supremely!
O let me see Your face!

2.
In You, I'm safe, Lord Jesus!
By You, I am redeemed!
To God, I am brought near;
It's more than I had dreamed.
By Your own precious blood
I'm cleansed and sanctified!
And soon You will present me
To Yourself as the bride.

In You, I find forgiveness!
I'm honoured by Your grace!
In You, I'm blessed supremely!
O let me see Your face!

Tunes: Hankey.

Psalm 119.105-106
NUN. Thy word is a lamp unto my feet, and a light unto my path.
I have sworn, and I will perform it, that I will keep thy righteous judgments.

15th January.

CMD (with refrain).

When We Survey that Ruggèd Cross.

When we survey that ruggèd cross,
The nails, the gall and spear,
We wonder at Thy faithfulness
And blood that brings us near.
We see the tempest and the flood
Of all God's wrath divine
Beat down upon Thy holy soul
That we with Thee might shine.

O Lord, with joy, we now praise Thee
For dying on the tree.
And ever, as the ages roll,
Our love we'll bring to Thee.

What agony of heart was Thine!
What torments tore Thy soul!
The turmoil of those deep torrents
Above Thyself did roll!
The weeds were wrapped about Thy head!
Earth's bars imprisoned Thee!
Thou wast forsaken by Thy God,
To set sin's prisoners free.

O Lord, with joy, we now praise Thee
For dying on the tree.
And ever, as the ages roll,
Our love we'll bring to Thee.

Tunes: Providence, Ellacombe.

Jonah 2.5
The waters compassed me about, even to the soul: the depth closed me round about, the weeds were wrapped about my head.
I went down to the bottoms of the mountains; the earth with her bars was about me for ever: yet hast thou brought up my life from corruption, O LORD my God.

16th January.

87.87.

Gathered to Your name, Lord Jesus.

1. Gathered to Your name, Lord Jesus;
Your blest presence we would claim;
On Yourself our hearts would focus
From Your cradle to Your reign.

2. 'Twas Your grace that brought You down,
From the glorious heights above,
To Bethlehem's tiny town;
Where we read that "God is love!"

3. 'Twas Your love that led You onward
To the cross of Calvary.
There we see God's blessing stored
In Your blood shed so freely.

4. Yours the cost and Yours the suff'ring
Yours the cross of deepest shame.
There we see Your God departing
As His wrath upon You came.

5. 'Twas the glory of the Father
Raised You from the sculpted tomb!
Seated on His throne, as Saviour,
Death is robbed of all its gloom!

6. You are coming soon, Lord Jesus,
Our poor bodies to redeem.
Then made like You, for Your glory,
We'll display the light You beam.

7. When You come as Lord and King
Then Your saints with You shall reign.
All the earth will bow before You;
And we'll all adore Your name.

Tunes: Sussex, Day By Day, Rathbun, Gott Will's Machen, Mariners, Cross of Jesus.

Romans 6.4

Therefore we are buried with him by baptism into death: that like as Christ was raised up from the dead by the glory of the Father, even so we also should walk in newness of life.

17th January.

88.88.

Lord Jesus, We Remember Thee.

1. Lord Jesus, we remember Thee
In all Thy shame and agony.
We see Thy suff'ring on the tree
And, Saviour, we adore Thee.

2. Deep darkness swirled about Thy head
As for our sins Thy blood was shed;
And there Thy God turned back from Thee
As Thy soul's torment set us free.

3. O Calvary! Cruel Calvary!
The hill on which our Saviour died.
O Calvary! Cruel Calvary!
The place where Christ was crucified.

4. With joy we hail Thee, risen Lord;
The Son of God in majesty!
And now triumphant o'er the grave
Thine is the power to help and save.

5. Lord Jesus, we'll remember Thee
Until Thy blessèd face we see.
'Tis then we'll know Love's mystery
As we eternally worship Thee.

Based on "Jesus! We remember Thee" by Samuel Trevor Francis.
Tune: His Wondrous Ways.

1Corinthians 11.23 -25
For I have received of the Lord that which also I delivered unto you, that the Lord Jesus the same night in which he was betrayed took bread: and when he had given thanks, he brake it, and said, Take, eat: this is my body, which is broken for you: this do in remembrance of me. After the same manner also he took the cup, when he had supped, saying, This cup is the new testament in my blood: this do ye…

18th January.

86.86.

Upon the Field Where Summer's Rain.

1.
Upon the field where summer's rain
Has stained the grass so green;
The lion and the lamb lie down
And peace – God's peace is seen.

2.
O see the leopard with the kid!
The cow and bear as one!
And know a child shall lead them on
Where peace – God's peace is won!

3.
Then hear Creation shout with joy
As God's own sons are shown.
And see the glory of His grace
Where peace – God's peace is known.

4.
A righteous sceptre rules the scene;
The King is on His throne.
'Tis Shiloh, by His precious blood,
Brings peace – God's peace, alone.

Tunes: Nativity, Westminster (Turle), St. Agnes, Belmont, Tyrone, Beatitudo, Bishopthorpe.

Isaiah 11.6-7

The wolf also shall dwell with the lamb, and the leopard shall lie down with the kid; and the calf and the young lion and the fatling together; and a little child shall lead them. And the cow and the bear shall feed; their young ones shall lie down together: and the lion shall eat straw like the ox. And the sucking child shall play on the hole of the asp, and the weaned child shall put his hand on the cockatrice' den.

19th January.

66.66D.

Upon Golgotha's Hill.

1. Upon Golgotha's hill,
A shadow veils the ground;
The shadow of a cross
To which my Lord was bound.
The crown that pierced His head
Was plaited with sharp thorn;
The nails that pierced His limbs
Were hammered home with scorn.

2. Upon Golgotha's hill,
Stood the accursèd tree.
'Twas there that God's dear Son
Yielded His life for me.
Now His most precious blood
Speaks of new life to me.
I can draw near to God
As one who is sin-free.

3. Upon Golgotha's hill
I see the cross of shame;
And there upon its head
I read my Saviour's name.
'Jesus of Nazareth'
Tells of the Lord who saves.
Rejected here by men,
His love my heart enslaves!

Tunes: 66.66D: Invitation (Maker), Denby. 12.12.12.12: Lausanne, Corbet, The Blessed Home, Harvington.

Matthew 27.33-34
And when they were come unto a place called Golgotha, that is to say, a place of a skull, They gave him vinegar to drink mingled with gall: and when he had tasted thereof, he would not drink.

20th January.

99.99.

Wonderful Maker! Wonderful Son!

1. Wonderful Maker! Wonderful Son!
Wonderful all the work You have done!
Wonderful Saviour! Wonderful cross!
Where You endured all suff'ring and loss!

2. Wonderful Shepherd! Wonderful Lamb!
Wonderful name: I AM THAT I AM!
Wonderful Priest and wonderful Friend!
Wonderful worship knowing no end!

3. Wonderful Saviour, wonderful Lord,
Wonderful name for ever adored.
Wonderful Captain! Wonderful King!
To You our hearts as presents we bring.

4. Wonderful Builder! Wonderful Head!
Wonderful Church that You have prepared.
Wonderful comfort! Wonderful rest!
In heav'nly glory – supremely blessed!

5. Wonderful Jesus! Wonderful Man!
Wonderful wisdom found in God's plan!
Wonderful Bridegroom! Wonderful love!
Wonderful bond in heaven above!

Tunes: Adelaide, St. Cecilia (Sewall).

Isaiah 9.6-8

For unto us a child is born, unto us a son is given: and the government shall be upon his shoulder: and his name shall be called Wonderful, Counsellor, The mighty God, The everlasting Father, The Prince of Peace. Of the increase of his government and peace there shall be no end, upon the throne of David, and upon his kingdom, to order it, and to establish it with judgment and with justice from henceforth even for ever. The zeal of the LORD of hosts will perform this.

21st January.

CMD.

Come, Hear the Voice that to You Calls.

1. Come, hear the voice that to you calls
Return unto Your God!
The evil that you do this day
Demands my chastening rod!
Refrain:
And though your sins scarlet should be,
They'll shine as white as snow.
Though they be red with crimson dye,
As white as wool they'll glow.

2. Guide those oppressed and judgment seek;
The fatherless defend!
Come, plead the faithful widows' cause!
Do well and don't pretend!
Refrain:
And though your sins scarlet should be,
They'll shine as white as snow.
Though they be red with crimson dye,
As white as wool they'll glow.

3. Both willing and obedient be
And blessings will abound.
But know the sword hangs over those
In deep rebellion found.
Refrain:
And though your sins scarlet should be,
They'll shine as white as snow.
Though they be red with crimson dye,
As white as wool they'll glow.

4. Your trespasses, I shall forgive,
I'll send them far away;
And as those chosen in my love
I'll keep you day by day.
Refrain:
And though your sins scarlet should be,
They'll shine as white as snow.
Though they be red with crimson dye,
As white as wool they'll glow.

Tunes: Providence, Landas.

Isaiah 1.16-18

Wash you, make you clean; put away the evil of your doings from before mine eyes; cease to do evil; learn to do well; seek judgment, relieve the oppressed, judge the fatherless, plead for the widow. Come now, and let us reason together, saith the Lord: though your sins be as scarlet, they shall be as white as snow; though they be red like crimson, they shall be as wool.

22nd January.

88.88D.

You Made Me Love You, Jesus, Lord.

1. You made me love You,
Jesus, Lord,
Your name for ever be adored.
You left the joys of heaven
above
To come to earth in all Your
love.
In a mean manger, You were
laid,
Born of that faithful virgin
maid.
The Christ of David's line You
were!
The Son of God, our blest
Saviour!

2. You made me love You,
Jesus, Lord,
Your name for ever be adored.
A perfect life, You lived while
here;
The sinless Man who knew no
fear.
You bore the burdens of the
poor;
And for the sick You had a
cure.
You brought the dead to life
again;
While knowing that You must
be slain.

3. You made me love You,
Jesus, Lord,
Your name for ever be adored.
You bore my sins to Calvary;
And there You hung upon the
tree.
'Twas there deep darkness
bound Your soul;
'Twas there You died to make
me whole.
My heart is broken by Your cry:
"Eli, lama, sabachthani?"

4. You made me love You,
Jesus, Lord,
Your name for ever be adored.
Your grave was marked out in
God's plan
Before You died for ruined
man;
But death is robbed of all its
power
And life - eternal life can
flower!
For from the glory up above
You're pouring forth Your light
and love.

Tunes: Sweet Hour, He Leadeth Me, Nazareth, St. Crispin, Bucklebury.

1Peter 1.8
Whom having not seen, ye love; in whom, though now ye see him not,
yet believing, ye rejoice with joy unspeakable and full of glory:

23rd January.

CMD.

We Would Not See Thee Dying, Lord.

1.
We would not see Thee dying, Lord,
On the accursed tree.
Nor in the grey tomb lying, Lord,
Wrapped up so fragrantly.
But we would see Thee up above
In all Thy majesty.
For there, exalted on God's throne,
Thy glory we shall see.

2.
We would not stand on Calvary
Shedding our tears for Thee.
We'd look into the empty tomb
And see Thy victory.
We know that thence our hope begins
And peace o'er us is cast!
'Tis to Thyself we look above
And see Thy love is vast.

3.
Sin, Satan, death and Hell are slain!
The Victor's crown is Thine!
Yet, still the work is not complete
Till we are seen as Thine.
Soon Thou shalt come, the Lord of all,
And say to us, "Arise!"
Our bodies changed, we'll fly to Thee
Beyond the clouded skies.

4.
"All praise and honour be to Thee
Thou Son of God most high!
All riches, power and glory be,
To Thee, O Lord!" we cry.
"Worthy, O Lamb of God, art Thou
Of our untiring praise!
And we will worship and adore,
Thyself, through endless days.

Tunes: Beaufort, All Saints, Fair Haven, I Bring My All To Thee.

1Corinthians 15.53-55

So when this corruptible shall have put on incorruption, and this mortal shall have put on immortality, then shall be brought to pass the saying that is written, Death is swallowed up in victory. O death, where is thy sting? O grave, where is thy victory? The sting of death is sin; and the strength of sin is the law. But thanks be to God, which giveth us the victory through our Lord Jesus Christ.

24th January.

66.66D.

Lord Jesus, At Thy Feet.

1.
Lord Jesus, at Thy feet,
We bow in all our sin.
Tears of repentance flow
And shame lies deep within;
But Thou, the Lord of all,
Whose precious blood was shed,
Wilt make us fit for heaven
And be our living Head.

2.
Lord Jesus, at Thy feet,
We sit to hear Thy word.
Help us to understand,
That truth may be preferred.
May Thy commands be kept;
Thy sayings guarded too;
May every word of Thine
Come to our hearts anew.

3.
Lord Jesus, at Thy feet,
We kneel to worship Thee.
The Saviour blest, Thou art
Who died to set us free.
The fragrance of Thy worth
From Thine own suff'rings stream,
Filling the church with praise -
Proclaiming Thee Supreme.

Tunes: 66.66D: Invitation (Maker), Denby. 66.66: Holy Guide, St. Cecilia, Eccles.

Luke 7.38
And stood at his feet behind him weeping, and began to wash his feet with tears, and did wipe them with the hairs of her head, and kissed his feet, and anointed them with the ointment.

Luke 10.39
And she had a sister called Mary, which also sat at Jesus' feet, and heard his word.

John 12.3
Then took Mary a pound of ointment of spikenard, very costly, and anointed the feet of Jesus, and wiped his feet with her hair: and the house was filled with the odour of the ointment.

25th January.

76.76D.

Cleanse Us From All Our Sin, Lord.

1. Cleanse us from all our sin, Lord,
Wash us as white as snow;
And in Thy precious blood, Lord.
Give us Thy love to know.
Free us from pride and passion;
From anger and deceit.
Fill our poor heart with praises
While at Thy mercy seat.

2. Cleanse us from all our sin, Lord,
Wash us as white as snow;
And feed us by Thy word, Lord,
So we like Thee may grow.
Then fit us for Thy service,
To work in Thy blest will;
Make us a faithful witness –
Thy precious word instill.

3. Cleanse us from all our sin, Lord,
Wash us as white as snow;
May Thy Spirit within, Lord,
Empower us to know
The glories of Thy God
Shining in wondrous grace;
And soon in Heaven above
We'll praise Thee face to face.

Tunes: Greenland, Thornbury, Aurelia, Ewing, Petition, Passion Chorale.

Isaiah 1.18
Come now, and let us reason together, saith the LORD:
though your sins be as scarlet,
they shall be as white as snow;
though they be red like crimson,
they shall be as wool.

26th January.

76.76.

Father, the Blood was Sprinkled.

1.
Father, the blood was sprinkled
Upon my sin-sick soul.
The blood of Thine own Son
Has cleansed me - made me whole!

2.
The cedar and the scarlet,
The hyssop and the clay,
Were stained by heavenly blood
By waters clear as day.

3.
So we see Christ as righteous;
In all His dignity.
We see Him meek and lowly
Perfect in His body.

4.
The slain bird tells of Jesus
Dying at Calvary.
The living bird reminds me
He's raised my Lord to be.

5.
Soon, He shall come to take me
Up to His home above.
Then I shall stand a trophy
To all His grace and love.

6.
Father, we'll bow in worship,
Sincere and ever true;
We'll own Thy worth and ways
As we His glory view.

Tunes: 76.76: River City, Cara. 76.76D: Ahnfelt, Greenland, Penlan, Missionary Hymn, Aurelia, Day of Rest, Ellacombe, Angel's Story.

Leviticus 14.4-7

Then shall the priest command to take for him that is to be cleansed two birds alive and clean, and cedar wood, and scarlet, and hyssop:
and the priest shall command that one of the birds be killed in an earthen vessel over running water:
as for the living bird, he shall take it, and the cedar wood, and the scarlet, and the hyssop, and shall dip them and the living bird in the blood of the bird that was killed over the running water:
and he shall sprinkle upon him that is to be cleansed from the leprosy seven times, and shall pronounce him clean, and shall let the living bird loose into the open field.

27th January.

CM.

To Be With Him, the Living One.

1.
To be with Him, the living One,
In courts of heav'nly light,
Where God's eternal glory shines,
Will be our great delight.

2.
To be near Him who gave Himself
In love upon the tree
Will fill our hearts with wondrous joy
For we, His face, shall see.

3.
To be like Him in every way
That manhood can proclaim,
Will bring much honour to our souls
And glory to His name.

4.
To know we're His for evermore
Will lift our voice in praise.
To hear that we're His one desire
Will all our fears erase.

5.
O Lord, to see the blest reward
In heaven kept for me,
Can never reach the matchless thought
Of being there with Thee.

Tunes: Pisgah, Winchester (Old), Belmont, Chimes, Horsley, Irish, Nativity, St. Agnes, Westminster (Turle), Abridge.

Song 7.10
I am my beloved's, and his desire is toward me.

28th January.

CMD.

Father, It is Joy to Know.

1.
Father, it is a joy to know
By Jesus' blood, we're clean.
The sin that led us to the grave
Is now, by grace, unseen.
Refrain:
'Twas grace that brought the Saviour down
'Twas grace that met our need.
'Twas grace that led Him to the cross
'Twas grace that made Him bleed.

2.
Father, it is a joy to know
That righteousness is ours.
'Twas purchased by the blood of Christ
That all our sin devours.
Refrain:

3.
Father, it is a joy to know
That we may come boldly
Into Thy presence at the throne
And pray with liberty.
Refrain:

4.
Father, it is a joy to know
That we with Christ shall dwell.
And then thy home of heavenly light
Shall with our praises swell.
Last Refrain:
'Twas grace that brought the Saviour down
'Twas grace that met our need.
'Twas grace that raised Him from the dead;
All by Thy love decreed.

Tunes: Landas, Providence, Bethlehem, Release, Forest Green, Minerva, No King But Christ.

2Corinthians 8.9

For ye know the grace of our Lord Jesus Christ, that, though he was rich, yet for your sakes he became poor, that ye through his poverty might be rich.

Hebrews 4.16

Let us therefore come boldly unto the throne of grace, that we may obtain mercy, and find grace to help in time of need.

29th January.

10,10.10.10.

The Peal of Thy Voice, Blessèd Lord, We'll Hear.

1.
The peal of Your voice, blessèd Lord, we'll hear
Piercing the clouds - commanding and so clear.
"Rise up, my bride, 'tis time to fly away;
Stand at my side on this triumphant day."

2.
Hear the archangel calling for Your own;
Children of Abra'am rise up to God's throne.
The trumpet's blast Gentiles shall call to rise
And join El Shaddai way beyond the skies.

3.
Those who believe and on this earth remain
Shall receive bodies for that heavenly plain.
Immortal bodies, glorious and pure;
So powerful and evermore secure.

4.
Lord Jesus, come and take Your bride away;
Present her to Yourself with joy today.
The church You love, shall own Your rightful sway
And in the glory all Your grace display.

Tunes: Woodlands, Penetentia, De Reef, Field, Ellers, Morecambe.

Song 2.10-13
My beloved spake, and said unto me,
Rise up, my love, my fair one, and come away.
For, lo, the winter is past, the rain is over and gone;
the flowers appear on the earth;
the time of the singing of birds is come, and the voice of the turtle is heard in our land;
the fig tree putteth forth her green figs, and the vines with the tender grape give a good smell.
Arise, my love, my fair one, and come away.

30th January.

66.86.

Without One Sin Between.

1. Without one sin between,
We'll see Him face to face;
And in His glory, we shall find
The wonders of His grace.

2. Without one sin between,
We'll see Him as He is;
The Son of God in heav'nly light
Will greet us with a kiss.

3. Without one sin between
We'll see Him, Lord of all;
And at His Name shall every knee
Before His presence fall.

4. Without one sin between
By grace, we'll like Him be.
We'll stand, the subjects of His love,
And know its mystery.

5. Without one sin between,
We'll stand in bodies bright;
Immortal, powerful and pure
We'll walk in robes of white.

6. Without one sin between
We'll praise Him and adore;
The fragrance of love's ointment sweet
On His blest head, we'll pour.

Tunes: 66.86: Lake Enon, St. Ethelwald, Cambridge, Energy.

Rev 19.8

And to her was granted that she should be arrayed in fine linen, clean and white: for the fine linen is the righteousness of saints.

31st January.

66.66.88.88.

Who Freed us From the World?

1.
Who freed us from the world
And its seductive way?
Who saved us with His arm
And by our side will stay?
'Tis the Lord, the King eternal!
'Tis the Lord of heaven and earth!
'Tis the Lord, the Prince of glory!
'Tis the Lord of precious worth!

2.
Who took us for His own
A people saved by grace?
Who is this mighty God
Whose mercy we can trace?
'Tis the Lord, the King eternal!
'Tis the Lord of heaven and earth!
'Tis the Lord, the Prince of glory!
'Tis the Lord of precious worth!

3.
Who was the Lord of all
That led us to the land?
Sheltered our failing souls
With His most tender hand?
'Tis the Lord, the King eternal!
'Tis the Lord of heaven and earth!
'Tis the Lord, the Prince of glory!
'Tis the Lord of precious worth!

Tunes: None found.

Titus 2:14

Who gave himself for us, that he might redeem us from all iniquity, and purify unto himself a peculiar people, zealous of good works.

1st **February.**

87.87 or 87.87D.

Christ is Risen! Hallelujah!

1. Christ is risen! Hallelujah!
Christ is risen from the dead!
Christ is risen! Hallelujah!
Now He is our Lord and Head!

2. Christ is risen! Hallelujah!
Death has lost its vicious sting.
Christ is risen! Hallelujah!
He's the Heir of everything

3. Christ is risen! Hallelujah!
Sin's dominion is destroyed!
Christ is risen! Hallelujah!
All God's mercy is deployed.

4. Christ is risen! Hallelujah!
Satan's power is nullified!
Christ is risen! Hallelujah!
Now in heaven, He's glorified!

5. Christ is risen! Hallelujah!
Now our souls are justified!
Christ is risen! Hallelujah!
Praise the Lamb once crucified!

6. Christ is risen! Hallelujah!
Let His name be magnified!
Christ is risen! Hallelujah!
Love will soon be satisfied!

7. Christ is risen! Hallelujah!
He shall live eternally!
Christ is risen! Hallelujah!
Soon He'll come to set us free!

8. Christ is risen! Hallelujah!
He, as King of kings shall reign!
Christ is risen! Hallelujah!
From His life comes all our gain!

Tunes: 87.87: Gott Wills Machen,. 87.87D: Beecher, Hymn to Joy..

Luke 24.5-7

And it came to pass, as they were much perplexed thereabout, behold, two men stood by them in shining garments:

and as they were afraid, and bowed down their faces to the earth, they said unto them, Why seek ye the living among the dead?

He is not here, but is risen: remember how he spake unto you when he was yet in Galilee, saying,

The Son of man must be delivered into the hands of sinful men, and be crucified, and the third day rise again.

2nd February.

CMD.

Come, Let Us From the Rooftops Shout.

1. Come, let us from the rooftops shout,
"Christ is raised up today!"
It's time to celebrate His worth
And own His rightful sway.
He left His home of heav'nly light
To die on Calvary.
Now He is raised in glory bright
To live eternally.

2. Come, let the bells of triumph sound
As Christ is raised this day!
The Strong Man wears the Victor's crown
And Satan's sent away.
Sin, death and Hell are all vanquished
As we His pow'r survey.
Love, righteousness and mercy flow
As we His grace display.

3. Come, lift your voice in praise of God
For Christ is raised this day.
The Firstfruits of all them that sleep
Shall God rightly display.
He is the Firstborn from the dead;
The Church's living Head.
He is the mighty Son of God
Who suffered in our stead.

4. Lord Jesus, we would praise Thy name
For Thou art Lord of all.
We watch in prayer and wait for Thee
To thrill us with Thy call.
Then we shall rise with Thee to be
In Thy blest home above.
For ever, we shall worship Thee
And bask in all Thy love!

Tunes: Bethlehem, Release, Ellacombe, Landas, No King But Christ, Forest Green, Jesus is God, Warrior.

1Corinthians 15.54-56
So when this corruptible shall have put on incorruption, and this mortal shall have put on immortality, then shall be brought to pass the saying that is written,
Death is swallowed up in victory. O death, where is thy sting? O grave, where is thy victory?
The sting of death is sin; and the strength of sin is the law. But thanks be to God, which giveth us the victory through our Lord Jesus Christ.

3rd February.

87.87D.

By His Own Blood, Christ Has Entered.

1. By His own blood, Christ
has entered
Into Heaven up above;
And as those redeemed by
grace
We shall bask in all His love.
Tell us once more of His
sorrow!
Show His pain upon the tree!
Speak of blood that is most
precious!
Of the blood that set us free!

2. The blood of the Lamb shall
ever
Be effective and endure.
Gold and silver could not save
us,
For its value is unsure.
'Tis that blood, so rich and
noble,
That redeems the sinful soul!
'Tis the blood that sanctifies us!
'Tis the blood that makes us
whole!

3. See the blood poured out in
mercy;
See God's judgement turn to
grace!
There upon the cross of torment
Love is found in Jesus' face.
And in those long hours of
darkness,
His soul took on all our sin;
There the curse of God fell on
Him
As our hearts He sought to win.

4. In the blood, we find
salvation
And our souls are justified.
Adopted by God the Father
We shall soon be glorified.
Yes, redeemed our bodies shall
be
As our dear Lord calls us nigh.
Made like Christ, we'll sing His
praises
In the Father's house on
high.

Tunes: Shipton, Mount of Olives, Deerhurst, Here is Love, Love Divine (Stainer), Hymn to Joy, Woodside, Alleluia (Wesley), Everton.

1Peter 1.18-20

Forasmuch as ye know that ye were not redeemed with corruptible things, as silver and gold, from your vain conversation received by tradition from your fathers; but with the precious blood of Christ, as of a lamb without blemish and without spot: who verily was foreordained before the foundation of the world, but was manifest in these last times for you...

4th February.

CMD.

O Lord, To Thee We Lift Our Voice.

1.
O Lord, to Thee we lift our voice
In songs of grateful praise;
The tiny grain sown liberally
Thy glory now displays.
Shining with gold upon the field
Thy power we survey;
And in its fruitful ear we find
The wisdom of Thy way.

2.
O Lord, Thy blessing is secure;
And thanks to Thee we bring.
The firstfruits of the land are Thine
As to Thy grace we cling.
We looked to Thee for wind and rain
And golden sunshine too;
We looked to Thee for life and growth
And now Thy blessing view.

3.
O Lord, the firstfruits tell of Thee
As risen from the dead.
And waved before the Father's face
There all Thy worth is read.
But soon another harvest shall
Be ripened on this earth.
Then to Thyself, we shall be reaped
As souls of heavenly birth.

Tunes: Bethlehem, Ellacombe, Warrior, Forest Green, Minerva.

1Corinthians 15.20-21
But now is Christ risen from the dead, and become the firstfruits of them that slept. For since by man came death, by man came also the resurrection of the dead.

5th **February.**

CMD.

We're Gathered to Your Name, Dear Lord.

1.
We're gathered to Your name, dear Lord,
Upon this wedding day;
We seek a blessing from Yourself
In a most happy way.
The bridegroom with his bride desire
Your presence with them here;
And as they make their solemn vows
Remove all doubt and fear.

2.
They seek to marry in You, Lord,
To trust You and obey.
They seek the wisdom of Your will
And by Your side would stay.
Fill them with love, Your love, blest Lord,
The love that knows no end.
And may their union prove to be
So strong that none can rend.

3.
O Lord, may they on You depend
In joy and sorrow too;
And in the confines of their home
May they give placc to You.
So as they serve You here below
May meekness mark their way;
And may their pilgrimage be blessed
In each and every day.

4.
Blest Lord, how happy You shall be
With Your bride at your side.
The bride You purchased with Your blood
When You were crucified.
Though once a Man of sorrows here,
You are now glorified;
And with Your bride in glory bright,
Your love is satisfied.

Tunes: Release, No King But Christ, None But Christ, Bethlehem, Jesus is God, Minerva, All Saints, Goshen, Tyrol.

John 3.29.

He that hath the bride is the bridegroom: but the friend of the bridegroom, which standeth and heareth him, rejoiceth greatly because of the bridegroom's voice: this my joy therefore is fulfilled.

6th February.

87.87D.

Please, Grant Us Your Presence, Father.

1.
Please, grant us Your presence, Father,
As in Eden's land of old
When marriage was a pure picture
Like as silver framed in gold.
Adam Your Christ represented,
In deep sleep, a rib he lent;
And You made Eve - a fine help meet!
They then joined with Your consent.

2.
Please, grant us Your presence, Father,
In giving away this bride;
May all her joys soon be fulfilled
At her dearest bridegroom's side.
There You see Your own dear Son
With His most belovèd bride.
And measure out His vast love
As He, for her, has once died.

3.
Please, grant them Your presence, Father,
Keep them safe beneath Your wing.
Let no hindrance spoil their marriage;
Grant to them Your rich blessing.
Walk with them on life's long journey
In sorrows and in joys too;
Help them through each storm of testing
To be wise, faithful and true.

4.
Please, grant them Your presence, Father,
When their journey is well run;
When in Heaven's brightest glory
They shall be like Your blest Son.
Then they'll cast their crowns before You
Boldly proclaiming Your worth;
And they'll bless You for the guidance
That You gave them here on earth.

Tunes: Everton, Hymn to Joy, Here is Love, Deerhurst, Beecher.

Ephesians 5.31b
…And they two shall be one flesh.

7th February.

76.76D.

Oh, Who Can Make the Sun Rise?

1.
Oh, who can make the sun rise,
And sprinkle grass with dew?
Oh, who can make a rainbow
Red, yellow, green and blue?
Oh, who can make the snow fall
Like feathers light and white?
Oh, who can make the flowers
With colours clear and bright?

Refrain:
Only our God can do this!
It's all in His good plan!
Only our God can do this
As only His love can!

2.
Oh, who can make the sun set
And sprinkle night with stars?
Oh, who can make the planets
Like Mercury and Mars?
Oh, who can make the moon shine
Just like a silver ball?
Oh, who can make the pine tree
Grow up so straight and tall?
Refrain:

3.
Oh, who can make the grain grow
And sprinkle earth with rain?
Oh, who can make the mountains
And the soft, fertile plain?
Oh, who can keep the whole world
Spinning around in space?
Oh, who can keep His children
In His loving embrace?
Refrain:

Tunes: Hankey, Oh, House of Many Mansions

Job 38.4-7

Where wast thou when I laid the foundations of the earth? declare, if thou hast understanding. Who hath laid the measures thereof, if thou knowest? or who hath stretched the line upon it? Whereupon are the foundations thereof fastened? or who laid the corner stone thereof; when the morning stars sang together, and all the sons of God shouted for joy?

Or who shut up the sea with doors, when it brake forth, as if it had issued out of the womb?

When I made the cloud the garment thereof, and thick darkness a swaddling-band for it, and brake up for it my decreed place, and set bars and doors, And said, Hitherto shalt thou come, but no further: and here shall thy proud waves be stayed?

8th February.

CMD.

The Bible is the Word of God.

1. The Bible is the Word of God;
The book we hold most dear.
It tells of our salvation
In words so true and clear.
It tells us all of Jesus Christ,
The Son of God on high.
It tells us of the wondrous love
That brought Him here to die.

2. The Bible is a picture book
So full of history.
Its science and its literature
Are found in poetry.
Its letters are so full of life
And keep us in God's way.
Its lessons tell us how to act,
To trust and to obey.

3. The Bible is a book of songs
That cheers our pathway here.
It tells us that our God is love
And we should never fear.
We find that Jesus is our Lord
As the Good News is taught.
We know we're saved through Him alone
And by Him we are bought.

4. We thank You for the Bible, Lord,
And all we find therein.
We thank You that Your precious blood
Now cleanses from all sin.
We thank You for the church You build;
For daily cleansing too.
We thank You for that day to come
When we Your glory view.

Tunes: Bethlehem, I Bring My All To Thee, Landas, No King But Christ, Release

Hebrews 4.12

For the word of God is quick, and powerful,
and sharper than any twoedged sword, piercing even to the dividing asunder of soul and spirit, and of the joints and marrow, and is a discerner of the thoughts and intents of the heart.

2Timothy 3.16

All scripture is given by inspiration of God, and is profitable for doctrine, for reproof, for correction, for instruction in righteousness…

9th February.

CMD.

There's History and Geography.

1.
There's History and Geography,
Science and music too;
Plain parables and prophecy
They all belong to You.
Refrain:
You are the wisdom of God's way
You are His living Word.
You speak the truth so faithfully
Salvation is assured!

2.
There's literature and poetry
Design and building too;
There's number work and government;
They all belong to You.
Refrain:

3.
There's Physics and Biology
Within Your pages too;
Astronomy and counselling,
That all belong to You.
Refrain:

4.
But most of all, we find in You
We can be cleansed from sin;
And fitted out with righteousness
God's Spirit dwells within.
Final refrain:
O Lord, we thank You for Your word
That speaks of Your dear Son.
We thank You for Your blessings too
Through all that He has done.

Tunes: Bethlehem, Ellacombe, No King But Christ, Warrior.

1Corinthians 2.9-13

But as it is written, Eye hath not seen, nor ear heard, neither have entered into the heart of man, the things which God hath prepared for them that love him. But God hath revealed them unto us by his Spirit: for the Spirit searcheth all things, yea, the deep things of God. For what man knoweth the things of a man, save the spirit of man which is in him? even so the things of God knoweth no man, but the Spirit of God. Now we have received, not the spirit of the world, but the spirit which is of God; that we might know the things that are freely given to us of God. Which things also we speak, not in the words which man's wisdom teacheth, but which the Holy Ghost teacheth; comparing spiritual things with spiritual.

10th February.

88.88 or 88.88D.

When Do the Children with Joy Sing?

1. When do the children with joy sing?
At Easter time! At Easter time!
When do church bells their anthems ring?
When Christ is praised at Easter time!

2. When was it that my Saviour died?
At Easter time! At Easter time!
When was it He was crucified?
'Twas during one sad Easter time!

3. When was it Jesus His blood shed?
At Easter time! At Easter time!
Where did He suffer in our stead?
'Twas on a cross at Easter time!

4. When was my Lord put in the tomb?
At Easter time! At Easter time!
When was the grave robbed of its gloom?
'Twas during one glad Easter time!

5. When was God's Lamb raised from the dead?
At Easter time! At Easter time!
Where is the pow'r of God now read?
In Christ's new life at Easter time!

6. When do we find blessings abound?
At Easter time! At Easter time!
Where is our hope of glory found?
In Christ raised up at Easter time!

Tunes: Church Triumphant, Winchester (New), Abends, Nazareth.

Isaiah 53.5
But he was wounded for our transgressions, he was bruised for our iniquities: the chastisement of our peace was upon him; and with his stripes we are healed.

11th February.

66.66D.

What Kind of Child were You?

1.
What kind of child were You
By angels' voices named?
What kind of child were You
Who all the ages framed?
What kind of boy were You.
Seeking Your Father's will?
What kind of boy were You
The universe to fill.

2.
What kind of man were You
Commanding wind and sea?
What kind of man were You
Who set the captives free?
What kind of Lamb were You
Who died at Calvary?
What kind of Lamb were You
Offered by God's decree?

3.
What kind of Lord are You
Now risen from the grave?
What kind of Lord are You
Who has the power to save?
You are the Man of dreams,
The Father's only Son.
You are the Man of dreams
Whose battle is well won.

4.
Your name is Wonderful,
The Mighty God of old.
Your name is Wonderful
More precious than fine gold.
Your name is Counsellor,
The Prince of Peace we see.
Your name is Counsellor,
Source of eternity.

Tunes: Invitation, Denby.

Luke 8.25

And he said unto them,
Where is your faith?
And they being afraid wondered, saying one to another,
What manner of man is this! for he commandeth even the winds and water, and they obey him.

Luke 2.46

And it came to pass, that after three days they found him in the temple,
sitting in the midst of the doctors,
both hearing them, and asking them questions.
And all that heard him were astonished at his understanding and answers.

12th February.

66.66D.

Lord, I Can See the Stars.

1.
Lord, I can see the stars
In all their beauty shine.
I see Venus and Mars
And know Your work's divine!
The beauty of the skies
And of the earth below,
Is seen by mortal eyes
And all Your glories show.

Refrain:
Tell me, my precious Lord,
The wisdom of Your way.
Tell me, my precious Lord,
Your purposes this day.

2.
Lord, I can see the cross
Where You, my Saviour, died.
I see the shame and loss
When You were crucified.
Your suffering on the tree
I cannot understand.
Yet, 'twas Your love for me
Achieved what God had
planned.
Refrain:

3.
Lord, I can serve You here
Led by Your wondrous word.
Lord, I can worship You
As by Your Spirit stirred.
Yet, I would seek to know
The point of suffering;
That I, Your praise might show
In all the songs I sing.
Refrain:

4.
All of your suffering
Has come from Adam's sin.
Death comes in many forms
And works away within.
So, in my government,
My judgement always stands!
But in my grace, I shall
Mould You with loving hands.
Final refrain:
So, my most precious child,
Know this thing is from me.
It works out for Your best
Now and eternally.

Tunes (for verses only): Invitation (Maker), Denby, Lausanne, Corbet.

Genesis 3.19
In the sweat of thy face shalt thou eat bread, till thou return unto the ground;
for out of it wast thou taken: for dust thou art, and unto dust shalt thou return.

13th February.

99.99.

Thoroughly Faithful! Thoroughly Wise!

1. Thoroughly faithful! Thoroughly wise!
You are our God, the God of the skies.
Mighty in power! Unchanging too!
These are the virtues that we can view.

2. Thoroughly tender! Thoroughly kind!
You care for us in body and mind.
Your love is lasting! Your love is true!
There is no turning shadow in You.

3. Thoroughly gracious! Thoroughly good!
Thoroughly righteous! Free from falsehood!
Holy Your presence, You're always near!
You are our Father, we shall not fear!

4. You are eternal! The Lord of Time!
You know all things and You are sublime!
Help us to trust You in everything.
Knowing You're for us makes our hearts sing!

5. Father of glory, open our eyes!
Father of mercies, help and advise!
Father of Spirits, our lives maintain!
Father in heaven, hallowed Your name!

Tunes: Adelaide, St. Cecilia (Sewall), Moody.

Exodus 34. 5-7
And the LORD descended in the cloud, and stood with him there, and proclaimed the name of the LORD.
And the LORD passed by before him, and proclaimed, The LORD, The LORD God,
merciful and gracious, longsuffering, and abundant in goodness and truth,
Keeping mercy for thousands, forgiving iniquity and transgression and sin…

14th February.

76.76.

O Lord, Carry Our Burdens.

1.
O Lord, carry our burdens
And in our sorrows share;
Give us the joy of knowing
The wonder of Your care.

2.
When life is filled with trial
And we are in despair;
Give us the joy of knowing
The wonder of Your care.

3.
When friends we knew desert
us
And colleagues stop and stare;
Give us the joy of knowing
The wonder of Your care.

4.
When poverty attacks us
And cupboards are so bare;
Give us the joy of knowing
The wonder of Your care.

5.
When illness strikes with
venom
And life seems so unfair;
Give us the joy of knowing
The wonder of Your care.

6.
When sin with stealth deceives
us
And we're in Satan's snare;
Give us the joy of knowing
The wonder of Your care.

7.
Lord, when our spirits sink
Help us turn to prayer,
And we shall joy in knowing
The wonder of Your care.

Tunes: Vulpius, Cara, Matrimony, River City.

1Peter 5.6-7
Humble yourselves therefore under the mighty hand of God, that he may exalt you in due time: casting all your care upon him;
for he careth for you.

Romans 5.3-5
And not only so, but we glory in tribulations also: knowing that tribulation worketh patience; and patience, experience; and experience, hope: and hope maketh not ashamed;
because the love of God is shed abroad in our hearts by the Holy Ghost which is given unto us.

15th February.

76.76D.

Lord, Friendship is a Treasure.

1.
Lord, friendship is a treasure
That we are pleased to know;
For by Your word, blest Saviour,
We find Yours here below.
We are no longer servants;
But those drawn close to You.
With heads upon Your bosom,
We know what You will do.

2.
Lord, help us to obey You,
To glorify Your name!
And as Your friends, proclaim You
Yahweh! Jesus the Same!
So make Your friendship blossom
Like flowers in a field;
And may its fruit then give us
A most abundant yield.

3.
Lord, friendly words are music
To every listening ear.
We sit at Your feet, hearing
The words that bring us cheer.
Your deeds of friendship tell us
Of Your endearing love.
They weave us robes of linen
We'll wear in heav'n above.

4.
You're closer than a brother
Supporting us each day.
Your friendship has no measure
Along the narrow way.
Your kindness is abundant.
Almighty is Your power.
Your will is so delightful
And keeps us hour by hour.

5.
Lord, friendship is a token
Of love more strong than death.
It's seen in all Your suffering
And in Your "final" breath.
O help us know its value.
As we kneel down to pray.
Grant us to know its virtues
And pass it on today.

Tunes: Ahnfelt, Ewing, Greenland, Lymington, Angel's Story.

John 15.13-14
Greater love hath no man than this, that a man lay down his life for his friends. Ye are my friends, if ye do whatsoever I command you. Henceforth I call you not servants; for the servant knoweth not what his Lord doeth: but I have called you friends; for all things that I have heard of my Father I have made known unto you..

16th February.

76.76D.

Oh, Have You Seen My True Love?

1. Oh, have you seen my true love
In the blue skies above?
His heart is in the sunshine;
It's filled with His great love.
His face is in the moonlight
His power in the stars.
Oh, let me see my true love
In Venus, Earth and Mars!

2. Oh, have you heard my true love
Speaking in the cool breeze?
His voice sings at the lakeside
My worries to appease.
He teaches me in wisdom
I know to be divine.
Oh, let me hear my true love
As I on Him recline.

3. Oh, have you felt my true love
Touch you with tender care?
The hand that held the leper
Will all your burdens share.
The Word who all things made
Will strengthen you each day.
Oh, let me feel my true love
And near His side I'll stay.

Tunes: Greenland, Ahnfelt, Passion Chorale, St. Edith, Thornbury, Wolvercote, Day of Rest, Ewing,

Psalm 19.1-3

To the chief Musician, A Psalm of David. The heavens declare the glory of God; and the firmament sheweth his handywork day unto day uttereth speech, and night unto night sheweth knowledge. There is no speech nor language, where their voice is not heard.

17th February.

CMD.

Blest Lord, You See Each Sparrow Fall.

1. Blest Lord, You see each sparrow fall
Down to the ground and die.
So if a sparrow knows Your care
Then, how much more shall I.
Lord, men despise the tiny bird;
They think it has no worth;
But You, O Lord, have high regard
For all in heaven and earth.

2. Blest Lord, the ravens of the field
Can neither reap nor sow;
Yet, in the goodness of Your care
You give them food to grow.
Lord, if this bird of ill repute
Is subject to Your care;
Then let us all with joy give thanks
And all Your love declare.

3. Blest Lord, You see the lilies grow;
They do not toil or spin:
Yet, with great beauty, they're arrayed;
Thy power is seen therein.
So if the lowly lily's clothed
In such a glorious way;
Then we shall never naked be,
But covered every day.

4. Blest Lord, You made the lilies shine
In all their glory bright.
You gave the humble sparrow life
And in its wings put flight.
You made the raven black as night
And used it in Your will.
You made us in Your image, Lord,
And so You love us still.

Tunes: No King But Christ, Release, Tyrol, Bethlehem, Ellacombe.

Luke 12.6-7

Are not five sparrows sold for two farthings, and not one of them is forgotten before God? But even the very hairs of your head are all numbered. Fear not therefore: ye are of more value than many sparrows.

Luke 12.27

Consider the lilies how they grow: they toil not, they spin not; and yet I say unto you, that Solomon in all his glory was not arrayed like one of these.

18th February.

CM.

Our Father, When We're Well and Strong,

1.
Our Father, when we're well and strong,
Rejoicing in each day;
Help us to think upon those tired
And weary of the way.

2.
Father, we thank Thee for Thy gifts
Of joy and happiness;
But help us think upon the sick
And those in deep distress.

3.
O Father, we would know Thy word
That comfort we might bring
To those who don't know what to do
In all their suffering.

4.
Father, grant us a heart of love
That good deeds may be done;
Give us the grace to watch and pray
For each beloved one.

Tunes: Pisgah, Irish, St. Agnes, Westminster (Turle), Beatitudo, Belmont.

Isaiah 58.6-7
Is not this the fast that I have chosen?
To loose the bands of wickedness, to undo the heavy burdens, and to let the oppressed go free, and that ye break every yoke?
Is it not to deal thy bread to the hungry, and that thou bring the poor that are cast out to thy house? when thou seest the naked, that thou cover him; and that thou hide not thyself from thine own flesh?
Then shall thy light break forth as the morning, and thine health shall spring forth speedily…

19th February

CM.

O Come and Worship Christ the Lord!

1.
O come and worship Christ the Lord!
For He is love! Pure love!
Worthy the name that's over all!
Yes, He is love! Pure love!

2.
O come and praise God's only Son!
For He is love! Pure love!
He has our great salvation won!
Yes, He is love! Pure love!

3.
O come and thank the Holy One!
For He is love! Pure love!
How great the things that He has done!
Yes, He is love! Pure love!

4.
O come and crown Him as the King!
For He is love! Pure love!
To Him our hearts we'll gladly bring!
Yes, He is love! Pure love!

(Written for children).

Tunes: St. Agnes, Pisgah, Irish, Westminster (Turle), Winchester (Old), Nativity, Beatitudo, Christmas Eve, Belmont, Chimes.

1John 4.-9
Beloved, let us love one another: for love is of God;
and every one that loveth is born of God, and knoweth God.
He that loveth not knoweth not God; for God is love.
In this was manifested the love of God toward us, because that God sent
his only begotten Son into the world,
that we might live through him.

20th February.

CM or CMD.

The Lord's My Shepherd, Shall I Want?

1.
The Lord's my Shepherd, shall
I want?
No! He'll my needs supply.
Food, shelter, clothing, He'll
provide;
His own, He won't deny.

2.
The Lord's my Shepherd, shall
I sin?
No! He was crucified!
So, cleansed, I might have part
with Him
Who, for our sins, once died.

3.
The Lord's my Shepherd, shall
I stray?
No! He will be my Guide!
And when the road is rough and
steep,
He will not leave my side.

4.
The Lord's my Shepherd, shall
I fear?
No! He's my Strength and Stay!
And when dark shadows press
my soul,
He'll keep me day by day.

5.
The Lord's my Shepherd, shall
I strive?
No! My Saviour is He!
When enemies surround the
camp
I'll see His victory.

6.
The Lord's my Shepherd, shall
I fret?
No! Goodness follows me!
And in God's house for
evermore,
My dwelling place shall be.

Tunes: 86.86: Westminster (Turle), St. Agnes, Irish, Abends, Abridge.
86.86D: No King But Christ, Land of Rest, None But Christ, Bethlehem.

Psalm 23.2-5
A Psalm of David.
The LORD is my shepherd; I shall not want. He maketh me to lie down in green pastures: he leadeth me beside the still waters.
He restoreth my soul: he leadeth me in the paths of righteousness for his name's sake. Yea, though I walk through the valley of the shadow of death, I will fear no evil: for thou art with me; thy rod and thy staff they comfort me.

21st February.

65.65.

Father, at the Evening.

1. Father, at the evening
Of another year,
We bless and we thank You
For love so sincere.

2. Faithful were Your mercies
Freeing us from fear.
Tender was Your pity
Wiping every tear.

3. Bountiful in goodness,
You brought us good cheer.
By Your loving nature,
You have kept us near.

4. Father, at the dawning
Of another year:
Keep us in Your presence!
Your blest will make clear!

5. Lead us, righteous Father,
In the path of peace.
Make our lives more fruitful!
Make our love increase!

6. May Your Son be precious
To our heart and mind!
May Your Spirit help us
Fellowship to find!

Tunes: 65.65: Armentrout, Ernstein, North Coates, Quietude, Castle Eden..

James 1.17
Every good gift and every perfect gift is from above, and cometh down from the Father of lights, with whom is no variableness, neither shadow of turning.

22nd February.

77.77D.

Father, Keep Me Day by Day.

1. Father, keep me day by day;
Lead me in the narrow way.
Keep me faithful; keep me true;
For I now belong toYou.
In life's dangers, make me brave
Knowing You are strong to save;
And when sin entices me,
Help me to resistant be.

2. Father, keep me day by day,
Lead me in the narrow way.
Keep me close to Your blest side
That in love I may abide.
In life's sorrows, comfort me;
In despair, Your strength I'd see;
And when all seems dark and bleak
Give me grace Your mind to seek.

3. Father, keep me day by day,
Lead me in the narrow way.
With joy let me tell of You;
Show me all that I must do;
Then each burden I must bear
Will be lightened by Your care
Till the day I fly above
To those mansions steeped in love.

Inspired by "Father, Lead me Day by Day" by John Page Hopps, 1834-1912). Tunes: Hollingside, Messiah, New St. Andrew.

Jude 1.24
Now unto him that is able to keep you from falling, and to present you faultless before the presence of his glory with exceeding joy,
to the only wise God our Saviour, be glory and majesty, dominion and power, both now and ever.
Amen.

23rd February.

CMD.

You Are the Mighty God Who Made.

1.
You are the Mighty God who made
The universe we see.
You are the noble Prince of peace
Who died on Calv'ry's tree.
You are our Saviour, Priest and King
And Lord of everything.
You are the Man of God's own heart -
Of you, we gladly sing.

2.
You are Alpha and Omega,
Who revealed God below.
You are the First and You're the Last
The I AM we now know.
You are the Beginning of all
And so You are the End.
You are the Lover of our souls,
Our Redeemer and Friend.

3.
You are this dark world's shining light
Of God, the Chosen One
You are the Way, the Truth and Life
You are God's only Son.
You are the Shepherd of the sheep
Who came in by God's door.
All glory, honour, praise and pow'r
Be Yours for evermore!

4.
You are the dearest thing to me;
I long to see Your face.
The face once marred at Calvary
Now shining with God's grace.
I'll cast my crown before Your throne
As I adore Your name.
Humbly, I'll kiss Your holy feet
And own: "You are the Same"!

Tunes: No King But Christ, Minerva, Bethlehem, Landas, Jesus is God.

Colossians 1.16-18
For by him were all things created, that are in heaven, and that are in earth, visible and invisible, whether they be thrones, or dominions, or principalities, or powers: all things were created by him, and for him: And he is before all things, and by him all things consist. And he is the head of the body, the church: who is the beginning, the firstborn from the dead; that in all things he might have the pre-eminence.

24th February.

10.10.10.10.

I'll Always Love You As Day Passes Day.

1. I'll always love You as day passes day.
I'll always love You, my Guide in the way.
I'll always love You, Saviour, most divine.
I'll always love You and on You recline.

2. I'll always love You, God's belovèd Son.
I'll always love You for the work You've done.
I'll always love You for the grief You bore.
I'll always love You, My Lord and Mentor.

3. Your presence, Lord, is perfume to my soul;
Your kisses, sweet as wine, my heart console;
Your smiling eyes betray a will to love.
And Your embrace lifts me to heights above.

4. I'll always love You for You first loved me.
I'll always love You - dying on the tree.
I'll always love You whose love set me free.
I'll always love You as You live for me.

5. I'll always love You, Your beauty's sublime.
I'll always love You through the mists of Time.
I'll always love You as Jesus, my Lord.
I'll always love You, the Christ so adored.

6. You are the brightness of our God on high
And it's Your blood that to Him brought us nigh.
We see You seated on the Father's throne
Till that blest day when You come for Your own.

Tunes: Penetentia, Ellers, Maori, Toulon, Skara, Glory to Jesus.

1John 4.18-19
There is no fear in love; but perfect love casteth out fear: because fear hath torment. He that feareth is not made perfect in love.
We love him, because he first loved us.

25th February.

77.77.

Father, Hear Me As I Pray.

1.
Father, hear me as I pray
At the start of each new day.
Give me knowledge of You, Lord
That Your name might be adored.

2.
Father, hear me as I pray
Handing to You each new day.
With Your love, please fill my heart;
That I may with You have part.

3.
Father, hear me as I pray,
Keep me from all sin this day.
Help me walk in righteousness;
May salvation be my dress.

4.
Father, hear me as I pray,
Giving thanks to You each day.
Every good and perfect gift
Comes from You, my soul to lift.

5.
Father, hear me as I pray
For provisions in the day.
Yes, You know my every need
And will guide me, as I plead.

6.
Father, hear me as I pray,
For those smitten by the day.
Heal the sick; strengthen the weak;
Let those suff'ring, comfort seek.

7.
Father, hear me as I pray,
For those serving You today.
May their work be kind and true;
May it always honour You.

8.
Father, hear me as I pray,
For all troubled in this day.
Lift their burdens; dry their tears;
And remove their guilt and fears.

9.
Father, hear me as I pray
For all known to me this day.
May they each be born anew;
May they each Your will pursue.

Tunes: 77.77: St. Bees, Innocents, Monkland, Calvary (Monk), Confidence (Ousely), Buckland Evelyn (Ashford).

26th February.

66.66D.

I Sent My Only Son.

1.
I sent my only Son
From glorious heights above.
I sent my only Son
The object of my love.
I sent my only Son
To Bethl'em's manger bare.
I sent my only Son
Because I really care.

2.
I sent my only Son
By men to be despised.
I sent my only Son
To earth to be baptized.
I sent my only Son
To die on Calv'ry's tree.
I sent my only Son
To make you all sin-free.

3.
I sent my only Son
Into a cold, dark tomb.
I sent my only Son
To rob death of its gloom.
I sent my only Son
To rise with pow'r divine.
I sent my only Son
In heavenly light to shine.

4.
And, now, I'm sending you
To be a shining star.
And, now, I'm sending you
To sinners near and far.
And, now, I'm sending you
To lead souls to my side.
And, now, I'm sending you
With all my grace supplied.

Tunes: 12.12.12.12: Corbet. 66.66:Quam Dilecta, St. Cecilia, Eccles.

John 3.16-18
For God so loved the world, that he gave his only begotten Son, that whosoever believeth in him should not perish, but have everlasting life.
For God sent not his Son into the world to condemn the world; but that the world through him might be saved.
He that believeth on him is not condemned: but he that believeth not is condemned already, because he hath not believed in the name of the only begotten Son of God.

1John 4.14
And we have seen and do testify that the Father sent the Son to be the Saviour of the world.

27th February.

76.76D.

O Lord, We See You Weeping.

1.
O Lord, we see You weeping
Close to the cold, dark tomb.
Death snatched a loved one
from You
And hearts to grief give room.
Your groans of deepest sorrow
Tell of the pain sin wrought.
Your tears of tender pity
Allied with souls distraught.

2.
O Lord, we see You weeping
Here in this place of woe.
Death snatched a loved one
from us
And our distress, You know.
Our agony and anguish
Express our crushing loss.
And now we know the feelings
Of Mary at Your cross.

3.
O Lord, we see You standing
Both raised and glorified.
The Lamb of God in
heaven;
The Lamb once crucified.
You are the Resurrection,
And You're the Life, we know.
You took the path to Glory
Where all God's blessings flow.

4.
O Lord, we see You standing,
With arms stretched out, above.
Your child You will
receive
In all Your joy and love.
And though we sorrow greatly,
We know that s/he'll be blessed
For s/he'll be ever with You
And in Your presence – rest!

Written upon hearing of the sudden death of a young Christian.
Tunes: Thornbury, Ewing, St. Edith, Greenland, Passion Chorale, Webb, Wolvercote, Aurelia, Commemoration, Crucifix, Angel's Story, Ahnfelt.

John 11.34-35
And said, Where have ye laid him? They said unto him, Lord, come and see. Jesus wept.

2Corinthians 5.6-8
Therefore we are always confident, knowing that, whilst we are at home in the body, we are absent from the Lord:
(for we walk by faith, not by sight:)
We are confident, I say, and willing rather to be absent from the body, and to be present with the Lord.

28th February.

85.85.

Come and Help Us! Come and Help Us!

1. "Come and help us! Come and help us!"
Is the urgent cry
Of those distant, searching sinners
All about to die.

2. Let us help them! Let us help them!
Take it from the Lord.
'Tis His will that we should reach them
With His holy word.

3. Shall we fail Him! Shall we fail Him!
Saints of God, arise!
Armed with faith and hope and love,
Say your fond goodbyes.

4. "Jesus loves you! Jesus loves you!"
These, your words shall be.
"He who is a mighty Saviour
Died at Calvary."

5. "Blood that's precious! Blood that's precious!
Washes white as snow!
Change your ways and trust Him fully -
All His blessings know!"

6. Till He cometh! Till He cometh!
Serve Him cheerfully;
For the Lord who died to save us
Our reward shall be!

Tunes: 85.85: Cairnbrook. 85.85D: Sinclair

Rev 3:11

Behold, I come quickly: hold that fast which thou hast, that no man take thy crown.

29th February.

76.76D.

O Lord, the Torch Now Flickers.

1.
O Lord, the torch now flickers
Held in the hands of few.
The torch that once blazed brightly
Needs saints faithful and true.
It bears the Gospel message
To those in distant lands.
It bears the precious promise
Of breaking Satan's bands.

2.
O Lord, the torch now flutters,
The torch once borne by those
Who spent their lives revealing
The Christ who died and rose.
But now, in deepest darkness
The light of life seems dim
For few are those that labour;
And few that speak of Him.

3.
O Lord, the adversary
Has veiled the eyes of men.
And he who would deny Thee,
Defies Thee yet again.
O Lord, by Thy blest Spirit
Raise up a torch so bright,
That Satan and his forces
Flee, screaming, from the fight.

4.
O Lord, wake up Thy servants
To bear the torch today;
And may their faith breed courage
To show lost souls Thy way.
Sustain them in Thy mercy;
Help them to faithful be;
And by Thy Spirit's guidance
May they toil on for Thee.

Tunes: Ahnfelt, Lymington, Thornbury, Webb, Mountain, Day of Rest, St. Edith, Ewing, Greenland, Aurelia, Passion Chorale.

Matthew 9.36-37
But when he saw the multitudes, he was moved with compassion on them, because they fainted, and were scattered abroad, as sheep having no shepherd. Then saith he unto his disciples, The harvest truly is plenteous, but the labourers are few…

John 4.35
Say not ye, There are yet four months, and then cometh harvest?
behold, I say unto you,
Lift up your eyes, and look on the fields;
for they are white already to harvest.

1st March.

CM.

Go Forth and Tell Lost Souls of Me.

1. Go forth and tell lost souls
of Me
And of my Father's love.
Draw them into God's family
That they might dwell above.

2. Go forth and tell lost souls
of Me;
Tell them I'm God's dear Son;
The One who dwelt in glory
bright
Before the world begun.

3. Go forth and tell lost souls
of Me;
The Word who all things made;
And found in fashion as a man
Was in a manger laid.

4. Go forth and tell lost souls
of Me;
My birth, my life, my cross.
Trust in me as your one
resource
And count this world but dross.

5. Go forth and tell lost souls
of Me;
Of my redeeming blood.
The ransom for their souls is
paid
By its most precious flood.

6. Go forth and tell lost souls
of Me;
And resurrection power.
And with a meek and lowly
heart
Speak of new life this hour.

7. Go forth and tell lost souls
of Me;
Of majesty and might.
Show them the victory is won
And Satan's lost the fight.

8. Go forth and tell lost souls
of Me;
Of all my love and grace.
Then in that glorious day to
come,
They'll see Me face to face.

Tunes: CMD: Bethlehem, No King But Christ, Landas, Minerva. CM: Bishopthorpe, Westminster (Turle), Nativity, Pisgah, St. Agnes.

Matthew 28.19-20
Go ye therefore, and teach all nations, baptizing them in the name of the Father, and of the Son, and of the Holy Ghost:
teaching them to observe all things whatsoever I have commanded you: and, lo, I am with you alway, even unto the end of the world.
Amen.

2nd March.

76.76D.

A Prayer for Our Brother.

1. Father, we miss our brother,
His smile and quiet way;
We miss him in the Gospel
And miss him when we pray.
Draw close to him, dear Father,
In this, his time of need.
Put loving arms around him
And comfort him, we plead.

2. Father, we miss our brother,
His faith is sorely tried.
Please, take away his worries;
Let wisdom be his guide.
And may his soul remember
That Christ for him once died
That he might be well fitted
To be part of his bride.

3. Father, we miss our brother,
For those he loves, we feel.
Please, meet them in their sorrow
And wounded hearts, please heal.
We'll trust in You, blest Father,
With all that we hold dear.
Please strengthen Your belovèd
Removing all his fear.

4. Father, we'd see our brother
Among us once again.
Freed from his every burden;
Freed from his grief and pain.
Oh, may we with rejoicing
See his dear face again;
And may his soul find solace
In hearts where Christ has reign.

Tunes: Ewing, Passion Chorale, Thornbury, Greenland.

Isaiah 35.10 and 55:7

And the ransomed of the LORD shall return, and come to Zion with songs and everlasting joy upon their heads:
they shall obtain joy and gladness, and sorrow and sighing shall flee away…
Let the wicked forsake his way, and the unrighteous man his thoughts: and let him return unto the LORD, and he will have mercy upon him; and to our God, for he will abundantly pardon.

Jeremiah 24.7

And I will give them an heart to know me, that I am the LORD: and they shall be my people, and I will be their God: for they shall return unto me with their whole heart.

3rd March.

CMD.

O Lord, Please Look Upon our Land.

1. O Lord, please look upon our land
In such a sorry state.
So full of wickedness and strife,
Of violence and of hate.
O, watch and keep the trusting soul
From sin and its torment.
Stretch forth Thy mighty hand to save
The poor and innocent.

2. The government, planted by Thee,
We ask Thee now to bless.
Grant it Thy wisdom from above
To rule in righteousness.
O, watch and keep the trusting soul;
May Thy peace fill his heart.
Stretch forth Thy mighty hand to save
And all Thy love impart.

3. O Lord, the proud are scattered now;
Riches have flown away!
And in this time of greatest need
Mammon has lost its sway.
O, watch and keep the trusting soul;
Provide for him each day.
Stretch forth Thy mighty hand to save
And lead him in Thy way.

4. O Lord, the humble, Thou shalt bless;
The hungry, Thou shalt feed.
And when the homeless cry to Thee,
Thou shalt their pleading heed.
O, watch and keep the trusting soul;
Let him Thy presence know.
Please, turn this land from sin and death
Keep it from every foe.

5. O Lord, we magnify Thy name
And joy before Thy face.
We praise Thee for Thy faithfulness,
For mercy and for grace.
Our lips rejoice in Thee to sing
The Lord of hosts on high;
The God of heaven and of earth,
On Whom we all rely.

Tunes: Bethlehem, Release, No King But Christ, Forest Green.

Luke 15.1
…He hath scattered the proud in the imagination of their hearts.

4th March.

CM or CMD.

I'm Saved to Serve Through Jesus' Blood!

1. I'm saved to serve through
Jesus' blood!
I'm saved by grace alone!
No works that I could ever do
Could for my sins atone!
It's only faith my fears could
calm;
Faith in the Son of God!
He gave Himself that I might be
Shielded from judgment's rod.

2. I'm saved to serve! A priest
of God!
I'm saved to sympathise
With all who are by sorrow
bound –
Depressed by tears and sighs.
I'm saved to give prayerful
support
To those by trials torn.
I'm saved to help each needy
soul
And weep with those who
mourn.

3. I'm saved to serve! A saint
of God!
To Him, I now belong.
I'm sanctified in Jesus' name
To God, I now belong.
I know He can delight in me
As in His only Son.
And in His purpose, I have part
In all that Christ has won.

4. I'm saved to serve! A
worshipper
Of the Father on high!
For it's the blood of God's own
Lamb
By which I may draw nigh.
Into His presence, I would
come
And humbly bow the knee.
For in the cross of Christ, I see
The love He has for me.

5. I'm saved to serve! In this
wide world;
But what I do is small.
Yet, with the Lord of Hosts at
hand,
By Him, I can do all.
And through the darkness and
the strife
For God, I'll labour on,
Until the day of rapture comes
When I shall see His Son.

Tunes: No King But Christ, Bethlehem, Ishpeming, Land of Rest, Jesus is God, Landas, Goshen, Warrior.

Romans 14.18
For he that in these things serveth Christ is acceptable to God, and approved of men.

5th March.

76.76D.

Lord Jesus, We Remember.

1. Lord Jesus, we remember
Yours was a lowly birth;
The stable and the manger
Both hid Your holy worth.
But angels spoke of glory;
A King was born that day.
The Chosen One of God
Would all His love display.

2. Lord Jesus, we remember
Your lonely path of love;
A Stranger on this planet
Whose home was high above!
Your righteousness and mercy,
Your power and kindness too,
All worked for Mankind's
blessing!
To God faithful and true!

3. Lord Jesus, we remember,
That on the cross You died.
The grief and sorrow suffered
When You were crucified.
We see Your pain and anguish
On the accursèd tree.
There God Himself forsook
You
That we might be sin-free.

4. Lord Jesus, we remember
The tomb for You prepared.
The scented linen bindings
That once Your body snared.
Yet, in God's mighty power,
You left them lying there!
Now in the light of Heaven
Most glorious robes, You wear!

5. Lord Jesus, we remember
That You will come again.
You'll take us up to Glory –
That we with You might reign.
And in the Father's mansions,
Our hearts will be set free;
We'll worship and adore You!
We'll praise Your majesty!

Tunes: Aurelia, Greenland, Day of Rest, Ewing, Penlan, Wolvercote, Missionary Hymn.

Ecclesiastes 12.1

Remember now thy Creator in the days of thy youth, while the evil days come not, nor the years draw nigh, when thou shalt say, I have no pleasure in them…

Genesis 40.14

But think on me when it shall be well with thee…

6th March.

CM.

Forgiveness Comes From God Above.

1. Forgiveness from God above
There is no other source.
The Father who has sent His Son
His justice must enforce.

2. Forgiveness comes with Your dear name,
Jesus, the Lord of all.
And never shall our God above
A single one recall.

3. Forgiveness comes through Your own blood
Shed on Golgotha's tree.
'Twas there, forsaken of Your God,
You were made sin for me.

4. Forgiveness comes by faith alone –
Faith in the work You've done.
Our sins You've borne upon the tree;
Your love our hearts has won.

5. Forgiveness comes to us today
As Your words clearly tell.
With souls redeemed, we praise Your name,
For You've saved us from Hell.

6. Forgiveness comes with blessings too
From our God up above.
Yes, every good and perfect gift
Is given in His love.

7. Forgiveness comes with Your command
To go forth with Your word.
Give us the grace to tell this world
Of You, the risen Lord!

Tunes: Winchester (Old), Nativity, St. Agnes, Westminster (Turle), Pisgah, Irish, Beatitudo, Belmont.

Colossians 1.14

In whom we have redemption through his blood, even the forgiveness of sins…

Acts 26.18

To open their eyes, and to turn them from darkness to light, and from the power of Satan unto God…

that they may receive forgiveness of sins, and inheritance among them which are sanctified by faith that is in me.

7th March.

66.66D.

Lord Jesus, Unto You We bring a Note of Praise.

1.
Lord Jesus, unto You
We bring a note of praise
For love as strong as death
Must all our voices raise!
We're washed in Your own blood!
Yes, cleansed from every sin!
You've made us royal priests
By Your Spirit within.

2.
All glory be to You
Who rose up from the grave!
All pow'r and riches too,
For You are strong to save!
And when You come as King,
The earth will cease its groan!
All shall give place to You
And to Your righteous throne.

3.
May God who is, and was,
And shall be evermore,
Grant us pure hearts of love
To praise You and adore.
And may His grace and peace
To us for ever flow,
So when to You we bow
Your glories we shall know.

Tunes: Corbet, Invitation (Maker), Denby, Lausanne.

Song 1.6

Set me as a seal upon thine heart, as a seal upon thine arm: for love is strong as death; jealousy is cruel as the grave: the coals thereof are coals of fire, which hath a most vehement flame.

8th March.

10.10.10.10.

Let All the Saints, Who are by Grace Most Blessed.

1.
Let all the saints, who are by grace most blessed
Rejoice in Thee, the Lord of peace and rest;
Let them proclaim the name that they've professed
Till found in glory in Thy beauty dressed.

2.
Thou art the Son, the Father's pure delight!
Thou art the Word who brought us into light!
Thou art our Rock, our Fortress and our Might!
Thou art the Head in whom we all unite!

3.
Thou art the Christ, God's own anointed One!
Thou art the Maker of the earth and sun!
Thou art the Shepherd and the Corner-stone
Thou art the Lamb who fought the fight alone!

4.
Lord, give us strength to stand in this dark day;
And when the fight is fierce, Thy will obey!
Help us to walk with Thee along the way.
And, when the path is rough, we will not stray!

5.
Lord, we look on to see Thee in the air;
Thy shout will free us from all earthly care!
There, in new bodies, Thy likeness we'll bear
And, with great joy, our love for Thee declare.

Tunes: Eventide, Ellers, Woodlands, Penetentia, Maori, Omaha, Skara.

Ephesians 1.7-8
In whom we have redemption through his blood, the forgiveness of sins, according to the riches of his grace; wherein he hath abounded toward us in all wisdom and prudence…

9th March.

86.86D.

Father, Please, Teach Us How to Pray.

1.
Father, please, teach us how to pray
In Jesus' precious name.
Thy children, we draw near the throne
And there, Thy blessings claim.
Into Thy presence, we now come
With reverence and fear.
And in the sacrifice of Christ
Find blood that brings us near.

2.
Father, please teach us how to sit
At Jesus' holy feet.
As children, we would hear His word
That we might be complete.
Into His presence, we now come
In true humility.
And here with hearts yearning to learn
Find truths that set us free.

3.
Father, please teach us how to walk
In Jesus' sinless way.
As children, we would seek to be
Like Christ from day to day.
So through the prayers we lift to Thee,
And knowledge of Thy word,
Help us to grow in love and grace
With endless life assured.

Tunes: Jesus is God, Land of Rest, Landas, Bethlehem, Ellacombe, Minerva, Release, Warrior.

Hebrews 4.16
Let us therefore come boldly unto the throne of grace, that we may obtain mercy, and find grace to help in time of need.

10th March.

76.76D.

All glory, Laud and Honour.

1.
All glory, laud and honour
To Christ upon the throne
Where righteousness and
judgment
Are by His sceptre shown.
We'll worship and adore Him
As those saved by His grace;
And, privileged, we'll serve
Him
In glory, face to face.

2.
The earth shall cease her
groaning,
Displaying all her store.
The desert lands shall blossom,
And nations turn from war.
Yes, "Peace!" shall be the
watchword
Of man and creature too;
For mighty is the power
That we in Christ shall view.

3.
The true God will be
worshipped;
Idolatry shall cease.
The people shall dwell safely;
Their ages will increase.
Oppression will be banished;
The needy shall be filled.
The land shall yield her bounty
As fertile ground is tilled.

4.
All kings shall fall before Him,
To Him their tribute
bring;
And Zion, His blest people,
Shall lift her voice and sing.
His name shall be remembered
As sunrise greets the day;
And splendour shall surround
Him
In beauty's bright array.

Tunes: St. Edith, St. Theodulph, Thornbury, Ewing, Greenland, Lymington, Passion Chorale, Ellacombe, Webb, Wolvercote.

Isaiah 32.17-18
And the work of righteousness shall be peace; and the effect of righteousness quietness and assurance for ever. And my people shall dwell in a peaceable habitation, and in sure dwellings, and in quiet resting places…

Isaiah 35.1
The wilderness and the solitary place shall be glad for them; and the desert shall rejoice, and blossom as the rose.

11th March

CMD.

Delivered From the Law, Dear Lord.

1. Delivered from the law, dear
Lord,
Rescued by blood alone;
Lead us by Thy blest Spirit,
Lord,
Let our hearts be Thy throne.
Brought into liberty by
Thee,
Each is a child of God.
Oh, give us grace to follow
Thee;
And keep us in Thy care.

2. Delivered from that dark
domain,
Where Satan ruled through sin;
We now belong to Thee, dear
Lord,
Who died our souls to win.
Partakers with the saints in
light,
We joy before Thy face.
We bow before the Father's
love
And wonder at Thy grace.

3. Delivered from this evil
world,
We would its pleasures shun.
Oh, help us look to Thee above
Till all our work is done.
A burden of death, we might
bear
Wherever, we may go;
But, Lord, Thy victory, we
claim
That freedom we may know.

4. Delivered from the wrath to
come,
We wait for Thee, dear Lord.
Help us to watch in praise and
prayer
As Thy name is adored.
'Tis then we shall be like Thee,
Lord,
And for Thy glory so.
Please, mould us to Thine
image now
While we serve Thee below.

Tunes: Bethlehem, Release, Forest Green, No king But Christ, Jesus is God, Ellacombe, Land of Rest, Landas, Warrior.

1Thessalonians 1.9-10
For they themselves shew of us what manner of entering in we had unto you, and how ye turned to God from idols to serve the living and true God; and to wait for his Son from heaven, whom he raised from the dead, even Jesus, which delivered us from the wrath to come.

12th March.

66.66D.

Jesus is Son of God!

1. Jesus is Son of God!
The Son of God most high!
Jesus is Son of God
Who came to earth to die!
Jesus was born a baby
To a young virgin maid!
Jesus was born a baby!
God in a manger laid!

2. Jesus the carpenter!
A carpenter by trade.
Jesus the carpenter
By whom the worlds were made
Jesus was a true servant
Serving His God above!
Jesus was a true servant
Serving His own in love!

3. Jesus the Son of man!
Lower than angels made.
Jesus the Son of man!
His blood our ransom paid!
Jesus the Lamb of God!
Who died because of sin!
Jesus the Lamb of God!
Himself so pure within!

4. Jesus is Lord of all!
Now risen from the dead!
Jesus is Lord of all!
He is the church's Head!
Jesus is our dear Bridegroom!
Who'll come for us one day!
Jesus is our dear Bridegroom
Who'll take His bride away!

5. Jesus is King of kings!
He'll reign in righteousness!
Jesus is King of kings!
And this world He will bless!
Jesus is our blest Saviour
And our Redeemer too!
We'll praise Him now and ever
And soon His glory view!

Tunes: Thornbury, Passion Chorale, St. Theodulph, Lymington, Greenland, Petition.

John 5:18 and 9:35-37
Therefore the Jews sought the more to kill him, because he not only had broken the sabbath, but said also that God was his Father, making himself equal with God…
Jesus heard that they had cast him out; and when he had found him, he said unto him, Dost thou believe on the Son of God?
He answered and said, Who is he, Lord, that I might believe on him?
And Jesus said unto him, Thou hast both seen him, and it is he that talketh with thee.

13th March.

CM.

The Word of Life Art Thou, O Lord.

1. The Word of Life art Thou, O Lord,
Both heard and seen on earth.
Handled by those who are Thine own
Who knew Thy precious worth.

2. A light that shines in a dark place,
The word of prophecy.
We know that it will lead us on
For it must speak of Thee.

3. The worlds were framed by Thy blest word,
And formed from things concealed.
But 'tis the power of Thy word
That holds up all revealed.

4. Thy word endures for evermore,
Tempered with righteousness.
It speaks the truth in terms of love
And tells of Thy goodness.

5. Its promises are just and sure;
Its words, faithful and true.
It brings the Gospel to all men
And in it life we view.

6. It says we're reconciled to God
Through blood that Thou hast shed.
As Wisdom, it declares Thy name
And by it, we are fed.

Tunes: Pisgah, Westminster (Turle), Winchester (Old), Beatitudo.

Hebrews 11.3
Through faith we understand that the worlds were framed by the word of God, so that things which are seen were not made of things which do appear.

14th March.

CM.

Lord, May the Treasures of Thy Word.

1. Lord, may the treasures of Thy word
Wisdom to us impart;
And by Thy Spirit in us form
A true and loving heart.

2. Lord, may the treasures of Thy word
Assure the soul each day.
Grant us the knowledge of Thy will
And lead us in Thy way.

3. Lord, may the treasures of Thy word
Reveal to us Thy Son.
Oh, may His glories fill our sight -
Besides the work He's done.

4. Lord, may the treasures of Thy word
Thyself, as Father show;
That we might worship Thee while here
And all Thy blessings know.

5. Lord, may the treasures of Thy word
Teach us to watch and pray;
For Jesus soon shall come again
And snatch us all away.

6. Lord, may the treasures of Thy word
Tell us of life above.
Speak of Thy house of joy and peace;
The home of perfect love.

Tunes: CM: Pisgah, Nativity, St. Agnes, Westminster (Turle), Winchester (Old), Irish, Belmont, Beatitudo.

Colossians 2.3
...To the acknowledgement of the mystery of God, and of the Father, and of Christ; in whom are hid all the treasures of wisdom and knowledge.

15th March.

CMD.

The Scriptures are Inspired by Thee.

1. The scriptures are inspired by Thee,
The great, eternal God.
They tell how sinful souls are won
And how our path be trod.
They teach us of Thy precious Son,
The Word who flesh became.
They tell us all that He has done
In bringing us Thy name.

2. The scriptures are applied by Thee
Through Thy blest Paraclete.
And when we're led away by sin
Conviction brings retreat.
They straighten up the path we take
And shed light on our way.
They keep us all in righteousness
And train us day by day.

3. The scriptures are well used by Thee
To make us all complete;
And in Thy wisdom, we are led
To Thy pure mercy seat.
O Lord, let Thy word fill our hearts
That we may be prepared
To do good works by Thy command
That all Thy love be shared.

Tunes: I Bring My All To Thee, Bethlehem, Ellacombe, Jesus is God,
No King But Christ, Release, All Saints.

2Corinthians 4.6-7
For God, who commanded the light to shine out of darkness, hath shined in our hearts, to give the light of the knowledge of the glory of God in the face of Jesus Christ.
But we have this treasure in earthen vessels, that the excellency of the power may be of God, and not of us.

16th March.

66.66D.

Lift Up Your Banner, Lord.

1. Lift up Your banner, Lord,
We'll gather to Your side.
The battle runs its course
In fields blood-stained and wide.
The faithful hear Your voice
And stand at Your command
The devil and his hordes
Attack Your loyal band.

2. We fight the fight of faith!
We stand to meet the foe!
Our armour is of God
And onward we shall go.
We'll fight for God above!
We'll fight for You, His Son!
We'll fight for the pure word!
We'll fight till vict'ry's won!

3. We'll fight with all our might!
We'll fight for all that's right!
We'll fight with saints in light!
We'll fight in darkest night!
Although the battle's long
And we may weary grow.
Grant us Your wisdom, Lord,
That we Your peace may know.

Tunes: Invitation (Maker), Denby

Song 5.9-10
What is thy beloved more than another beloved,
O thou fairest among women?
what is thy beloved more than another beloved, that thou dost so charge us?
My beloved is white and ruddy,
the chiefest among ten thousand.

17th March.

10.10.10.10.

How Wonderful that by Faith I Can See.

1.
How wonderful that by faith I can see
The love eternal that God has for me.
Before the universe was brought to be,
The holy God had set His mark on me.

2.
How wonderful that He sent His own Son
Into this world where sin its course had run.
There on the cross, upon Golgotha's hill,
He bled and died God's purpose to fulfil.

3.
How wonderful that He rose from the grave
And, from the glory, He's mighty to save.
There, He is seated on God's righteous throne
Until He comes, with joy, to claim His own.

4.
How wonderful that I His face shall see!
How wonderful the love He'll pour on me!
How wonderful to share His glory bright!
How wonderful to live in heav'nly light!

Tunes: 10.10.10.10: Woodlands, Penetentia, Ellers.

Psalm 40.5-7

Many, O LORD my God, are thy wonderful works which thou hast done, and thy thoughts which are to us-ward:
they cannot be reckoned up in order unto thee:
if I would declare and speak of them, they are more than can be numbered.
Sacrifice and offering thou didst not desire; mine ears hast thou opened: burnt offering and sin offering hast thou not required.
Then said I, Lo, I come: in the volume of the book it is written of me…

18th March.

88.88D

Lord, When I Stand Before Thy Throne.

1.
Lord, when I stand before Thy "throne"
And see the things that I have done;
Thy righteous judgement, I shall own;
And claim the vict'ry Thou hast won.
Yes, though my work lacked faith that's real
And all my labours lacked Thy zeal;
Thou in Thy mercy shalt reveal
That which Thy love may always seal.

2.
Lord, when I stand before Thy throne,
Thy comeliness shall rest on me.
'Tis then, I'll know as I am known
'Tis then, I fully blessed shall be;
And when I see Thee as Thou art
Then thee I'll love with all my heart.
O Lord, with joy, I shall have part
In all Thy wisdom can impart.

3.
Lord, when I stand before Thy throne,
Then I shall see Thy majesty;
The Lamb who bore the cross alone
Is worthy of all love in me.
Lord, Thou shalt reign as King of kings
And earth her bounty to Thee brings;
While, in the shadow of Thy wings,
My spirit of Thy glory sings.

Tunes: Duane St., Sweet Hour, Nazareth.

2Corinthians 5.10
or we must all appear before the judgment seat of Christ; that every one may receive the things done in his body, according to that he hath done, whether it be good or bad.

19th March.

CMD.

We Who are Weary Come to You.

1. We who are weary come to You,
The living, loving Lord.
Our heavy burdens, You will bear
As You our cries have heard.
And so You give us rest, blest Lord,
The rest that gives us strength.
And for the honour of Your name
Yourself, we'll serve at length.

2. We who are weary, come to You;
Your yoke, with joy, we wear.
We learn from You, the lowly One
As in Your work, we share.
We find "grace" written in Your heart;
We find meekness in You.
And in the tasks, You set for us,
We find that You are true.

3. In You, we find pardon and peace
Along with joy and love.
We know You as our Saviour dear,
The Son from God above.
All honour, praise and glory be
To You upon the throne.
All riches, wisdom, pow'r and might
Be Yours, and Yours alone!

Tunes: All Saints, Release, Warrior, Bethlehem, Landas, Land of Rest,, Jesus is God.

Matthew 11.28-30
Come unto me, all ye that labour and are heavy laden, and I will give you rest.
Take my yoke upon you, and learn of me; for I am meek and lowly in heart: and ye shall find rest unto your souls.
For my yoke is easy, and my burden is light.

20th March.

65.65.

Patience!

1.
Patience! Quiet patience
For both young and old!
Patience! Quiet patience
Casts in Jesus' mould!

2.
Patience with the angry;
Patience with the loud;
Patience with the troubled;
Patience with the proud;

3.
Patience with the tearful;
Patience with the weak;
Patience with the weary;
Patience we shall seek!

4.
Patience! Quiet patience
Enduring and calm!
Patience! Quiet patience
Is a healing balm!

Tunes: Eudoxia, Quietude, Armentrout, Castle Eden, See the Shining Dewdrops, North Coates, Ernstein.

Romans 5.3-6
And not only so, but we glory in tribulations also: knowing that tribulation worketh patience;
and patience, experience; and experience, hope:
and hope maketh not ashamed;
because the love of God is shed abroad in our hearts by the Holy Ghost which is given unto us.
For when we were yet without strength, in due time Christ died for the ungodly.

21st March.

76.76.

We Come to Thee, our Father.

1.
We come to Thee, our Father,
To seek Thy holy mind.
Fill us with Thy great wisdom;
And help us to be kind.

2.
Open our eyes to see Thee
In Jesus Christ, our Lord.
And may our hearts behold Thee
Through all Thy works and word.

3.
May we be pure and honest,
Both faithful and discreet.
May we be strong in battle
And free from sin's deceit.

4.
Keep us from pride and anger;
Make us sincere and true.
Fill us with Thy compassion;
Mark us with Thy virtue.

5.
As led by Thy blest Spirit,
We'd honour Thee above.
Adoring, we would worship;
Expressing all our love.

Tunes: River City, Cara, Matrimony, Vulpius.

1Peter 1.22
Seeing ye have purified your souls in obeying the truth through the Spirit unto unfeigned love of the brethren, see that ye love one another with a pure heart fervently…

22nd March.

76.76D.

O Lord, We Would Be Zealous.

1.
O Lord, we would be zealous
In all our hands may do
Until that day of glory
When we Thyself shall view.
Oh, may our faith be strengthened,
And virtue mark our way;
Help us to grow more like Thee
Increasingly each day!

2.
O Lord, we would be like Thee
In all we say and do;
We'd mirror all Thy features
And all Thy grace pursue.
May self-control so guide us
That we may "all" endure;
May piety and kindness
Lead us to love that's pure.

3.
O Lord, we would be with Thee
And never leave Thy side;
Thy calling drew us to Thee -
Chosen to be Thy bride.
Please, help us to be faithful;
To be fruitful for Thee;
And seek that glorious entry
Into eternity.

Tunes: Ewing, Greenland, Lymington, Thornbury, Ellacombe, Mountain, Passion Chorale, St. Edith.

Colossians 3.17
And whatsoever ye do in word or deed, do all in the name of the Lord Jesus, giving thanks to God and the Father by him.

23rd March.

76.76D.

O Father, We'd Remember.

1.
O Father, we'd remember
Those happy hours and days
When in our joy and singing
We gave to You our praise.
The things we learned about You;
The service we have done;
All stemmed from our blest Saviour -
Your own beloved Son.

2.
The friendships You have fashioned;
The blessing from each trial;
The kindness of Your servants
Who went the extra mile;
The strength You gave in weakness;
The healing and the calm;
All lift our hearts in worship
To You in song and psalm.

3.
And so the year has ended;
Our hope is yet deferred!
The Son, whom we expected,
Is bound by Your blest word!
O Father, may this new year
Be that which sets Him free!
Then all Your grace and glory
In His dear face, we'll see!

Tunes: Greenland, St. Edith, Thornbury, St. Theodulph, Ewing, Lymington, Passion Chorale.

Acts 1.7
And he said unto them, It is not for you to know the times or the seasons, which the Father hath put in his own power.

24th March.

76.76D.

Eternal is Thy Goodness.

1.
Eternal is Thy goodness
That blesses us each day.
Eternal is Thy power
That keeps us in the way.
Eternal is Thy wisdom
That leads us all in light.
Eternal is Thy love
That makes our lives so bright.

2.
Eternal is Thy mercy
That meets our every need.
Eternal is Thy judgement
Poured out on pride and greed.
Eternal is the Godhead
Of Father, Spirit, Son.
Eternal is the glory
That Thou for us hast won.

3.
Eternal is Thy Being
The "I AM THAT I AM".
Eternal is Thy word
That tells us of the Lamb.
We praise Thee, God our Father,
For all that Thou hast done.
We'll worship Thee with gladness
As endless ages run.

Tunes: Lymington, Greenland, Mountain, Passion Chorale, St. Edith.

Romans 1.20
For the invisible things of him from the creation of the world are clearly seen, being understood by the things that are made, even his eternal power and Godhead; so that they are without excuse…

25th March.

CM.

We Seek Thy Wisdom From Above.

1.
We seek Thy wisdom from above;
The wisdom steeped in love.
The wisdom that is pure as light;
Wisdom that clears our sight.

2.
We seek Thy wisdom from above;
The wisdom steeped in love.
The wisdom that will peace possess;
Wisdom with gentleness.

3.
We seek Thy wisdom from above;
The wisdom steeped in love.
The wisdom that is just and fair;
Wisdom with all its care.

4.
We seek Thy wisdom from above;
The wisdom steeped in love.
The wisdom that good fruit must bare;
Wisdom with mercy rare.

5.
We seek Thy wisdom from above;
The wisdom steeped in love.
That righteousness may mark us here;
And peace remove all fear.

6.
Lord, Thou art Wisdom from above,
The Wisdom steeped in love.
Its aspects are all seen in Thee
And we would like Thee be.

Tunes: Westminster (Turle), Pisgah, Nativity, Beatitudo, Arlington, Tyrone, St. Agnes, Belmont, Irish.

James 1.13 and 3.17 and Proverbs 3.13
Who is a wise man and endued with knowledge among you? let him shew out of a good conversation his works with meekness of wisdom… But the wisdom that is from above is first pure, then peaceable, gentle, and easy to be intreated, full of mercy and good fruits, without partiality, and without hypocrisy. And the fruit of righteousness is sown in peace of them that make peace.

Happy is the man that findeth wisdom, and the man that getteth understanding.

26th March.

66.66D.

"I'll live! I Shall Not Die"

1.
"I'll live! I shall not die"
What wondrous words are these!
"I'll live! I shall not die"
The mighty God to please.
"I'll live! I shall not die"
His wonders to proclaim.
"I'll live! I shall not die"
I'll praise His holy name.

2.
I was sorely chastened,
But death turned back from me.
I was sorely chastened,
God's purposes to see.
I was sorely chastened,
That I might proven be.
I was sorely chastened,
By love He set on me.

3.
I will yet praise the Lord
In truth and righteousness.
I will yet praise the Lord
Who heard me in distress.
I will yet praise the Lord,
My salvation and song.
I will yet praise the Lord
For I, to Him, belong.

4.
Save now, O Lord, I pray,
Send us prosperity.
Save now, O Lord, I pray,
Thy glory we would see.
Save now, O Lord, I pray,
Reveal Thy light once more.
Save now, O Lord, I pray,
That mercy may endure.

Tunes: Denby, Invitation (Maker).

Psalm 118.15-23

The voice of rejoicing and salvation is in the tabernacles of the righteous: the right hand of the LORD doeth valiantly.

The right hand of the LORD is exalted: the right hand of the LORD doeth valiantly. I shall not die, but live, and declare the works of the LORD. The LORD hath chastened me sore: but he hath not given me over unto death.

Open to me the gates of righteousness: I will go into them, and I will praise the LORD: this gate of the LORD, into which the righteous shall enter. I will praise thee: for thou hast heard me, and art become my salvation. The stone which the builders refused is become the head stone of the corner.

This is the LORD'S doing; it is marvellous in our eyes.

27th March.

76.76.

Help Us to Give, Blest Father.

1. Help us to give, blest Father,
As You most freely gave
Your own dear Son to save us
And lift us from the grave.

2. Help us to give our parents
Honour and joy and care.
Help us to give our friends
The faithfulness we share.

3. Help us to give our teachers
Attention and respect;
Help us to give our neighbours
The peace that they expect.

4. Help us to give the lonely
The joy of friendliness;
Help us to give the grieving
Comfort in their distress.

5. Help us to give the doubting
The surety of Your word;
Help us to give the lowly
The guidance of our Lord.

6. Help us to give the poor
The means for which they strive;
Help us to give the weak
The power to survive.

7. Help us to give sad sinners
The wondrous words of life;
Help us to give those burdened
Relief from care and strife.

8. But most of all, blest Father,
Help us to give to You
All power and praise and glory,
And love, so justly due.

Tunes: 76.76: Cara, Vulpius. 76.76D: Webb, Day of Rest, St. Theodulph, Greenland (Haydn), Eden (Boston).

Acts 20.33-35.

I have coveted no man's silver, or gold, or apparel. Yea, ye yourselves know, that these hands have ministered unto my necessities, and to them that were with me.

I have shewed you all things, how that so labouring ye ought to support the weak, and to remember the words of the Lord Jesus, how he said, It is more blessed to give than to receive.

Matthew 10.7-8

And as ye go, preach, saying, The kingdom of heaven is at hand. Heal the sick, cleanse the lepers, raise the dead, cast out devils: freely ye have received, freely give.

28th March.

76.76D.

Lord Jesus, Stand Among Us.

1.
Lord Jesus, stand among us
In resurrection power
And let this time of worship
Be a most holy hour.
Lord, help us to remember
The path You trod
below;
And lead us to the cross
Where You were deigned to go.

2.
We see You in the emblems –
Unleavened bread and wine.
The bread speaks of Your body;
You're human and divine!
The wine tells us of blessing –
A contract sealed with blood.
The Spirit is the witness
Of its pure, cleansing flood.

3.
Lord Jesus, we remember
The cradle, cross and curse.
We joy in Your salvation
And praise You in our verse.
At God's right hand, we see
You
Seated upon His throne!
The splendour of Your glory
Proves You're the Cornerstone.

4.
All honour, praise and glory
Are Yours, blest Lord, above.
The truth of Your blest Spirit
Tells us of all Your love.
You're altogether lovely!
A man of heavenly worth!
We worship and adore You,
The Lord of heaven and earth!

Tunes: Passion Chorale, Ellacombe, Wolvercote, Aurelia, Greenland (Haydn).

Matthew 18.20-22

For where two or three are gathered together in my name, there am I in the midst of them. Then came Peter to him, and said, Lord, how oft shall my brother sin against me, and I forgive him? till seven times? Jesus saith unto him, I say not unto thee, Until seven times: but, Until seventy times seven.

1Corinthians 11,25

After the same manner also he took the cup, when he had supped, saying, This cup is the new testament in my blood: this do ye, as oft as ye drink it, in remembrance of me.

29th March.

76.76.

You See the Word, Blest Saviour.

1. You see the word, blest Saviour,
Sown in the hearts of men.
You seek the fruit it carries
That truth may live again.

2. There on the trodden pathway
The seed lies crushed and still.
Your word is there rejected
And Satan has his fill.

3. Upon the shallow topsoil,
The word takes root and grows;
The heat of persecution -
A false faith will expose.

4. Among the thorns, it's scattered
And battles to survive;
But faithless care and greed
Your light and love deprive.

5. But, look again, dear Saviour,
The seed in faith-filled hearts
Springs up with health and vigour,
All blessing it imparts.

6. Your Spirit drills, blest Saviour,
The seed in a ploughed field.
It grows to God's great glory
The fruit of faith to yield.

Tunes: Lymington, River City, Cara, Day of Rest, Greenland.

Matthew 13.3-8
And he spake many things unto them in parables, saying, Behold, a sower went forth to sow…But other fell into good ground, and brought forth fruit, some an hundredfold, some sixtyfold, some thirtyfold.

30th March.

66.66D.

"Hosanna!" Lord, We Cry.

1. "Hosanna!" Lord, we cry,
"So save us now!" we pray.
Our foes lie round about us
And hunt us down like prey!
The Stone that we rejected
Now comes in majesty!
His precious name, we bless,
And share His victory!

2. Your wondrous work's completed
You cast away our fear.
Rejoicing marks the moment
For You have drawn us near.
The Saviour You have sent us
Holds us in His blest hand.
The light of life, You give!
Your love will ever stand!

3. This is Your day, O Lord,
The day of righteousness.
Glory to You, we'll bring
Who always sought to bless.
So lift your heads, you gates,
The everlasting doors.
Your King will enter in;
The Son our soul adores.

Tunes: Lymington, British Grenadiers, Greenland, Ellacombe, St. Edith, Thornbury, Knowhead, Lancashire, Llangfyllin, Web.

Matthew 21.9
And the multitudes that went before,
and that followed, cried, saying,
Hosanna to the Son of David:
Blessed is he that cometh in the name of the Lord;
Hosanna in the highest.

31st March.

76.76D.

Lord Jesus, Lead the Singing.

1. Lord Jesus, lead the singing
Among Thine own while here.
Thy God is good and gracious
And drives away our fear.
O let us sing His praises
In accents loud and clear.
In distress and rejoicing
We know that He is near.

2. The Lord's our Rock and Helper
And ever takes our part.
Our foes shall quake before Him
And from our coasts depart.
Our trust is in the Lord
Who arms us for the fight.
Our trust is in the Lord;
We'll stand for what is right!

3. Lord Jesus, Thou'rt exalted
To His right hand above.
The Saviour of poor sinners
And Messenger of love.
God was Thy strength and song
As Thou this earth didst tread;
And now in glory bright,
Though art the church's Head.

4. The Stone despised, rejected,
The cross was Thine to bear.
Now risen and ascended
There is no-one so fair.
The house of God is growing
Under Thy hand of grace.
Yet, in the midst of glory,
Thou hast prepared our place.

5. This day of great rejoicing
Was by Thy Father made.
We bow to Him in worship;
The One by Thee displayed.
We'll shout our glad hosannas
When Thou dost come as King.
We'll own that Thou art worthy,
Our hearts, to Thee we'll bring.

Tunes: Thornbury, Passion Chorale, Webb, St. Edith, Greenland,

Hebrews 2.11-13
For both he that sanctifieth and they who are sanctified are all of one: for which cause he is not ashamed to call them brethren, saying,
I will declare thy name unto my brethren, in the midst of the church will I sing praise unto thee.
And again, I will put my trust in him. And again, Behold I and the children which God hath given me.

1st April.

66.66D.

I Need a Saviour, Lord.

1.
I need a Saviour, Lord,
For I am full of sin.
I need a Saviour, Lord,
To cleanse my soul within.
Your blood alone can save!
Can wash away sin's stain.
Your blood alone can save
And take away my pain.

2.
I need a Saviour, Lord,
To keep me in God's way.
I need a Saviour, Lord,
To still my fears each day.
Your rod alone can save;
Can beat the lion down.
Your rod alone can save;
Till I shall gain my crown.

3.
I need a Saviour, Lord,
My body to transform.
I need a Saviour, Lord,
Great wonders to perform.
Your power alone can save;
And lift us up above.
Your power alone can save
And acts for those You love!

4.
You are my Saviour, Lord,
There is no-one like You.
You are my Saviour, Lord,
Your beauty I would view.
Your blood, your rod and power
Make my salvation sure.
But it's love, only love
That prompts me to adore.

Tunes: Denby, Invitation (Maker).

Romans 10.9-10
That if thou shalt confess with thy mouth the Lord Jesus, and shalt believe in thine heart that God hath raised him from the dead, thou shalt be saved. For with the heart man believeth unto righteousness; and with the mouth confession is made unto salvation.

1John 1.7-9
But if we walk in the light, as he is in the light, we have fellowship one with another, and the blood of Jesus Christ his Son cleanseth us from all sin.
If we say that we have no sin, we deceive ourselves, and the truth is not in us. If we confess our sins, he is faithful and just to forgive us our sins, and to cleanse us from all unrighteousness.

2nd April.

76.76D.

Let's Shout our Glad Hosannas.

(A hymn for the Jew when Christ shall come as King).

1. Let's shout our glad hosannas
To Christ, our Lord and King;
For He has come to save us!
To Him our praise we bring.
In the LORD's name, He cometh
Our enemies to slay;
And through His power and glory
We shall be free this day!

2. The Christ, we once rejected,
Shall sit upon the throne;
And of the house of our God,
He is the Corner Stone.
The earth shall cease her groaning
And as the rose shall bloom;
While peace shall fill the valleys
With life's own sweet perfume.

3. God's Son shall hold the sceptre;
In righteousness, He'll reign.
Oppression will be banished!
The poor their needs shall gain!
All pride will be abolished;
And war shall be no more.
The King of grace and glory
Shall evermore endure!

Tunes: Lymington, Day of Rest, Thornbury, Greenland, Ellacombe, Ahnfelt, Mountain, Passion Chorale.

Psalm 118.22-26

The stone which the builders refused is become the head stone of the corner. This is the LORD'S doing; it is marvellous in our eyes… Blessed be he that cometh in the name of the LORD: we have blessed you out of the house of the LORD.

3rd April.

76.76D.

It is Your Power, Blest Father.

1.
It is Your power, blest Father,
That keeps me close to You;
And by the faith You've given
Salvation I shall view.
So lead me on, blest Father,
Let me Your presence know;
And grant me this assurance,
You'll never let me go.

2.
It is Your peace, blest Father,
That keeps my heart and mind.
It comes through the Lord Jesus
Who gentle is, and kind.
So take my hand, blest Father,
That I Your love may know;
And grant me this assurance,
You'll never let me go.

3.
Faithful You art, blest Father,
From evil me to keep.
And You with faith shalt gird me
That I may stand, not weep.
So strengthen me, blest Father,
That I Your arm may know;
And grant me this assurance,
You'll never let me go.

4.
Exceeding joy, blest Father,
Is found in You above.
When I am brought before You
As one rescued by love.
And faultless in Your presence,
I shall Your glory know.
There I shall raise this chorus,
You did not let me go.

Tunes: Greenland, St. Edith, Webb.

Psalm 27.8-11

When thou saidst, Seek ye my face; my heart said unto thee, Thy face, LORD, will I seek. hide not thy face far from me; put not thy servant away in anger: thou hast been my help; leave me not, neither forsake me, O God of my salvation. When my father and my mother forsake me, then the LORD will take me up. Teach me thy way, O LORD, and lead me in a plain path, because of mine enemies.

Romans 15.33 and 5.1

Now the God of peace be with you all. Amen.

Therefore being justified by faith, we have peace with God through our Lord Jesus Christ…

4th April.

76.76D.

I Cannot Do Without Thee.

1. I cannot do without Thee
My Shepherd, Priest and King.
I need Thy strength and wisdom
And love that makes me sing.
'Tis then the world will see
Thee
In all humility.
'Tis then the world will know
Thee:
Thyself, in me, they'll see.

2.
I cannot do without Thee,
My Shepherd in life's way;
The path is long and weary;
I need Thee every day.
Thy staff gives me assurance
Along the narrow trail.
Thy rod gives me the
knowledge
That enemies will fail.

3. I cannot do without Thee,
My Great High Priest on high;
Once, here as Man of Sorrows,
Thou for my sin didst die.
Now, knowing all my
weakness,
Draw me close to Thy breast.
And through Thy loving
kindness,
Grant me Thy peace and rest.

4. I cannot do without Thee,
The Lord of hosts – my King.
I'll humbly bow before Thee
And songs of worship bring.
Thy glory is resplendent!
Thy majesty's sublime!
Thine eye is ever for us
For Thou hast made us Thine!

Tunes: Thornbury, Ewing, Ahnfelt, Day of Rest, Greenland, Lymington.

John 10.11

I am the good shepherd: the good shepherd giveth his life for the sheep.

Hebrews 13.20

Now the God of peace, that brought again from the dead our Lord Jesus, that great shepherd of the sheep, through the blood of the everlasting covenant…

1Peter 5.4

And when the chief Shepherd shall appear, ye shall receive a crown of glory that fadeth not away.

5th April.

8.11.8.11.8.10.8.9.

God Brought Me Up! He Brought Me Up!

1.
God brought me up! He brought me up
From an horrible pit; from the miry clay.
God brought me up! He brought me up
From the depths of death; from the trench of sin.
God set my feet! He set my feet
On the firmest rock; in the steadfast way
God set my feet! He set my feet
On Salvation's ground; life's path within.

2.
God tuned my mouth! He tuned my mouth
With the greatest song; with that lively strain.
God tuned my mouth! He tuned my mouth
To speak His worth; to praise His name.
And so you see! And so you see
The music in me; and the joy to gain.
And so you see! And so you see
The peace of trust - His blessings claim!

Tunes: None known.

Psalm 40.1-6

To the chief Musician, A Psalm of David. I waited patiently for the LORD; and he inclined unto me, and heard my cry. He brought me up also out of an horrible pit, out of the miry clay, and set my feet upon a rock, and established my goings. And he hath put a new song in my mouth, even praise unto our God: many shall see it, and fear, and shall trust in the LORD.

Blessed is that man that maketh the LORD his trust, and respecteth not the proud, nor such as turn aside to lies. Many, O LORD my God, are thy wonderful works which thou hast done, and thy thoughts which are to us-ward: they cannot be reckoned up in order unto thee: if I would declare and speak of them, they are more than can be numbered.

Sacrifice and offering thou didst not desire; mine ears hast thou opened: burnt offering and sin offering hast thou not required.

6th April.

CMD.

Thy King Is Set, Most Blessèd God.

1.
Thy King is set, most blessèd God,
Upon Thy holy hill.
There with Thy goodness ever blessed
His throne, Thy power shall fill.
Thou'st crowned Him with the purest gold
And gave Him length of days.
His joy, it is, to trust in Thee
And walk in all Thy ways.

2.
In Thy salvation, I rejoice
And praise Thee in the way.
While in Thy mercy, I will trust
Most surely, day by day.
And as I suffer here below
With tears of grief and pain;
Yet, I shall share His royal throne
And with my Saviour reign.

Tunes: Jesus is God, Bethlehem, Landas, No King But Christ, Warrior.

Psalm 2.1-11

Why do the heathen rage, and the people imagine a vain thing? The kings of the earth set themselves, and the rulers take counsel together, against the LORD, and against his anointed, saying, let us break their bands asunder, and cast away their cords from us. He that sitteth in the heavens shall laugh: the Lord shall have them in derision. Then shall he speak unto them in his wrath, and vex them in his sore displeasure. Yet have I set my king upon my holy hill of Zion. I will declare the decree: the LORD hath said unto me, Thou art my Son; this day have I begotten thee. Ask of me, and I shall give thee the heathen for thine inheritance, and the uttermost parts of the earth for thy possession. Thou shalt break them with a rod of iron; thou shalt dash them in pieces like a potter's vessel. Be wise now therefore, O ye kings: be instructed, ye judges of the earth.Serve the LORD with fear, and rejoice with trembling.

7th April.

CMD.

As a Bright Light, Send Out Your Truth.

1. As a bright light, send out Your truth
To lead me in the way.
O bring me to Your presence, Lord,
For there, it is, I'd stay.
To Your own table, I would go
Where I'd remember You.
My joy, yea, my delight expressed
In worship sweet and true.

2. My soul is thirsting for You, Lord,
For You're my strength and stay;
And as a deer for water pants
Is my desire to pray.
Though tears have been my food all day
And troubled is my soul;
I'll worship in Your presence, Lord,
For You have made me whole.

3. One day, I'll see You face to face,
My Lord, my Priest, my King;
And in Your presence, I shall give
Myself, an offering.
With hymns and songs and shouts of praise
The span of heaven shall ring.
You are the Object of my joy;
To You, my love, I bring.

Tunes: No King But Christ, Warrior, Landas, Jesus is God.

Psalm 16.6-9
The lines are fallen unto me in pleasant places; yea, I have a goodly heritage. I will bless the LORD, who hath given me counsel: my reins also instruct me in the night seasons. I have set the LORD always before me: because he is at my right hand, I shall not be moved. Therefore my heart is glad, and my glory rejoiceth: my flesh also shall rest in hope.

8th April.

87.87D.

Father of Lights, our Blessed God.

1.
Father of Lights, our blest God,
Evermore Thy name endures!
Father of Christ - living Lord,
Evermore Thy name endures!
Father, Source of every thing,
Evermore Thy name endures!
Father of most tender mercies,
Evermore Thy name endures!

2.
Father of both peace and glory,
Evermore Thy name endures!
Father of all, who dwells in us,
Evermore Thy name endures!
Father of both grace and goodness,
Evermore Thy name endures!
Father too of consolation,
Evermore Thy name endures!

3.
Father of life and of spirits,
Evermore Thy name endures!
Father of all love and truth,
Evermore Thy name endures!
Father in Thee wisdom dwells
Evermore Thy name endures!
Father robed in righteousness,
Evermore Thy name endures!

Tunes: Beecher, Hymn to Joy.

Psalm 135.13-14 and Psalm 72.17
Thy name, O LORD, endureth for ever; and thy memorial, O LORD, throughout all generations….His name shall endure for ever:

9th April.

12.11.12.11.

Oh, the Riches of Wisdom and Knowledge of Thee.

1.
Oh, the riches of wisdom and knowledge of Thee
Are deeper, O God, that the deepest, blue sea.
Thy judgments are true and most righteous, I see
Thy thoughts and Thy ways are far too high for me;

2.
For all things come from Thee, and through Thee as well,
And all things are to Thee and that I can tell.
So to Thee the glory for ever belongs.
And for Thy pure presence, my yearning soul longs.

Tune: Jewels

Romans 11.33-36
O the depth of the riches both of the wisdom and knowledge of God! how unsearchable are his judgments, and his ways past finding out! For who hath known the mind of the Lord? or who hath been his counsellor? Or who hath first given to him, and it shall be recompensed unto him again? For of him, and through him, and to him, are all things: to whom be glory for ever. Amen.

Revelation 5.11-12
And I beheld, and I heard the voice of many angels round about the throne and the beasts and the elders: and the number of them was ten thousand times ten thousand, and thousands of thousands; saying with a loud voice, Worthy is the Lamb that was slain to receive power, and riches, and wisdom, and strength, and honour, and glory, and blessing.

Psalm 104
O LORD, how manifold are thy works! in wisdom hast thou made them all: the earth is full of thy riches. So is this great and wide sea, wherein are things creeping innumerable, both small and great beasts.

Romans 16.27
To God only wise, be glory through Jesus Christ for ever. Amen.

10th April.

10.7.10.7.

Give Us the Will to Walk in Light.

1. Give us the will to walk in light
So Thy glory may be seen.
Empower us to act for Thee
In this ungodly scene.

2. Add Thy great wisdom to our hearts
That we Thy mind might glean
Make us firm in faith and love
That we on Thee might lean.

3. Give us the strength to serve Thee here;
May all Thy work be done!
Give us the grace Thy word to spread
And glorify Thy Son.

4. O, grant us peace within our souls
When clouds of darkness rise;
And lead us on to that blest home
So far beyond the skies.

Tunes: Golden Key.

1John 1.7-10

But if we walk in the light, as he is in the light, we have fellowship one with another, and the blood of Jesus Christ his Son cleanseth us from all sin.
If we say that we have no sin, we deceive ourselves, and the truth is not in us. If we confess our sins, he is faithful and just to forgive us our sins, and to cleanse us from all unrighteousness.
If we say that we have not sinned, we make him a liar, and his word is not in us.

John 11.9-10

Jesus answered, Are there not twelve hours in the day? If any man walk in the day, he stumbleth not, because he seeth the light of this world. But if a man walk in the night, he stumbleth, because there is no light in him.

11th April.

CM.

Dear Lord, Your Word is Like a Fire.

1. Dear Lord, Your word is like a fire
Trying our lives each day.
As gold refined our faith would be
Your glory to display.

2. Your word is like a hammer, Lord,
It breaks the rock in two.
So every barrier to life
Is broken, Lord, by You.

3. Your word is like that precious seed
Sown in the hearts of men.
The good soil by Your Spirit tilled
Brings forth its fruit again.

4. Your word is like a two-edged sword;
With energy and power.
It reads our motives and our thoughts
And keeps us hour by hour.

5. Your word is like a lamp, blest Lord,
It leads us day by day.
And when the path is rough and steep
It lightens up the way.

6. O Lord, we bless You for that word -
The word of truth and grace.
We thank You that it has displayed
Your glories in Christ's face.

Tunes: Irish, Nativity, Pisgah, Beatitudo, Bishopthorpe, Belmont, Glasgow.

Jeremiah 23:29

Is not my word like as a fire? saith the LORD; and like a hammer that breaketh the rock in pieces?

12th April.

87.87.

Come, Ye Saints, the Sight is Glorious.

1.
Come, ye saints, the sight is glorious,
See the Lord in triumph rise!
He it is who made and saved us;
Our Redeemer, just and wise.

2.
We're the people of His pasture;
He the Shepherd who once died.
Through His death, we are forgiven;
By His life, we're justified.

3.
Come into His holy presence,
Bringing glory to His name.
His kindness is everlasting,
And His love remains the same.

Tunes: Gott Wills Machen, Sussex, Oxford (Stainer), Cross of Jesus.

Ezekiel 34.12-16

As a shepherd seeketh out his flock in the day that he is among his sheep that are scattered; so will I seek out my sheep, and will deliver them out of all places where they have been scattered in the cloudy and dark day. And I will bring them out from the people, and gather them from the countries, and will bring them to their own land, and feed them upon the mountains of Israel by the rivers, and in all the inhabited places of the country. I will feed them in a good pasture, and upon the high mountains of Israel shall their fold be: there shall they lie in a good fold, and in a fat pasture shall they feed upon the mountains of Israel. I will feed my flock, and I will cause them to lie down, saith the Lord GOD.

Isaiah 40.11

He shall feed his flock like a shepherd: he shall gather the lambs with his arm, and carry them in his bosom, and shall gently lead those that are with young.

13th April.

76.76D.

Time was Filled with Trouble.

1.
That time was filled with trouble
When Thou to earth didst come.
The Babe of Bethl'em's manger
Thou art God's lovely Son.
Born of the virgin maiden
In true humanity.
Yet, sent by God the Father,
We see divinity.

2.
The cross held all the trouble
That man's sin had accrued.
'Twas there Thy God forsook Thee
In dreadful solitude.
Thy soul was made an offering
That sin might be destroyed.
There, Thou didst take the judgement
That grace might be deployed.

3.
The gate of hope was opened
By Thy great sacrifice.
Our liberty was granted
As Thou didst pay the price.
We wait for Thy blest coming
With Thee, we'd have our part.
Forever, Thou'rt the object
Of our adoring heart.

4.
The rest of God remaineth
And we may enter in;
For Thou has drawn us to Him
By vanquishing our sin.
In heaven, His peace is flowing;
And mercy marks His throne.
His joy is never ending
Where Thy dear name is known.

Tunes: Lymington, Aurelia, Greenland (Haydn), Thornbury, St. Edith.

Hebrews 4.3-5 and Hebrews 4.9-10
For we which have believed do enter into rest, as he said,
As I have sworn in my wrath, if they shall enter into my rest: although
the works were finished from the foundation of the world.
For he spake in a certain place of the seventh day on this wise,
And God did rest the seventh day from all his works.
And in this place again, If they shall enter into my rest...
There remaineth therefore a rest to the people of God.
For he that is entered into his rest,
he also hath ceased from his own works,
as God did from his.

14th April.

CMD.

Marvellous Mercies, O My God.

1.
Marvellous mercies, O my God,
Are found in Thee alone.
Mercies that saved my sinful soul
And made me all Thine own.
So take my body, blessed Lord,
A holy offering;
And may my life be Thine to live
Through joy or suffering.

2.
Renew my mind, most blessèd Lord,
That I the world may shun;
My thinking by Thy power transform;
And Thy will shall be done.
Its goodness shall assure my soul
In every circumstance;
Its counsel is most wise and true;
And shall my life enhance.

Tunes: No King But Christ, Land of Rest, Landas, Jesus is God, Bethlehem, Warrior, Tyrol.

Romans 12.1-6
I beseech you therefore, brethren, by the mercies of God, that ye present your bodies a living sacrifice, holy, acceptable unto God, which is your reasonable service. And be not conformed to this world: but be ye transformed by the renewing of your mind, that ye may prove what is that good, and acceptable, and perfect, will of God.
For I say, through the grace given unto me, to every man that is among you, not to think of himself more highly than he ought to think; but to think soberly, according as God hath dealt to every man the measure of faith.
For as we have many members in one body, and all members have not the same office: So we, being many, are one body in Christ, and every one members one of another.

15th April.

CM.

Banished by Thee, O Lord, I see.

1. Banished by Thee, O Lord, I see
Myself, by sin, undone.
A flaming sword now keeps the way
Man's judgement has begun.

2. Dark Death - the wages paid by sin,
Seeks out my life to take;
And in a moment of despair
Right thoughts in me awake.

3. Thou gav'st Thine only Son to die;
Made sin upon the tree.
And through His blood so freely shed
Thy cleansing love I see.

4. O Lord, I'd trust His precious name
And own for me, He died.
I know He bore away my sins
When He was crucified.

5. Accepted in Thy lovely Son,
I bow before Thy throne.
Eternal life is mine to claim
In Christ, in Christ alone!

6. The Tree of Life is there for me
Its fruits shall grow in me.
And in the wonder of Thy home
I'll live eternally.

Tunes: Pisgah, Abridge, Beatitudo, Bishopthorpe, Irish.

John 3.16
For God so loved the world,
that he gave his only begotten Son, that whosoever believeth in him
should not perish, but have everlasting life.

16th April.

CM.

Sion, Mountain of our God.

1. Sion, the mountain of our God,
In faith, we come to Thee.
Exalted in the heav'ns above,
God's glory shines from Thee.

2. Jerusalem, city of peace,
In faith, we come to Thee.
The cross of Christ has brought us here;
His love has set us free.

3. Angels of our most mighty Lord,
In faith we, to you, come.
We share your ministry of grace
And joy in God's dear Son.

4. Church of the firstborn writ in heav'n
In faith, we come to Thee.
We worship Christ our Lord and Head
And praise His victory.

5. Our God, the righteous Judge of all,
To Thee, in faith, we come.
We know Thee as our Father here
Through all that Christ has done.

6. Spirits of men, just and complete,
In faith, we come to you.
In days gone by, your lives we see
And all your service too.

7. Lord Jesus Christ, our Go-between,
In faith, we come to Thee.
Seated at God's right hand on high
Thy majesty, we see.

8. O, blood of sprinkling, precious blood,
In faith we, to Thee, come.
The value of Christ's sacrifice
Is that which makes us one.

Tunes: Westminster (Turle), Pisgah, Belmont, Nativity, Tyrone.

Hebrews 12.22-23

But ye are come unto mount Sion, and unto the city of the living God, the heavenly Jerusalem, and to an innumerable company of angels, to the general assembly and church of the firstborn, which are written in heaven, and to God the Judge of all, and to the spirits of just men made perfect,

17th April.

66.66D.

You Are My Great Shepherd.

1.
You are my great Shepherd
Providing all for me.
So I shall never want
Such is Your care for me.
Your hands provide the rest
Of pleasant pastures green.
Your wisdom leads me on
By waters still and clean.

2.
Your love restores my soul
When I have turned away.
Your Spirit draws me back
When I have gone astray.
For Your name's sake, You guide
My soul in righteousness.
Your presence is my joy
When I'm in deep distress.

3.
Your rod and staff keep me.
No evil shall I fear.
A table You prepare
Though enemies are near.
You cleanse my head with oil
Like prophet, priest and king.
Your blessings flood my cup
To You my heart I bring.

4.
Soon, I shall dwell with You
In that bright scene above.
There I, Your face, shall see
And know Your pow'r and love.
Your mercy and goodness
Shall always follow me!
Your mercy and goodness
Shall be my praise and plea!

Tunes: 66.66D Invitation (Maker), Denby.

Psalm 23
A Psalm of David.
The LORD is my shepherd; I shall not want.
He maketh me to lie down in green pastures: he leadeth me beside the still waters.
He restoreth my soul: he leadeth me in the paths of righteousness for his name's sake.
Yea, though I walk through the valley of the shadow of death, I will fear no evil: for thou art with me; thy rod and thy staff they comfort me.
Thou preparest a table before me in the presence of mine enemies: thou anointest my head with oil; my cup runneth over.
Surely goodness and mercy shall follow me all the days of my life: and I will dwell in the house of the LORD for ever.

18th April.

88.88D.

Born to Sing of Our Creator.

1. Born to sing of our Creator;
Born to sing of all His power;
He has measured every mountain
Formed the sun and wind and shower.
Mark the chain of endless ages
Formed by His direct command!
Mark the span of heaven's glory
And all else that He has planned.

2. Born to sing of our Redeemer!
Born to sing of matchless grace!
He once left His throne in heav'n
That we all might see God's face!
Mark His life of deep devotion;
See Him carry grief and shame;
Mark the sacrifice appointed;
Worship Him, the Lord the Same!

3. Born to sing of God's salvation;
Born to sing of sins forgiven;
He chose us in His Beloved;
And has blessed us in His Son.
Mark that home of heavenly splendour
By our Lord for us prepared!
Mark the time of God's appointing
When that dwelling place is shared.

Tunes: Hymn to Joy, Here is Love, Beecher, Deerhurst, Shipton.

Isaiah 40.13
Who hath measured the waters in the hollow of his hand, and meted out heaven with the span, and comprehended the dust of the earth in a measure, and weighed the mountains in scales, and the hills in a balance? Who hath directed the Spirit of the LORD, or being his counsellor hath taught him?

19th April.

77.77.

Lord, By Love My Heart You Won.

1.
Lord, by love, my heart You won;
Lord, mould me just like Your Son;
Lord, Your Spirit's work be done;
May the race of faith be run.

2.
Lord, for ever in me dwell;
Lord, by my side - all is well;
Lord, before me - fill my sight,
Let me see Your glorious light.

3.
Lord, in sorrow, comfort me;
Lord, in peril, my strength be;
Lord, in conflict, be my shield;
To Your will help me to yield.

Tunes: Buckland, St Prisca, St. Bees.

Psalm 46.1-7 and 10-11
To the chief Musician for the sons of Korah, A Song upon Alamoth. God is our refuge and strength, a very present help in trouble.
Therefore will not we fear, though the earth be removed, and though the mountains be carried into the midst of the sea; though the waters thereof roar and be troubled, though the mountains shake with the swelling thereof. Selah.
There is a river, the streams whereof shall make glad the city of God, the holy place of the tabernacles of the most High.God is in the midst of her; she shall not be moved: God shall help her, and that right early.
The heathen raged, the kingdoms were moved: he uttered his voice, the earth melted.The LORD of hosts is with us; the God of Jacob is our refuge. Selah…
Be still, and know that I am God: I will be exalted among the heathen, I will be exalted in the earth. The LORD of hosts is with us; the God of Jacob is our refuge. Selah.

20th April.

CM.

'Twas in the Womb of Mary Mild.

1.
'Twas in the womb of Mary mild
Your body was prepared.
The body You would freely give
In love You always shared.

2.
'Twas in Gethsemane of old,
Where sorrow gripped Your soul,
Submitting to Your Father's will,
You bowed to His control.

3.
'Twas on the cruel cross of old
Your spirit was released
Into Your Father's precious hands
That joy might be increased.

4.
Your spirit, soul and body, Lord,
Your manhood proved below.
And now eternally in heav'n
God's blessings You bestow.

Tunes: CM: Beatitudo, Pisgah, St. Agnes, Belmont. CMD: Bethlehem, Ishpeming, Land of Rest, No King But Christ, Release.

Hebrews 10.5-9
Wherefore when he cometh into the world, he saith, Sacrifice and offering thou wouldest not, but a body hast thou prepared me:In burnt offerings and sacrifices for sin thou hast had no pleasure. Then said I, Lo, I come (in the volume of the book it is written of me,) to do thy will, O God. Above when he said, Sacrifice and offering and burnt offerings and offering for sin thou wouldest not, neither hadst pleasure therein; which are offered by the law; then said he, Lo, I come to do thy will, O God. He taketh away the first, that he may establish the second.

21st April.

76.76.

As Thy Redeemed, Lord Jesus.

1.
As Thy redeemed, Lord Jesus,
We would remember Thee,
Until that day, Lord Jesus,
Thou'lt come to set us free.

2.
We see Thee in the Glory,
The Father's great delight.
We trace Thine own down-
stooping
To meet us in our plight.

3.
The manger, we remember,
Where swaddled Thou wast
laid.
Emmanuel, God with us,
In this small world Thou'st
made.

4.
We gauge Thy love's one
object
To do Thy Father's will.
Hated, despised, rejected,
His plan Thou wouldst fulfil.

5.
The garden, we remember
Where Thou prostrate didst
fall.
Thine agony and anguish
Thy faithfulness recall.

6.
The cross, with all its passion,
The curse of God laid
bare.
For in those hours of darkness
Thy soul was made sin there.

7. 'Tis here, we pause and
wonder
At love so vast and free.
'Tis here, with hearts adoring,
We gladly bow to Thee.

Tunes: 76.76: Cara, Vulpius, Matrimony, River City 76.76D: Webb, Thornbury, St. Theodulph, Aurelia, Penlan, St. Edith, Ellacombe.

2Timothy 2.8-12

Remember that Jesus Christ of the seed of David was raised from the dead according to my gospel: wherein I suffer trouble, as an evil doer, even unto bonds; but the word of God is not bound.
Therefore I endure all things for the elect's sakes, that they may also obtain the salvation which is in Christ Jesus with eternal glory.
It is a faithful saying: For if we be dead with him, we shall also live with him: if we suffer, we shall also reign with him.

22nd April.

66.66.

When He Brings Forth His Own.

1.
When He brings forth His own
The people of His choice
Praise ye! Praise ye the Lord!
Praise Him with heart and
voice.

2.
When His goodness is shown
And His mercies are seen
Praise ye! Praise ye the Lord!
On His blest bosom lean.

3.
When His people are freed
And brought back to their land
Praise ye! Praise ye the Lord!
For this is what He planned.

4.
When broken hearts are healed
And bleeding wounds are
bound
Praise ye! Praise ye the Lord!
Praise Him while He is found.

5.
When barren - children bear,
And keep their house and home
Praise ye! Praise ye the Lord!
And never from Him
roam.

6.
When men delight in Him
Obeying His commands
Praise ye! Praise ye the Lord!
Lift up your holy hands.

7.
When poor are raised from dust
And needy souls supplied;
Praise ye! Praise ye the Lord!
And in His word abide.

8.
When sinners are devoured
And wicked are no
more
Praise ye! Praise ye the Lord!
His blessèd name adore.

Tunes: 12.12.12.12: Corbet, Lausanne, Harvington. 66.66D: Denby, Invitation. 6.6.6.6: Eccles, Holy Guide, Ibstone, St. Cecilia (Hayne).

Matthew 11.4-6
Jesus answered and said unto them,
Go and shew John again those things which ye do hear and see: the blind receive their sight, and the lame walk, the lepers are cleansed, and the deaf hear, the dead are raised up, and the poor have the gospel preached to them.
And blessed is he, whosoever shall not be offended in me.

23rd April.

CM.

As Members of Thy Body, Lord.

1.
As members of Thy body, Lord,
We're by Thy Spirit one.
We thank Thee for this
fellowship,
Through all that Thou hast
done.

2.
As members of Thy body, Lord,
We praise Thy God above.
He's given us a special place
Along with gifts of love.

3.
As members of Thy body, Lord,
On each we must depend.
And all are honoured by
Thyself
In work Thou dost commend.

4.
As members of Thy body, Lord,
We care for every
one.
The sorrow and rejoicing,
Lord,
We share in unison.

5.
As members of Thy body, Lord,
We bear our gifts with joy.
May each and every one of us
In love those gifts employ.

6.
As members of Thy body, Lord,
We by Thyself are led.
Give us the strength to do Thy
will –
Submitting to our Head.

Tunes: Pisgah, Belmont, Arlington, Abridge, Beatitudo, Christmas Eve, Irish, Nativity, St. Agnes.

1Corinthians 12.12

For as the body is one, and hath many members, and all the members of that one body, being many, are one body: so also is Christ. for by one Spirit are we all baptized into one body, whether we be Jews or Gentiles, whether we be bond or free; and have been all made to drink into one Spirit. For the body is not one member, but many. If the foot shall say, Because I am not the hand, I am not of the body; is it therefore not of the body? And if the ear shall say, Because I am not the eye, I am not of the body; is it therefore not of the body? If the whole body were an eye, where were the hearing? If the whole were hearing, where were the smelling? But now hath God set the members every one of them in the body, as it hath pleased him.

24th April.

66.66D.

There is One Body, Lord.

1.
There is one body, Lord,
The church for which thou'st died;
There is one body, Lord,
God's temple and Thy bride.
There is one Spirit, Lord,
Who binds us in Thy grace.
There is one Spirit, Lord,
Who shows us Thy blest face.

2.
There is one hope, blest Lord,
Thy coming with a shout.
There is one hope, blest Lord,
We shall not fear or doubt.
Jesus, Thou art the Lord
Who rose up from the grave.
Jesus, Thou art the Lord -
Mighty art Thou to save.

3.
There is one faith, blest Lord,
The faith that rests in Thee.
There is one faith, blest Lord,
By which we are set free.
There is one baptism
In which we died with Thee.
There is one baptism
Showing we side with Thee.

4.
There is one Father, Lord,
The Spring and Source of all.
There is one Father, Lord,
And we have heard His call.
So give us grace to live
In holy unity
Until that day of days
When with Thee we shall be.

Tunes: 12.12.12.12: Corbet, Lausanne, Harvington. :66.66D: Denby, Invitation (Maker).

Ephesians 4.4-8
There is one body, and one Spirit, even as ye are called in one hope of your calling;
one Lord, one faith, one baptism,
One God and Father of all, who is above all, and through all, and in you all.
But unto every one of us is given grace according to the measure of the gift of Christ.
Wherefore he saith,
When he ascended up on high, he led captivity captive, and gave gifts unto men.

25th April.

CMD.

Lord Jesus, Precious Corner Stone.

1. Lord Jesus, precious Corner Stone,
With joy, we worship Thee,
Once tried by Satan and the world,
You served God faithfully.
And though refused by builders here
Thy God exalted Thee.
He set Thee at the corner's head
And builds His house from Thee.

2. Lord Jesus, Thou art Lord of all,
The Chosen, Living Stone.
As blood-bought souls, we're sanctified,
We have been made Thine own.
Now living stones, on Thee, we rest
As our Foundation sure
A holy priesthood and God's house,
Our praise is prompt and pure.

3. Lord Jesus, our Shepherd, Thou art,
The Stone of Israel.
Lead us along the narrow way;
And all our fears dispel.
Feed us with Thy most precious word
And in our poor hearts dwell.
Let all Thy goodness and mercy
Show us that all is well.

Tunes: Bethlehem, Land of Rest, Forest Green, Ishpeming, Jesus is God, No King But Christ, Tyrol, Warrior.

1Peter 1.5
Ye also, as lively stones,
are built up a spiritual house,
an holy priesthood,
to offer up spiritual sacrifices,
acceptable to God by Jesus Christ.

26th April.

CM.

Believe His Words and Sing His Praise.

1.
Believe His words and sing His praise,
His name's Immanuel!
The Son of God who came to earth
As man with Man to dwell.

2.
Believe His words and sing His praise
For God's Right Arm is He.
Stretched forth in grace, He died for us;
His blood now sets us free.

3.
Believe His words and sing His praise
For He is Lord of all.
The powers of darkness He cast down
His mighty strength recall.

4.
Believe His words and sing His praise
He is the Cornerstone.
Refused by men, He sits above
A Prince upon God's throne.

5.
Believe His words and sing His praise
The Morning Star is He.
Soon, He will call us to Himself
And His dear face we'll see.

Tunes: Pisgah, Westminster (Turle), Nativity, St. Edmund (Hoyte).

Isaiah 51:5

My righteousness is near; my salvation is gone forth, and mine arms shall judge the people; the isles shall wait upon me, and on mine arm shall they trust.

27th April.

CMD.

Co-equal With th'Eternal God.

1.
Co-equal with th'eternal God,
Thou art the Source of all.
Creator of the universe,
We would Thy stoop recall.
We see Thee in a manger laid,
God here upon this earth.
We see Thee in the temple courts
Where men found out Thy worth.

2.
Co-equal with th'eternal God,
Thou art the Lord of all.
The Father's well beloved Son -
We would Thy path recall.
We see Thee there at Jordan's bank
Baptized with all Thine own.
We see Thee on the mountainside
Praying to God - alone.

3.
Co-equal with th'eternal God,
Thy name is Wonderful.
Eternal King and great I AM,
We would Thy pow'r recall.
We see Thee at Bethesda's pool
Healing a feeble soul.
We see Thee in a servant's form
Making the diseased whole.

4.
Co-equal with th'eternal God,
Thou art the Head of all.
The Amen and the First and Last -
We would Thy heart recall.
(PTO).

We see Thee in the upper room
Where love rested on Thee;
We see Thee in Gethsemane
In prayerful agony.

5.
Co-equal with th'eternal God,
Thou art the Heir of all.
The Rod of Jesse, David's Lord,
Thy pain we would recall.
We see Thee on that shameful tree
Where sin, Thy soul was made.
We see Thee in the stone-sealed tomb
For grace must be displayed.

6.
Co-equal with th'eternal God,
Thou art immutable.
Redeemer of the souls of men -
We would Thy name recall.
We love Thee, Jesus, for the worth
Which in Thyself we see.
We praise Thee for the mighty work
By which we are made free.

Tunes: Landas, Jesus is God, No King But Christ, Land of Rest.

John 1.1-3
In the beginning was the Word, and the Word was with God, and the Word was God. The same was in the beginning with God. All things were made by him; and without him was not any thing made that was made.

Philippians 2.5-6
Let this mind be in you, which was also in Christ Jesus:
Who, being in the form of God, thought it not robbery to be equal with God…

But unto the Son he saith, Thy throne, O God, is for ever and ever: a sceptre of righteousness is the sceptre of thy kingdom.

28th April.

CM.

We Hear Thy gracious Word, Blest Lord.

1. We hear Thy gracious word, blest Lord,
And come to think on Thee.
And in this bread and wine, dear Lord,
We would Thy glories see.

2. A body was prepared for Thee
As Thou didst come to earth.
And in that perfect life of Thine
We see Thy holy worth.

3. Yet in this bread before us now,
The bread, we sadly break,
We see Thy grief and agony
And eat, for Thy name's sake.

4. The cup of blessing is filled full -
A covenant of love!
And in its contents, joy we see
For man and God above!

5. Yet in Thy cup, we find the cost
Of blessing rich and free!
The wrath of God in judgement fell
On Thee upon the tree.

6. O Lord, we bless Thee for the grace
That came to Calvary.
And with our hearts with meekness bound
We praise and worship Thee.

Tunes: Westminster (Turle), Arlington, Belmont, St. Agnes, Pisgah.

1Corinthians 10.16
The cup of blessing which we bless, is it not the communion of the blood of Christ? The bread which we break, is it not the communion of the body of Christ?

29th April.

"You Are My Sunshine".

Born of the Virgin in Bethl'em's Stable.

1.
Born of the virgin in Bethl'em's stable;
Laid in a manger, a baby boy.
The Son of God and the King eternal!
God's most perfect Gift of joy.

Chorus:
You are My Saviour, my only Saviour.
O, let me show Your love for me.
You left Your home, Lord; Your home in Heaven
Came to earth to set me free.

2.
As Man of Sorrows, You were so tender;
So kind and gentle; so gracious too.
You bore our sickness - carried our anguish;
You're most caring, wise and true.
Chorus:

3.
You are God's dear Lamb! God's lovely Lamb!
So meek and lowly; so holy too.
You went to Calv'ry - died for our sin!
Cleansed by blood, we now love You.
Chorus:

4.
Now in the glory, You're Lord of all!
You sit at God's right hand above.
All riches, power, wisdom and blessing
Be to You for all Your love!
Chorus:

Tune: Written with the tune with "You are my sunshine" in mind.

30th April.

76.76D.

No Tears, No Zeal, No Labour!

1. No tears, no zeal, no labour!
Could Thy salvation win.
Only Thy gracious giving
Could save our souls from sin.
The Son of Thine affections,
The true and living Bread,
Has shown us all Thy glory
By all He did and said.

2. No tears, no zeal, no labour!
Could Thy salvation win.
Only Thy gracious giving
Could save our souls from sin.
The Lord of all creation,
The Son of God most high,
Was sent from brightest glory
Upon a cross to die.

3. No tears, no zeal, no labour!
Could Thy salvation win.
Only Thy gracious giving
Could save our souls from sin.
The blood poured out in
weakness,
Upon Golgotha's tree,
Springs up for our redemption –
The fee that sets us free.

4. No tears, no zeal, no labour!
Could Thy salvation win.
Only Thy gracious giving
Could save our souls from sin.
We thank Thee for the Saviour,
The precious, living Lord..
We thank Thee for our blessing,
Our Father, most adored.

Tunes: Thornbury, Lymington, Ewing, Ahnfelt, St. Theodulph, Day of Rest, Ellacombe, Aurelia, Greenland.

1John 4.14
And we have seen and do testify that the Father sent the Son to be the Saviour of the world.

1John 3.1
Behold, what manner of love the Father hath bestowed upon us, that we should be called the sons of God:
therefore the world knoweth us not, because it knew him not.

2Peter 1.17
For he received from God the Father honour and glory, when there came such a voice to him from the excellent glory,
This is my beloved Son, in whom I am well pleased.

1st May.

75.765

When I Sit Sad and Alone.

1.
When I sit sad and alone
When I am depressed;
Then the Lord steps in to help
And my soul is blessed.

2.
When by sin I am oppressed,
When doubts fill my mind;
Then the Lord steps in to help;
In Him, joy I find.

3.
When by illness I am bound;
When I'm racked with pain;
Then the Lord steps in to help -
His peace is my gain.

4.
When the saints the flesh display
And division looms;
Then the Lord steps in to help –
Fellowship then blooms.

5.
When the enemy is strong
Making all to fear;
Then the Lord steps in to help –
His strong arm is near.

6.
When my faith is tried by men,
Persecution reigns;
Then the Lord steps in to help -
His great love sustains.

7.
When my service seems so bland
When no fruit is seen;
Then the Lord steps in to help –
Whitened fields to glean.

8.
When I bow my knees to pray
And nought comes to mind;
Then the Lord steps in to help –
Many themes, I find.

9.
When I hear His precious word,
And refuse His claims;
Then the Lord steps in to help –
He, my soul sustains.

Tunes: Bruce, Guidance.

Psalm 90 v.10

The days of our years are threescore years and ten; and if by reason of strength they be fourscore years,
yet is their strength labour and sorrow; for it is soon cut off, and we fly away.

2nd May.

66.66D.

We're More Than Conquerors.

1.
We're more than conquerors
Through God who loves us so;
We're more than conquerors,
As He this world will show.
He, who gave His own Son
On our account to die
Fits us for heaven now -
In His bright home on high.

2.
We're more than conquerors
By our great God foreknown!
We're more than conquerors
Marked out to be His own.
He chose us in His Son
Before the world was made.
In time, He called us too -
Our joy shall never fade.

3.
We're more than conquerors
And shall be like His Son!
We're more than conquerors
For us the battle's won!
In God's light glorified;
Displayed in skies above;
With Christ, the Firstborn there;
The Object of our love.

Tunes: 66.66D: Invitation (Maker), Denby. 12.12.12.12: Corbet, Lausanne.

Romans 8.37.
Nay, in all these things we are more than conquerors through him that loved us.

3rd May.

66.66.

You Call Us Friends, Blest Lord.

1.
You call us friends, blest Lord
Because we keep Your word.
Give us the grace to know
Why Your love is preferred.

2.
Your love brought You to die
For those lost in their sin.
There is no greater love
That hardened hearts could win.

3.
Lord, now that we're Your friends,
And special friends indeed,
You tell us of Your plans
And meet our every need.

4.
You'll never leave our side;
You'll never let us down;
You'll lift us when we fall;
Your joy shall be our crown.

5.
Lord, You are faithful too,
And speak the truth in love.
The wounds You may inflict,
Lead us to God above.

6.
Lord, help us trust in You,
Give us Your will to know.
Please, draw us close to You,
That we in love might grow.

Tunes: 66.66: Ibstone, Eccles, Moseley. 66.66D: Denby, Invitation

John 15.13-15

Greater love hath no man than this, that a man lay down his life for his friends. Ye are my friends, if ye do whatsoever I command you. Henceforth I call you not servants; for the servant knoweth not what his lord doeth: but I have called you friends; for all things that I have heard of my Father I have made known unto you.

Proverbs 18:24

…And there is a friend that sticketh closer than a brother.

Zechariah 13:6

And one shall say unto him, What are these wounds in thine hands? Then he shall answer, Those with which I was wounded in the house of my friends.

4th May.

76.66.

Oh, Let the Words of My Mouth.

1.
Oh, let the words of my mouth,
And the thoughts of my heart,
Be pleasing in thy sight,
O Lord, omniscient.

2.
Oh, let the good that I do,
And all the things I give,
Be pleasing in Thy sight,
O Lord, beneficent.

3.
Oh, let the zeal that I have
For teaching Thy blest word,
Be pleasing in Thy sight,
O Lord, omnipotent.

4.
Oh, let the love that I hold
For all men and for Thee,
Be pleasing in Thy sight,
O Lord, omnipresent.

Tunes: Cara, Matrimony, Vulpius.

Psalm 19.13-14
Keep back thy servant also from presumptuous sins; let them not have dominion over me: then shall I be upright, and I shall be innocent from the great transgression. Let the words of my mouth, and the meditation of my heart, be acceptable in thy sight, O LORD, my strength, and my redeemer.

Proverbs 5.7
Hear me now therefore, O ye children, and depart not from the words of my mouth.

5th May.

CMD.

Blest Lord, We See Thee as the Lamb.

1.
Blest Lord, we see Thee as the Lamb,
Upon the cross of shame!
The Son of God! The great I AM!
How wonderful Thy name!
We hear Thy sob! We hear Thy cry!
When Thou didst bear the blame!
"Eli lama sabachthani!"
Thy dying words exclaim.

2.
We see Thine arms so widely spread,
Upon the cruel tree!
We see the scarring of Thy head,
Where Thou hast set us free!
'Twas there nails pierced Thy hands and feet,
Upon Golgotha's hill!
'Tis there where truth and mercy meet,
And that in God's good will!

3.
There peace and righteousness, we see -
The kiss of Calvary!
'Twas there God's judgement fell on Thee,
Such searing agony!
There, Thou the bitter cup didst drain,
The curse of Calvary!
Through Thy dark death, we blessing gain,
And have our part with Thee!

4.
There Thou hast suffered for our sin -
The cause of Calvary!
There love's last battle Thou didst win -
The cross of victory!
'Twas there that Satan's head was crushed,
Beneath thy wounded feet!
And from Thy side, pure blood has gushed -
The blood that makes us meet!

Tunes: No King But Christ, Bethlehem, Fair Haven, Ishpeming, Release, Warrior, Monora, Land of Rest, Landas,

Matthew 27.33-35
And when they were come unto a place called Golgotha, that is to say, a place of a skull, They gave him vinegar to drink mingled with gall: and when he had tasted thereof, he would not drink. And they crucified him, and parted his garments, casting lots…

6th May.

CMD.

Lord Jesus, from Your Blessèd Hand.

1.
Lord Jesus, from Thy blessèd hand
This loaf of bread, we take.
Obedient to Thine own command
We each of it partake.
It tells us of Thy life divine
Lived in the Father's will.
It tells us of Thy body giv'n
His purpose to fulfil.

2.
Lord Jesus, from Thy blessèd hand
We take this cup of wine.
It speaks of blessing from above
And tells us we are Thine.
It speaks of sufferings untold
Borne on that cross of shame.
It speaks of perfect righteousness
Found in Thy precious name.

Tunes: Bethlehem, All Saints, Jesus is God, Land of Rest.

1Corinthians 11.23
For I have received of the Lord that which also I delivered unto you, That the Lord Jesus the same night in which he was betrayed took bread:
And when he had given thanks, he brake it, and said,
Take, eat: this is my body, which is broken for you: this do in remembrance of me.
After the same manner also he took the cup, when he had supped, saying, This cup is the new testament in my blood: this do ye, as oft as ye drink it, in remembrance of me. For as often as ye eat this bread, and drink this cup, ye do shew the Lord's death till he come.
Wherefore whosoever shall eat this bread, and drink this cup of the Lord, unworthily, shall be guilty of the body and blood of the Lord. But let a man examine himself, and so let him eat of that bread, and drink of that cup.

7th May.

Nothing to do!

1.
Nothing to do!
There's nothing to do,
But trust, this day, in the dear Lord!
Nothing to do,
There's nothing to do,
But take Him at His holy word!

2.
Nothing to say!
There's nothing to say,
For Christ has died upon the tree.
Nothing to say!
There's nothing to say,
His death has made us all sin-free.

3.
Nothing to pay!
There's nothing to pay,
Christ paid the price upon the cross!
Nothing to pay!
There's nothing to pay,
Our blessing comes from His great loss!

4.
Nothing to fear!
There's nothing to fear,
God raised His Son up from the grave!
Nothing to fear!
There's nothing to fear,
He's willing and able to save!

5.
Nothing to doubt!
There's nothing to doubt,
He's coming soon for you and me.
Nothing to doubt,
There's nothing to doubt,
In heavenly glory, we shall be.

Written for children.

Tunes: Church Vigilant.

Luke 7.41-44
There was a certain creditor which had two debtors: the one owed five hundred pence, and the other fifty. And when they had nothing to pay, he frankly forgave them both. Tell me therefore, which of them will love im most? Simon answered and said, I suppose that he, to whom he forgave most. And he said unto him, Thou hast rightly judged. And he turned to the woman, and said unto Simon, Seest thou this woman? I entered into thine house, thou gavest me no water for my feet: but she hath washed my feet with tears, and wiped them with the hairs of her head.

8th May.

65.65.65.65.

The Summer is Ending.

1.
The summer is ending,
The harvest is due,
The message of Jesus
Is calling for you.
"O sinner, 'twas for you,
I died on the tree.
That you, through my blood,
From all sin might be free."

2.
The summer is ending,
The harvest is due,
The message of Jesus
Is calling for you.
"Come to me, you burdened,
And I'll give you rest.
I've loved you intensely;
To me, come - be blessed."

3.
The summer is ending,
The harvest is due,
The message of Jesus
Is calling for you.
"O sinner, I'll bless you
With gifts from above.
Salvation I'll bring you
With pardon and love."

4.
The summer is ending,
The harvest is due,
The message of Jesus
Is calling for you.
"Learn from my example,
Be gentle and meek.
To God look in all things
His good will to seek."

Tunes: Sankey, Hallel, Evelyns, Cradle Song, Happy Town of Salem.

Matthew 11.27-30
All things are delivered unto me of my Father: and no man knoweth the Son, but the Father; neither knoweth any man the Father, save the Son, and he to whomsoever the Son will reveal him. Come unto me, all ye that labour and are heavy laden, and I will give you rest. Take my yoke upon you, and learn of me; for I am meek and lowly in heart: and ye shall find rest unto your souls. For my yoke is easy, and my burden is light.

Isaiah 8.20
The harvest is past, the summer is ended, and we are not saved.

Matthew 9:37
Then saith he unto his disciples, The harvest truly is plenteous, but the labourers are few…

9th May.

10.10.10.10.

Bless'd be the God!

1.
Bless'd be the God!
Yes, blessèd be the God
The Father of our dear Lord
Jesus Christ.
He's 'gotten us!
Yes, He's begotten us
By mercy to a sure and living
hope.

2.
Bless'd be the God!
Yes, blessèd be the God
Who by His glory raised Christ
from the dead.
He's given us!
Yes, He has given us
A legacy reserved in heaven
above.

3.
Bless'd be the God!
Yes, blessèd be the God
Who marked us out for riches
long ago.
Inc'ruptible!
They will not fade away!
Our treasure's undefiled for
evermore.

4.
Bless'd be the God!
Yes, blessèd be the God
Who gave His Son to die for all
our sin.
He's Lord of lords!
The Saviour of our souls!
Our portion He will be,
eternally!

Tunes: Hold Thou My Hand, Help Me, Consolation (Mendelssohn), Albany.

Ephesians 3.3-7
Blessed be the God and Father of our Lord Jesus Christ, who hath blessed us with all spiritual blessings in heavenly places in Christ: according as he hath chosen us in him before the foundation of the world, that we should be holy and without blame before him in love:
Having predestinated us unto the adoption of children by Jesus Christ to himself, according to the good pleasure of his will,
to the praise of the glory of his grace, wherein he hath made us accepted in the beloved.
In whom we have redemption through his blood, the forgiveness of sins, according to the riches of his grace; wherein he hath abounded toward us in all wisdom and prudence…

10th May.

75.75.75.75.

Faith Will Soon Give Way to Sight.

1. Faith will soon give way to sight;
Hope shall run its course;
Love will evermore endure;
It's a vast resource.
Father, in Your great wisdom
Bless us day by day.
Fit us for the pilgrim way.
Teach us how to pray.

2. Faith will soon give way to sight;
Hope shall run its course;
Love will evermore endure;
It's a vast resource.
Father, speak to us this day.
Tell us of Your Son.
Show to us His suff'ring love
And the vict'ry won.

3. Faith will soon give way to sight;
Hope shall run its course;
Love will evermore endure;
It's a vast resource.
Father, we look for Your Son.
Let us hear His call.
Then we'll rise to heav'n above
Where life's wonderful.

Tunes: Guidance, Bruce.

1John 3.1-2

Behold, what manner of love the Father hath bestowed upon us, that we should be called the sons of God: therefore the world knoweth us not, because it knew him not.

Beloved, now are we the sons of God, and it doth not yet appear what we shall be: but we know that, when he shall appear, we shall be like him; for we shall see him as he is.

11th May.

CMD.

Rejoice in Prayer for All the Saints.

1. Rejoice in prayer for all the saints
Joy in their Christ-like growth;
Rejoice in love and in one mind;
Come, let's rejoice in both.
Joy in the Spirit's unity,
Guarding that bond of peace;
Rejoice that Christ has gone on high
Where praise shall never cease.

2. Rejoice in those who as lights shine
In this dark world of sin.
Rejoice in fellowship divine
And God's Spirit within.
Rejoice in His almighty power
That brings the dead to life.
Rejoice in those who pledge their lives
To serve in days of strife.

3. Rejoice in sacrificial love
That gives its all each day.
Joy in the Lord who gave Himself!
Rejoice in Him we pray!
Rejoice in weakness and defeat;
Rejoice when all is well.
Rejoice in grief and sorrow too -
In them God's purpose tell.

4. Rejoice in all the Father gives
To His belovèd Son.
Rejoice in all the majesty
That He, the Victor, won!
Rejoice that Christ shall come again
That we with Him might be.
Rejoice in that bright home above;
Rejoice eternally!

Tunes: No King But Christ, None But Christ.

Philippians 2.6-7; 2.18 and 4.4-7

Holding forth the word of life; that I may rejoice in the day of Christ, that I have not run in vain, neither laboured in vain. Yea, and if I be offered upon the sacrifice and service of your faith, I joy, and rejoice with you all. For the same cause also do ye joy, and rejoice with me.

Rejoice in the Lord alway: and again I say, Rejoice.
Let your moderation be known unto all men. The Lord is at hand.
Be careful for nothing; but in every thing by prayer and supplication with thanksgiving let your requests be made known unto God. And the peace of God, which passeth all understanding, shall keep your hearts and minds through Christ Jesus.

12th May.

66.4.6666.4.

Our Father God, to Thee.

1.
Our Father God, to Thee
We lift our songs with glee
For all Thy love.
Love that is crowned in Thee;
Love that shall ever be;
Love in Thy jubilee;
Love from above.

2.
Thou gav'st Thy Son to die;
This is the reason why –
To set us free.
Jesus, the Holy One,
Now sits upon Thy throne;
Praised now for all He's done
To honour Thee.

3.
There in Thy heav'nly light,We
see His glory bright,
And worship Thee.
We see Thee in His face,
Where we Thy beauty trace,
All in Thy matchless grace
Pure majesty!

4.
Protect us by Thy might;
Lead us in paths of light;
Keep us near Thee.
Soon our dear Lord will come
And take us to His home
Where in Thy great wisdom
Thy joy, we'll be.

Tune: UK National Anthem.

1John 3.1-3
Behold, what manner of love the Father hath bestowed upon us, that we should be called the sons of God:
therefore the world knoweth us not, because it knew him not.
Beloved, now are we the sons of God, and it doth not yet appear what we shall be: but we know that, when he shall appear, we shall be like him; for we shall see him as he is.
And every man that hath this hope in him purifieth himself, even as he is pure.

John 15.9-10
As the Father hath loved me, so have I loved you: continue ye in my love.
If ye keep my commandments, ye shall abide in my love; even as I have kept my Father's commandments, and abide in his love.

13th May.

CMD.

Love is the Kiss of Calvary.

1.
Love is the kiss of Calvary
Where Jesus died for me.
Peace is the warmth of Calvary
Where Jesus set me free.
Truth is the pow'r of Calvary
Fulfilling prophecy.
Mercy and righteousness are there
On the accursèd tree.

2.
Love is the heart of heaven above
Where Jesus lives for me.
Peace is the joy of heaven above,
Where Jesus prays for me.
Truth is the light of heaven above
The Lamb's its source, you see.
Mercy and righteousness are there
Seen in His majesty.

Tunes: Bethlehem, Ishpeming, Land of Rest, Providence, Jesus is God, Jesus is God.

Romans 5.6-9
For when we were yet without strength, in due time Christ died for the ungodly. For scarcely for a righteous man will one die: yet peradventure for a good man some would even dare to die.
But God commendeth his love toward us, in that, while we were yet sinners, Christ died for us.
Much more then, being now justified by his blood, we shall be saved from wrath through him.

Romans 8.35
Who shall separate us from the love of Christ? shall tribulation, or distress, or persecution, or famine, or nakedness, or peril, or sword?

14th May.

CM.

Rise Up, My Soul, and Sing with Joy.

1. Rise up, my soul, and sing with joy
For Christ may come today!
Watch out for Him in skies above
While walking in His way.

2. Redemption's hour is closer now
Than e'er it's been before.
To hear His voice and see His face!
What saint can ask for more?

3. I'm nearer to that judgement seat
Where all, He shall reveal.
There stands a prize for labours done
When I, before Him, kneel.

4. I'm closer to that legacy
Reserved beyond the sky.
A heritage that's pure as light,
And shall not age or die.

5. I'm nearer to that wedding day
When I shall be His bride.
For ever, I shall love the Son
Once mocked and crucified.

6. I'm closer to the Father's house,
The home of light and love.
I'll soon be in that place prepared
In glory up above.

Tunes: St. Agnes, Westminster (Turle), Beatitudo, Beulah.

Romans 8.22-24
For we know that the whole creation groaneth and travaileth in pain together until now.
And not only they, but ourselves also, which have the firstfruits of the Spirit, even we ourselves groan within ourselves, waiting for the adoption, to wit, the redemption of our body.
For we are saved by hope: but hope that is seen is not hope: for what a man seeth, why doth he yet hope for?

John 14.2
In my Father's house are many mansions: if it were not so, I would have told you. I go to prepare a place for you.

15th May.

88.88.

Our Eyes Look Up to Thee Above.

1. Our eyes look up to Thee above
Upon Thy throne – a throne of love.
And as we gaze upon Thy face
We see the beauty of Thy grace.

2. Our ears would listen to Thy word;
By Thy commands our hearts are stirred.
Thy purposes and counsels clear
Fill our souls and bring us near.

3. Our feet would walk in all Thy ways
Tracing the footsteps of Thy days.
The will of God was Thine to do;
Oh, help us to be faithful too.

4. Our hands would serve Thee every hour;
Grant to us all Thy zeal and power.
Let every work be marked by faith
And, in deep danger, keep us safe.

5. Our lips would speak the truth in love
Revealing wonders from above.
So help us witness faithfully
Speaking out boldly about Thee.

6. Lord Jesus, fill our hearts with praise
Throughout those everlasting days.
Then our dear Bridegroom, Thou shalt be
And we Thy bride eternally.

Tunes: 88.88: Tallis Canon, Federal Street. 88.88.88.88: Sweet Hour.

Hebrews 12,2-3
Looking unto Jesus the author and finisher of our faith; who for the joy that was set before him endured the cross, despising the shame, and is set down at the right hand of the throne of God. For consider him that endured such contradiction of sinners against himself, lest ye be wearied and faint in your minds.

1Peter 3.21
For even hereunto were ye called: because Christ also suffered for us, leaving us an example, that ye should follow his steps…

16th May.

76.76D.

Thy Love, O Lord, We've Tasted

1. Thy love, O Lord, we've tasted
A love that's bitter-sweet
For it was laced with sorrow,
Deep suff'ring and "defeat".
Yet, 'twas Thy love that bought us
When death's curse fell on Thee.
It was Thy love that blessed us;
A love that set us free.

2. Thy peace, O Lord, we've tasted
A peace that shall endure.
And when dark doubts surround us
Thy peace shall keep us pure.
When life's billows shall roar
And trials pierce our soul,
Thy peace shall be our refuge
And shall our hearts console.

3. Thy joy, O Lord, we've tasted
A joy that's deep within;
'Twas joy that bore the cross
Thy blessèd bride to win.
We know Thee as our Bridegroom
Our joy and crown art Thou.
And soon we shall be with Thee
With joy, to Thee we'll bow.

Tunes: Lymington.

Hebrews 6.4-5
For it is impossible for those who were once enlightened,
and have tasted of the heavenly gift,
and were made partakers of the Holy Ghost,
And have tasted the good word of God, and the powers of the world to come.

17th May.

66.66D.

You're the First, Lord Jesus.

You're the First, Lord Jesus,
And then You are the Last.
The God of every age,
The present, future, past.
You are the Beginning,
The Source of everything.
You are the Ending too,
Newness of life You bring.

A – You are the Amen
The Lord, who makes it so;
B – You are most beloved,
The Son of God we know.
C – You're the Christ of God
Who sits at His right hand.
D – You are the Dayspring
The light that God had planned.

E – You are eternal,
Yahweh, the great I AM.
F – You are the Firstborn,
The Head of every man.
G – You're God who's for us
The true Emmanuel.
H – You're Heir of all things
Who snatched our souls from hell.

I – You are God's image,
A dye faithful and true.
J – Your name is Jesus
And, Saviour, we love You.
K – You are Israel's King
And You will reign supreme.
L – You are the Lamb
Who shall the world redeem.

M – You're the mighty God,
And Wonderful's Your name.
N – You're the Nazarene
Who bore the cross of shame.
O – You're the Offering
Whose fragrance rose to God.
P – You're the Prince of Peace
Who suffered judgement's rod.

R – You're the ransom paid
To save our souls from sin.
S – You're the living Stone
Who gives us life within.
T – You're the Teacher who
The Father's heart has shown.
U – The Unspeakable
Sent down from God's just throne.

W – The Word of life
Who came to earth to die.
X – You were crucified,
Your death has brought us nigh.
Z – You're the Omega
Who showed us God's good will.
Yes, You are the All in All -
With love our hearts You fill.

Tunes: Invitation (Maker), Denby,

Revelation 1.8
I am Alpha and Omega, the beginning and the ending, saith the Lord, which is, and which was, and which is to come, the Almighty.

Revelation 22.13-14
And, behold, I come quickly; and my reward is with me, to give every man according as his work shall be. I am Alpha and Omega, the beginning and the end, the first and the last. Blessed are they that do his commandments, that they may have right to the tree of life, and may enter in through the gates into the city.

18th May.

CM.

Lord, Thou art Love, the Purest Love.

1. Lord, Thou art love, the purest love
That man could ever trace.
The wonder of that love divine
Is seen in all Thy grace.

2. Love in Thy lonely life below;
Love in the path of shame;
Love brought Thee grief and sorrow here;
All glory to Thy name!

3. Love bowed to Thine own Father's will
In dark Gethsemane.
Love led Thee on to Calvary
Where Thou didst die for me.

4. Love nailed Thee to that cross of shame
Love had Thee crucified;
Love raised Thee from the gloomy grave;
And Thyself glorified.

5. Love sent the Holy Spirit down;
In love to form Thy bride.
Love from Thy pure and tender heart
Has brought me to Thy side.

Tunes: St. Agnes, Westminster (Turle), Beatitudo, Beulah.

Galatians 2.20
I am crucified with Christ: nevertheless I live; yet not I, but Christ liveth in me: and the life which I now live in the flesh I live by the faith of the Son of God, who loved me, and gave himself for me.

Ephesians 5.2
And walk in love, as Christ also hath loved us, and hath given himself for us an offering and a sacrifice to God for a sweetsmelling savour.

19th May.

66.66.88.86.

Love! Love! Wonderful Love!

1. Love! Love! Wonderful love!
A love that is divine!
Love! Love! Wonderful love!
A love better than wine.
It saw me clothed in sin and shame;
It saw me so alone.
It saw me with a pitying eye,
And called me for its own.

2. Love! Love! Wonderful love!
A love that is divine!
Love! Love! Wonderful love!
A love better than wine.
It saw me wrecked, yes, dead within;
It saw my filthy state.
It washed me with God's holy word
And turned my soul from hate.

3. Love! Love! Wonderful love!
A love that is divine!
Love! Love! Wonderful love!
A love better than wine.
It told me of a sacrifice
That shone with righteousness.
It told me of a wounded Man
So full of tenderness.

4. Love! Love! Wonderful love!
A love that is divine!
Love! Love! Wonderful love!
A love better than wine.
It led me to a cross of shame
Where Christ was nailed for me.
And there, forsaken by His God,
He died to set me free.

5. Love! Love! Wonderful love!
A love that is divine!
Love! Love! Wonderful love!
A love better than wine.
The blood of love washed me from sin;
It brought me back to God.
It sent His Spirit to my heart;
In sonship my feet shod.

6. Love! Love! Wonderful love!
A love that is divine!
Love! Love! Wonderful love!
A love better than wine.
It dressed me in a righteous robe
And in salvation's light.
It set my mind on things above
And armed me for the fight.

7. Love! Love! Wonderful love!
A love that is divine!
Love! Love! Wonderful love!
A love better than wine.
It brings me to the Father's house
Where peace and joy must dwell.
It brings me to my Saviour's side
And tells me all is well!

Tunes: ?

Ephesians 3.18-21

May be able to comprehend with all saints what is the breadth, and length, and depth, and height;
and to know the love of Christ, which passeth knowledge, that ye might be filled with all the fulness of God.
Now unto him that is able to do exceeding abundantly above all that we ask or think, according to the power that worketh in us,
unto him be glory in the church by Christ Jesus throughout all ages, world without end.
Amen.

20th May.

CM.

Lord, Gathered to Thy Precious Name.

1.
Lord, gathered to Thy precious name,
We own Thy presence here.
Thy holy table, we surround
With reverential fear.

2.
Thy death, Lord Jesus, we declare,
Thy death upon the tree.
There Thou hast paid the price of sin
That we might be set free.

3.
Thy body broken in the bread;
Thy blood poured out as wine;
We thank Thee for these emblems, Lord,
That speak of love divine.

4.
'Twas grace and truth that brought Thee down;
Love beamed from Thee each day.
Through death, the Victor's crown is Thine;
Thy glory, we survey.

5.
Lord Jesus, Thou art soon to come
To take Thy bride away.
Before the throne in heaven above,
She will Thy grace display.

6.
All glory, riches, honour, power
To Thee, by right belong.
We'll praise Thee in Thy majesty
With an eternal song.

Tunes: CM: Beulah, Westminster (Turle), Nativity, St. Agnes, Beatitudo, Belmont, Irish, Pisgah.

2Corinthians 8.9
For ye know the grace of our Lord Jesus Christ, that, though he was rich, yet for your sakes he became poor, that ye through his poverty might be rich

Ephesians 1:7
In whom we have redemption through his blood, the forgiveness of sins, according to the riches of his grace…

21st May.

76.76.D.

You Did Not Leave Us Orphans.

1. You did not leave us orphans
When Your time came to die,
The Comforter was given,
When You ascended high.
He came to be among us;
He dwells in us today.
Sent by Your loving Father,
He keeps us in the way.

2. The world cannot receive Him,
It cannot see or know
The wonder of His Person
Or of His strength below.
He teaches us with wisdom,
With Your word fills our mind.
He comforts us in sorrow;
And, through Him, peace we find.

3. The Spirit glorifies You
Relaying all You say.
In truth, He leads and guides us;
Revealing You each day.
O, may we never grieve Him
By sins we should not do.
O, may we ever please Him
By being true to You.

Tunes: Greenland (Haydn), Lymington, Thornbury, St. Theodulph.

John 14.16-18

And I will pray the Father, and he shall give you another Comforter, that he may abide with you for ever;

even the Spirit of truth; whom the world cannot receive, because it seeth him not, neither knoweth him:

but ye know him; for he dwelleth with you, and shall be in you. I will not leave you comfortless: I will come to you.

22nd May.

76.76.

Closer than a Brother, Lord.

1. Closer than a brother, Lord,
I know You'll stand by me.
Faithful and true in all Your ways,
With love both full and free.

2. It's love that moves a righteous man
To die for his dear friend.
So human love is great, I see,
But leads to a sad end;

3. Yet, Lord, Your love surpasses all;
It brought You from on high.
It led You on to Calvary
For foes, like us, to die.

4. Your blood has washed us from all sin;
Removing judgement's rod.
It blesses us with peace and joy
And brings us back to God.

5. Now, Lord, Your love is in our souls
And we, in You, delight.
You bring us near and call us friends,
Now holy in Your sight.

Tunes: Westminster (Turle), Belmont, Beulah, St. Agnes, Irish.

John 15.14-15
Ye are my friends, if ye do whatsoever I command you. Henceforth I call you not servants; for the servant knoweth not what his lord doeth: but I have called you friends; for all things that I have heard of my Father I have made known unto you.
Ye have not chosen me, but I have chosen you, and ordained you, that ye should go and bring forth fruit,
and *that* your fruit should remain: that whatsoever ye shall ask of the Father in my name, he may give it you.

23rd May.

85.85D. with refrain.

Father, When My Friends Forsake Me.

1.
Father, when my friends forsake me,
You'll draw close to me;
When my colleagues turn against me,
You will stand by me.
When my soul is weak and wounded,
You will strengthen me;
When my spirit's joy is fading,
You'll encourage me.
Refrain:
Never can Your love diminish;
Never can Your care subside;
Never can Your power weaken;
Never will You leave my side.

2.
When my enemies surround me,
You will fight for me;
When the devil's darts are flying,
You my shield shall be.
When the storms of life are roaring,
You will shelter me.
When deep sorrows flood upon me,
You will comfort me.
Refrain:
Never can Your love diminish;
Never can Your care subside;
Never can Your power weaken;
Never will You leave my side.

Tunes:?

Romans 8.31
What shall we then say to these things? If God be for us, who can be against us?

24th May.

CMD.

You Glorified the Father, Lord.

1.
You glorified the Father, Lord,
While living on this earth.
In walk and word and wondrous work,
You showed us all His worth.
And now, by Him, You're glorified,
A Man at His right hand!
The majesty that shines from You,
Tells us of all He's planned.

2.
You glorified the Father, Lord,
Upon the cross of shame.
Made sin for us upon that tree
You bore God's wrath - our blame!
And yet, You made that offering
In love that knows no end.
The Father found His joy therein
And caused You to ascend.

3.
You glorified the Father, Lord,
In prayers made for Your own.
You asked that we might all be one
In glory you have won.
In You the Father ever dwells,
In perfect unity.
In us, we find You, precious Lord;
Yet with You, we would be.

Tunes: Jesus Is God, Landas, Ishpeming, Minerva, Belmont.

John 17:4
I have glorified thee on the earth: I have finished the work which thou gavest me to do.

25th May.

4.6.6.

Rejoice! Rejoice! Rejoice for Evermore!

Rejoice! Rejoice!
Rejoice for evermore!
And without ceasing pray!

Thank Him! Thank Him!
Thank Him for everything!
The Spirit's word obey!

Approve! Approve!
The prophet's word approve!
To good hold on firmly!

Live on! Live on!
In righteousness, live on!
At peace your mind shall be!

Tunes: ?

Psalm 5.11
But let all those that put their trust in thee rejoice: let them ever shout for joy, because thou defendest them: let them also that love thy name be joyful in thee.

Psalm 26:7
That I may publish with the voice of thanksgiving, and tell of all thy wondrous works.

Romans 2.18
And knowest his will, and approvest the things that are more excellent, being instructed out of the law;

Psalm 119.144
The righteousness of thy testimonies is everlasting: give me understanding, and I shall live.

26th May.

CMD.

A Little While - We'll See You, Lord.

1
A little while - we'll see You, Lord,
We'll see You face to face.
And in the glory of that hour
We'll wonder at You grace.
You left the Father's home, dear Lord,
To come to this sad earth.
The Rich One, who became so poor
Had such a lowly birth.

2.
A little while - we'll see You, Lord,
A Man of joy and peace.
And from the glory of that hour
Our praise will never cease.
In sorrow, You walked here below,
Mocked and rejected too.
For only those with broken hearts
Your love and mercy knew.

3.
A little while - we'll see You, Lord,
Son of our God most high.
And in the glory of that hour,
You heart will draw us nigh.
We'll see, in faith, those wounded hands
And torment of Your soul.
Then, we'll recall Your precious blood
Is that which made us whole.

4.
A little while - we'll see You, Lord,
The Heir of everything;
And in the glory of that hour
Our hearts their worship bring.
We'll then see You as Lord of lords;
We'll see You as the King.
We'll reign with You a thousand years
And of Your love we'll sing.

Tunes: Providence, Bethlehem, Minerva, No King But Christ, Landas.

John 16.19

Now Jesus knew that they were desirous to ask him, and said unto them, Do ye enquire among yourselves of that I said, A little while, and ye shall not see me: and again, a little while, and ye shall see me?

Revelation 3.11

Behold, I come quickly: hold that fast which thou hast, that no man take thy crown.

27th May.

76.76D.

Receive the Word with Gladness.

Receive the word with gladness;
Receive all things through prayer;
Receive the Spirit's power;
Receive God's love and care!
Receive His grace and pardon;
Receive the hope on high;
Receive life's crown in glory
Far out beyond the sky.

Tunes: Thornbury, Ahnfelt, Lymington, Greenland (Haydn), Mountain, St. Edith, St. Theodulph, Ellacombe, Ewing, Aurelia.

Psalm 24.1-6

A Psalm of David. The earth is the LORD'S, and the fulness thereof; the world, and they that dwell therein. For he hath founded it upon the seas, and established it upon the floods. Who shall ascend into the hill of the LORD? or who shall stand in his holy place? He that hath clean hands, and a pure heart; who hath not lifted up his soul unto vanity, nor sworn deceitfully. He shall receive the blessing from the LORD, and righteousness from the God of his salvation. This is the generation of them that seek him, that seek thy face, O Jacob. Selah.

Colossians 3.23-24

And whatsoever ye do, do it heartily, as to the Lord, and not unto men; knowing that of the Lord ye shall receive the reward of the inheritance: for ye serve the Lord Christ.

Ephesians 6.7-8

With good will doing service, as to the Lord, and not to men: knowing that whatsoever good thing any man doeth, the same shall he receive of the Lord, whether he be bond or free.

1Corinthians 5.10

For we must all appear before the judgment seat of Christ; that every one may receive the things done in his body, according to that he hath done, whether it be good or bad.

28th May.

76.76D.

Our Wickedness Was Dreadful.

1.
Our wickedness was dreadful,
O, Judge of all the earth.
We had no hope or future;
We had no joy or worth.
But Christ, in love and mercy
Came to us here below.
He died our judgement bearing
That true life we might know.

2.
We love the name of Jesus,
Thine own belovèd Son.
We love Thee as our Father
And for the victory won.
We praise Thee that the Saviour
Is crowned with glory now.
We bless Thee that in worship
Our knees before Him bow.

3.
One day, with clouds, He's coming
Over this world to reign.
Then every eye shall see Him
And tears shall fall as rain.
All men shall then remember
The piercing and the pain.
Wounded for their transgressions,
From Him their blessing came.

4.
But, Father, 'tis *our* portion
To be with Him above.
Soon He will call us to Him,
The climax of His love.
Oh, with our hearts' deep yearning,
To see His lovely face;
We will, with joy and gladness,
Embrace Him in Thy grace.

Tunes: Ahnfelt, Lymington, Thornbury, Ellacombe, Webb, Wolvercote, Greenland (Haydn), Angels' Story, Passion Chorale, Aurelia, Day of Rest,

Psalm 96.11
Let the heavens rejoice, and let the earth be glad; let the sea roar, and the fulness thereof.
Let the field be joyful, and all that is therein: then shall all the trees of the wood rejoice before the LORD:
for he cometh, for he cometh to judge the earth:
he shall judge the world with righteousness, and the people with his truth.

29th May.

74.74.77.4.

Jesus, Shepherd of Your Sheep.

1.
Jesus, Shepherd of your sheep,
Lead us along.
Jesus, Saviour of the weak,
Help us be strong.
Ever may Your presence cheer
us;
Ever may Your love endear us,
Ever may Your wisdom steer
us,
For You we long.

2.
Jesus, Lord of light and love,
Keep us secure.
Jesus, God's Son up above,
Our souls assure.
Ever may Your presence cheer
us;
Ever may Your love endear us,
Ever may Your wisdom steer
us,
For You we long.

3.
Jesus, Prophet, Priest and King,
Our faith increase.
Jesus, God of all living,
Grant us Your peace.
Ever may Your presence cheer
us;
Ever may Your love endear us,
Ever may Your wisdom steer
us,
For You we long.

4.
Jesus, Judge of all the earth,
Defend our cause.
Jesus, Man of heavenly worth,
Teach us Love's laws.
Ever may Your presence cheer
us;
Ever may Your love endear us,
Ever may Your wisdom steer
us,
For You we long.

Tunes: Ar Hyd Y Nos, Wynnstay.

Jude 1.24-25
Now unto him that is able to keep you from falling, and to present you faultless before the presence of his glory with exceeding joy, to the only wise God our Saviour, be glory and majesty, dominion and power, both now and ever. Amen.

Proverbs 23.19
Hear thou, my son, and be wise, and guide thine heart in the way.

30th May.

CMD.

In Jesus Christ, I Will Rejoice.

1. In Jesus Christ, I will rejoice,
For that's what Christmas means.
The birthday of God's own dear Son
Portrayed in glorious scenes.
The angels lift their voices high
In light that's clear and bright;
The shepherds haste to Bethlehem
To see the wondrous sight.

2. Surrendering to Jesus Christ
Fills Christmas time with joy.
Come, see Him in the manger laid,
A tiny, baby boy.
"Emmanuel" – God with us now!
The Gift of God unveiled!
Of everything, the Creator!
As Son of David hailed!

3. Worshipping the Lord Jesus Christ
Puts love in Christmas too.
"Jesus" - the Lord who saves our souls -
Is God's anointed Jew.
He travelled from the cattle stall
To bear a cross of shame.
From death, He rose in victory;
All glory to His name!

4. Come, bow your knees to Jesus Christ
And make Christmas your own.
Come, share in His inheritance,
His glory and His throne!
Know your most hateful sins forgiven!
Know peace with God above!
Know life in all its fullness here,
With mercy, truth and love!

5. I'm celebrating Jesus Christ,
So Christmas lives in me -
The coming of the Holy One,
Who made the blind to see.
For heaven's courts, He made me fit
Where with Him, I shall be,
I'm celebrating Jesus Christ,
And Christmas lives in me!

Tunes: Jesus is God, No King But Christ, Tyrol, Bethlehem, Release.

2Corinthians 9.15
Thanks be unto God for his unspeakable gift.

31st May.

10.10.10.10.

The Death Of The Cross! Oh, What Can It Mean?

1. The death of the cross! Oh, what can it mean?
The mind of Christ is central to this theme.
Equal with God, the great, eternal Son
His glory left, a bond- slave to become.

2. A body was prepared for Him down here,
And from the Father's will, He would not veer.
"Not my will, but Thy will alone be done!"
Such was the cry of God's beloved One.

3
The death of the cross! Oh, what can it mean?
Look closely at that solemn, closing scene
When bruised and battered, Christ hung from a beam,
So that our sinful souls, He might redeem.

4. There, God in justice, did not spare His Son!
He spent His wrath until His work was done!
Sin's judgement was exhausted on that tree
Pouring the love of God on you and me.

5. The death of the cross! Oh, what can it mean?
Christ's precious blood has washed us – made us clean!
He's reconciled us to His God on high.
In peace and joy, He now has brought us nigh.

6. Glory to God, our Father up above!
Glory to Christ, for all His wondrous love!
Glory to Him, who works in us on earth!
Let glory mark all those of heavenly birth!

Tunes: Eventide, Ellers, Toulon.

Romans 8.32
He that spared not his own Son, but delivered him up for us all, how shall he not with him also freely give us all things?

1st June.

87.87D.

Thou Art Coming Soon, Lord Jesus.

1.
Thou art coming soon, Lord Jesus,
'Tis a hope that cannot fail.
We rest on Thy faithful promise
Anchored safe within the vail.
In Thy Father's house, we'll praise Thee;
Worship at Thy holy feet;
For the grace Thy blood has brought us
Has redeemed and made us meet.

2.
Thou art coming soon, Lord Jesus,
From this earth, we'll then be freed.
Pain and sorrow, tears and anguish
Will be finished! One indeed!
No more death and no more crying,
Everything will be at rest.
In the joy of Thine own presence,
We shall evermore be blessed.

3.
Thou art coming soon, Lord Jesus,
We'll be raised and fly to Thee.
Bodies changed in but a twinkling
All Thy beauty, we shall see.
Dressed in bodies fit for glory.
Dressed in immortality.
Dressed in spirit and in power
Ever, we shall be like Thee .

Tunes: Hymn to Joy, Mount of Olives, Here is Love, Beecher, Shipton.

Revelation 3.11
Behold, I come quickly: hold that fast which thou hast, that no man take thy crown.

2nd June.

87.87D.

Father, Mockery, We Hear.

1.
Father, mockery, we hear
Of most cruel and wicked men.
Those who railed against Thy Son
Time and time and time again.
In Him, there was found no sin.
Silently, He sought to bless.
His object - Thy work to do
And Thy blest name to confess.

2.
Father, sounds of deepest sorrow
Came from dark Gethsemane
Where the cries of Thy Beloved
Pleaded earnestly with Thee.
Yet, in gravest grief and anguish,
We can trace Thy holy will.
And the tears shed in that hour
Thy mercy and truth distil.

3.
G od of love, we see Him suff'ring
High upon Golgotha's tree.
Israel's King, scorned and rejected,
And forsaken there by Thee.
In His wounded hands and feet
And His dear, tormented soul,
We find judgement is exhausted
And the grace that makes us whole.

4.
Father, His tomb's cold and empty
Thou hast raised Him from the dead.
At Thy side, He sits exalted
The Firstborn! The church's Head!
Now the silence may be broken:
"Serve the Lord!" is Thy command.
"Kiss the Son and know true life!
Know the purposes I've planned!"

Tunes: Mount of Olives, Here is Love, Hymn to Joy, Theodoret.

John 4.31-34
In the mean while his disciples prayed him, saying, Master, eat. But he said unto them, I have meat to eat that ye know not of. Therefore said the disciples one to another, Hath any man brought him ought to eat? Jesus saith unto them, My meat is to do the will of him that sent me, and to finish his work.

3rd June.

CMD.

You Came At First, So Long Ago.

1. You came at first, so long ago,
To save our souls from sin.
You gave Yourself that we might know
Your preciousness within.
Redeemed from all iniquity
We're special folk to you.
Oh, may we serve You faithfully
Till glory, we shall view.

2. You'll come again as our great God,
The Saviour that we love.
Your glory shall appear to all,
The glory from above.
That blessed hope now fills our heart
And, Lord, we long for You.
Soon, we shall see You as You are
The faithful and the true.

3. And as we wait, most gracious Lord,
For that triumphant day.
Help us to live pure lives while here
Within the narrow way.
Let righteousness shine as a shield;
Let godliness prevail.
May Your love mark our mind, we pray,
The love that will not fail!

Tunes: No King But Christ, Bethlehem, All Saints, Jesus is God, Minerva, Warrior.

Titus 2.13-14
Looking for that blessed hope, and the glorious appearing of the great God and our Saviour Jesus Christ; who gave himself for us, that he might redeem us from all iniquity, and purify unto himself a peculiar people, zealous of good works.

4th June.

CMD.

How Glorious Was House, blest Lord.

1.
How glorious Thy house, blest Lord,
That wondrous house of old.
A structure of great beauty, Lord,
With cedar, fir and gold.
And every door and every beam
Spoke of Thy glory, Lord.
And in its courts of heavenly light,
Thy name would be adored.

2.
How glorious Thy house, blest Lord,
Built by Thyself today.
The church in which Thy Spirit dwells
Shall Thy blest name display.
The pillar and the ground of truth,
It tells the world of grace.
The body that serves Thee on earth;
The bride that seeks Thy face

3.
How glorious Thy Father's house
Found there in heav'n above.
How wonderful the place prepared
For us by Thy great love.
It is the home of perfect peace;
Where we with Thee are blessed.
It is a home of light and love
A home of joy and rest.

Tunes: Ishpeming, Jesus is God, Bethlehem, Land of Rest.

John 14.1-2

Let not your heart be troubled: ye believe in God, believe also in me. In my Father's house are many mansions: if it were not so, I would have told you. I go to prepare a place for you.

5th June.

76.76D.

Lord, You Went On Together.

1.
Lord, You went on together,
The Father and the Son;
You went to make an off'ring
In will and purpose one.
We see the fire of judgement -
Wood of humanity;
We see the Lamb provided
Speak fragrantly of Thee.

2.
Lord, You went on together,
The Father and the Son;
You climbed the hill of Calvary
Where God's work would be done.
Obedient unto death,
We see Thy face so marred.
Thy hands and feet pierced for us,
Thy body bruised and scarred.

3.
Lord, You went on together,
The Father and the Son;
But God poured out sin's judgement
Upon His Holy One.
The Father did not leave Thee;
He knew Thy grief and pain.
He'd sent Thee as our Saviour
For our eternal gain.

Tunes: Ewing, Gerhardt, Lymington, Passion Chorale.

Genesis 22.6
And Abraham took the wood of the burnt offering, and laid *it* upon Isaac his son; and he took the fire in his hand, and a knife; and they went both of them together.

6th June.

76.76D.

We Find Grace in the Saviour.

1.
We find grace in the Saviour
Who came from heaven above;
We find grace is the lever
That moves Thy heart in love.
We find grace in our calling
To be Thy sons, O God;
We find grace in the off'ring
That saves from judgement's rod.

2.
'Tis grace that saved, yes, bought us
By blood that is divine;
'Tis grace that justifies us
And grace that makes us Thine.
'Tis grace that gave us life -
A life abundant here..
And grace shall speak in wisdom
To make Thy purpose clear.

3.
Grace teaches us Thy precepts
It teaches us to pray.
It gives us what is needed
And keeps us in the way.
And in affliction's fires
We find it full and free.
Thy grace, O God, is mighty
And strengthens one like me.

4.
In grace then let us grow
That we like Christ might be;
Then by the Spirit's power
We'll share His victory.
Accepted in the Son,
The Father draws us near;
And in that place prepared
We'll never want or fear.

Tunes: Angel's Story, Gerhardt, Mountain, Greenland, Passion Chorale, Thornbury.

Ephesians 2.8-10
For by grace are ye saved through faith; and that not of yourselves: it is the gift of God: not of works, lest any man should boast. For we are his workmanship, created in Christ Jesus unto good works, which God hath before ordained that we should walk in them.

John 1.14-16
And the Word was made flesh, and dwelt among us, (and we beheld his glory, the glory as of the only begotten of the Father,) full of grace and truth.

7th June.

66.66D.

We Have a God Who's Great.

1. We have a God who's great
And Jesus is His name.
In glory, He'll appear
To take away our shame.
Oh, what a blessèd hope
To be with Him above!
Oh, what a wondrous thought
To dwell with Him in love!

2. Our Shepherd too is great
And Jesus is His name.
He guides us day by day
And all His care ,we claim.
He shields us from the foe
And finds us when we stray.
Upon His word, we feed,
While in the narrow way.

3. We have a great High Priest
Who lives for us on high,
He is the Lord, the Same
He will our needs supply.
Each day, He prays for us,
Supports us by His grace.
With pow'r, He lends a hand
And leads us in faith's race.

4. There is a King who's great
And Jesus is His name.
He'll reign in righteousness
And God's heart shall proclaim.
Then shall this world be filled
With glory that's divine.
The Mighty God shall rule
And we, with Him, shall shine.

Tunes: 66.66D: Invitation (Maker), Denby. 66.66: St Cecilia (Hayne), Eccles, Quam Dilecta.

Matthew 1.20-23
But while he thought on these things, behold, the angel of the Lord appeared unto him in a dream, saying,
Joseph, thou son of David, fear not to take unto thee Mary thy wife: for that which is conceived in her is of the Holy Ghost.
And she shall bring forth a son, and thou shalt call his name JESUS: for he shall save his people from their sins.
Now all this was done, that it might be fulfilled which was spoken of the Lord by the prophet, saying,
Behold, a virgin shall be with child, and shall bring forth a son, and they shall call his name Emmanuel, which being interpreted is,
God with us.

8th June.

66.66.

The Half Has Not Been Told.

1.
The half has not been told
Of all Your glories, Lord,
Your presence, peace and power
Are all of one accord.

2.
We see God's glory, Lord,
Shine forth from Your dear face.
And in Your life down here
We find both love and grace.

3.
We see Your beauty, Lord,
As You hung on the tree.
The Holy One and True
Made sin to set us free.

4.
You are so faithful, Lord,
In all You do and say.
You are the Lord of life
Who keeps us every day.

5.
All praise to You be given
In earth and heaven above.
To You, we give our hearts,
And prosper in Your love.

Tunes: River City, Cara, Vulpius, Matrimony.

1Chronicles 9.6
Howbeit I believed not their words, until I came, and mine eyes had seen it: and, behold, the one half of the greatness of thy wisdom was not told me: for thou exceedest the fame that I heard.

9th June.

66.66.

Lord, You Feel All My Pain.

1.
Lord, You feel all my pain,
My griefs and sorrows too.
And in Your tender care,
You know just what to do.

2.
And when I fail You, Lord,
When faith has lost its hold;
My soul You will refine
And bring me forth as gold.

3.
When waves and billows roar
To flood my soul with doubt,
Your word will still the storm
And turn my mind about.

4.
Lord, I shall never fear
The hate and hurt of men
For You are always near,
My Strength - my great Captain.

5.
To You all praise be giv'n,
Riches and power too
For, purchased by Your blood,
We now belong to You.

Tunes: St. Cecilia (Hayne), Quam Dilecta, Ibstone, Eccles.

Hebrews 4.15
For we have not an high priest which cannot be touched with the feeling of our infirmities; but was in all points tempted like as we are, yet without sin.

10th June.

CMD.

Lord, Manifest in Flesh, We See.

1. Lord, manifest in flesh, we see
Our God, as Man below.
In word and walk and works You did
We see God's blessing flow.
Refrain:
The mystery of godliness
Has been revealed in You.
As every feature of our God,
We, in Your Manhood, view.

2. Lord, justified in Spirit here -
In Mary's womb conceived.
Then in Your life and in Your death
Your virtue was perceived.
Refrain:

3. Lord, angels sought to see God's face,
They found it in You here.
The light and love that You have brought
Removes all doubt and fear.
Refrain:

4. Lord, to the nations You were preached;
Your fame was spread abroad.
Now Jew and Gentile stand as one
And Your name is adored.
Refrain:

5. Lord, in this world of sin and shame
Lost souls have felt their need;
And trusting You with all their heart
They now follow Your lead.
Refrain:

6. Lord, You ascended up on high,
Welcomed in glory bright.
And as that Man enthroned above
You are the Lamp of light.
Refrain:

Tunes: Tyrol, Landas, Providence, Bethlehem, Ellacombe, Jesus is God.

1Timothy 3.16
And without controversy great is the mystery of godliness: God was manifest in the flesh, justified in the Spirit, seen of angels, preached unto the Gentiles, believed on in the world, received up into glory.

Ephesians 4.10
He that descended is the same also that ascended up…

11th June.

66.66.

There's No One Like You, Lord.

1.
There's no one like You, Lord;
Your friendship is secure.
You'll never let me down
For You are just and pure.

2.
You catch me when I fall,
You visit me in jail.
Your strength is there for me
Each time I come to fail.

3.
I don't need eyes to see
The love You have for me.
Your gentleness and care
My own delight shall be.

4.
No matter where I turn
Your word will be my guide.
And when You come for me,
Then I'll be glorified.

5.
No matter where I go,
Your presence is assured.
And by Your might and power
Each trial is endured.

6.
I will have part with You
Way out beyond the skies.
Your home of peace and rest
Will fill my longing eyes.

Tunes: St Cecilia, Holy Guide, Quam Dilecta, Moseley, Ibstone.

Song 5.10-16
My beloved is white and ruddy, the chiefest among ten thousand.
His head is as the most fine gold, his locks are bushy, and black as a raven.
His eyes are as the eyes of doves by the rivers of waters, washed with milk, and fitly set.
His cheeks are as a bed of spices, as sweet flowers: his lips like lilies, dropping sweet smelling myrrh.
His hands are as gold rings set with the beryl: his belly is as bright ivory overlaid with sapphires.
His legs are as pillars of marble, set upon sockets of fine gold: his countenance is as Lebanon, excellent as the cedars.
His mouth is most sweet:
yea, he is altogether lovely.
This is my beloved, and this is my friend,
O daughters of Jerusalem.

12th June.

77.77D.

Lord, I'd See Your Kingdom Come.

1.
Lord, I'd see Your kingdom come,
Gleaming, glistening glorious.
Let me scan its length and breadth;
And see love victorious.
Seed and harvest all year round;
Deserts as the rose are found.
Lions with the lambs lie down
Where God's blessing shall abound.

2.
Lord, I'd see Your kingdom come,
Gleaming, glistening glorious.
Let me scan its length and breadth;
And see love victorious.
Peace shall reign in righteousness
God is worshipped and adored.
Justice true shall run its course
To the praise of You, dear Lord.

3.
Lord, I'd see Your kingdom come
Gleaming, glistening glorious.
Let me scan its length and breadth;
And see love victorious.
Life is lengthened by Your hand,
Joy and hope Your praise shall sing
In the world that God had planned,
Kings shall bring their offering.
.

4.
Lord, I'd see Your kingdom come,
Gleaming, glistening glorious.
Let me scan its length and breadth;
And see love victorious.
Wonderful and Counsellor!
Mighty God and Prince of Peace!
Father of Eternity,
Praise for You shall never cease!

Tunes: St. Edmund Steggall, Safely Safely, Roland, New St. Andrew, Madrid (Carr).

Isaiah 11.6
The wolf also shall dwell with the lamb, and the leopard shall lie down with the kid; and the calf and the young lion and the fatling together; and a little child shall lead them.

13th June.

CMD.

The Baby in a Manger Laid.

1.
The Baby in a manger laid
Was swaddled firm and warm;
Emmanuel the holy name
Of God in human form.
Refrain:
All glory to the Lord most High!
All praise to Him ascend!
He came to earth to set us free
By love that knows no end!

2.
Some shepherds on the dark hillside
Were keeping watch by night;
The glory of the Lord shone round
And bathed them in its light.
Refrain:

3.
The angel of the Lord calmed them
And gave them wondrous news
He told them of a Saviour born –
A Saviour - Christ the Lord
Refrain:

4.
With haste the shepherds left their flocks
And to the manger came.
They saw the child of David's line
And Jesus was His name.
Refrain:

5.
With joy they spread the news abroad
Of all that had occurred.
While Mary thought about their words
God's people were assured.
Refrain:

Tunes: Bethlehem, Noel, Providence, Ellacombe, Forest Green, Jesus is God, Landas.

Luke 2.13-14
And suddenly there was with the angel a multitude of the heavenly host praising God, and saying, Glory to God in the highest, and on earth peace, good will toward men.

Luke 2.28
Then took he him up in his arms, and blessed God, and said, Lord, now lettest thou thy servant depart in peace, according to thy word: For mine eyes have seen thy salvation, which thou hast prepared…

14th June.

66.86.

Forever with the Lord!

1. Forever with the Lord!
O what a wondrous thought!
Jesus my Saviour comes for us
Wretches His blood has bought.

2. Forever with the Lord!
It's written in His word.
As He descends, His shout we'll hear
And rise with one accord.

3. Forever with the Lord!
What praise our souls shall fill.
To see the face of Him who died
In His blest Father's will.

4. Forever with the Lord!
And we shall like Him be
For in a twinkling, we'll be found
In bodies heavenly.

5. Forever with the Lord!
The Lord who loves us so.
And in His Father's house on high
His joy and peace, we'll know.

Tunes: Energy, Cambridge (Harrison), Lake Enon, Carlisle.

1Thessalonians 4.16-18
For the Lord himself shall descend from heaven with a shout,
with the voice of the archangel, and with the trump of God:
and the dead in Christ shall rise first:
then we which are alive and remain shall be caught up together with them in the clouds,
to meet the Lord in the air:
and so shall we ever be with the Lord.
Wherefore comfort one another with these words.

15th June.

77.77.

Rescued Through the Cross of Shame.

1.
Rescued through the cross of shame,
I must praise the Saviour's name.
See His blood poured out for me;
See the love that sets me free.

2.
Rescued now from judgement's rod,
I have peace! Yes, peace with God
Heaven's gates are opened wide;
Christ will take me for His bride.

3.
Rescued from the devil's power,
God gives strength for every hour.
Sin and death have lost their sting;
Of His vict'ry, I shall sing.

4.
Rescued from this world of strife,
I have joy and I have life.
Soon He'll come to take me home;
From Him nevermore to roam.

5.
Rescued from the storms of night,
Darkness is now turned to light.
Hope now rules my heart and mind;
In the Lord, my strength I find.

6.
Rescued to serve Him below,
I shall seek His will to know.
In the depth or in the height,
May my work of faith be bright.

Tunes: 77.77: St. Bees, Monkland, St. Prisca, Argyle, Buckland. 77.77D: St. Edmund Steggall, St. George's (Windsor), New St. Andrew, Hollingside, Benevento.

Colossians 1.12-13
Giving thanks unto the Father, which hath made us meet to be partakers of the inheritance of the saints in light: who hath delivered us from the power of darkness, and hath translated us into the kingdom of his dear Son…

16th June.

CMD.

Oh, Faithful is the Saying, Lord.

1.
Oh, faithful is the saying, Lord,
That You came here for me
And as the sinless Son of God
You died on Calvary's tree.
And every sin of mine was borne
In You upon that cross.
And all the blessings I possess
Came from Your shame and loss.

2.
Oh, faithful is the saying, Lord,
That we with You have died.
Our sinful selves hung on that cross
When You were crucified.
And so with You, we hope to dwell,
To live with You above.
While for the present, we would live
In all Your strength and love.

3.
Oh, faithful is the saying, Lord,
That exercise is fine;
It keeps our bodies fit and trim,
And helps our skin to shine.
But godliness is better far
It proves its worth in all.
So give us grace to do Your will
As we Your life recall.

4.
Oh, faithful is the saying, Lord,
That mercy set us free.
'Tis by Your grace, we're justified;
And heirs, with You, we'll be.
We're cleansed by Your most precious word
The Spirit is restored.
Eternal life is our reward,
And You, our Lord, adored.

Tunes: Bethlehem, No King But Christ, Landas, Land of Rest.

1Timothy 1.15
This is a faithful saying, and worthy of all acceptation, that Christ Jesus came into the world to save sinners; of whom I am chief.

2Timothy 2.11-12
It is a faithful saying: For if we be dead with him, we shall also live with him: if we suffer, we shall also reign with him: if we deny him, he also will deny us…

17th June.

76.76.

Lord Jesus, My Belovèd.

1.
Lord Jesus, my Belovèd,
The Father's only Son.
Thou, in Thy love's deep pity,
My humble heart hast won.

2.
Lord Jesus, my Belovèd,
Sweet myrrh unto my soul,
Thou'rt gentle, brave and faithful;
The Man who made me whole.

3.
Lord Jesus, my Belovèd,
Dwelling in brightest light;
How precious is Thy Person
In Thy blest Father's sight.

4.
Lord Jesus, my Belovèd,
Thy words and ways are love,
Sin, death and hell, Thou'st vanquished;
Thou'rt crowned in heav'n above.

5.
Lord Jesus, my Belovèd,
Speak peace to my poor mind.
For at Thy side in Glory
True wisdom, I shall find.

6.
Lord Jesus, my Belovèd,
My praise accept this day.
For Thou art ever lovely,
And bless'd in every way.

Tunes: 76.76: Cara, Matrimony, Eden (Boston). 76.76D: Lymington, Greenland (Haydn), Thornbury, St. Edith, Passion Chorale.

Song 1.13-14
A bundle of myrrh is my wellbeloved unto me; he shall lie all night betwixt my breasts. My beloved is unto me as a cluster of camphire in the vineyards of Engedi.

Song 2.3
3 As the apple tree among the trees of the wood, so is my beloved among the sons. I sat down under his shadow with great delight, and his fruit was sweet to my taste.

Song 2.9
My beloved is like a roe or a young hart: behold, he standeth behind our wall,..

18th June.

CMD.

O Lord, We See Thy Glory Bright.

1.
O Lord, we see Thy glory bright
Before the worlds were made.
The Father's joy! The Father's heart!
Was for Thyself displayed.
But Thou Thy heavenly home didst leave
To turn our night to day.
And Thou the Father's love hast shown
To us in every way.

2.
We see Thy wisdom and Thy power;
We hear Thy words of grace;
We see Thee bearing sorrows too
Our pain etched on Thy face.
We see Thine arms embrace the poor;
The dead Thy word obey.
In these, the Father's love Thou'st shown
To us in every way.

3.
We see Thee on the cross of shame
Bearing our sin and woe.
And there forsaken by Thy God
The depths of love didst show.
The anguish of Thy righteous soul
Was veiled upon that day.
Yet there, the Father's love was shown
To us in every way.

4.
Soon, we shall hear Thy wondrous voice
Call us to Thee above.
Once changed, we'll meet thee in the air,
And know the joy of love.
Thou wilt receive us as Thy bride
And with Thee we shall stay.
'Tis there, the Father's love will bless
Our lives in every way.

Tunes: Providence, Landas, Bethlehem.

Proverbs 8.29
When he gave to the sea his decree, that the waters should not pass his commandment:
when he appointed the foundations of the earth:
Then I was by him, as one brought up with him: and I was daily his delight, rejoicing always before him…

19th June.

88.88.

My Christian Friend, There's Work to Do.

1. My Christian friend, there's work to do.
And it's a job that's made for you.
Go, tiny one, and play your part
Great joy you'll bring to Jesus' heart.

2. Follow your Saviour, walk in love,
Send daily prayers to Him above.
Obey your parents in the Lord
Then His dear name will be adored.

3. Go to the old, bid them, "Good Day."
Jesus will give you words to say.
And when your friends come round to play,
Speak to them of the narrow way.

4. Take up the Spirit's mighty sword
Learn all you can of your blest Lord.
Stand for His name as best you can
Finding your place in His great plan.

5. When troubles come, you need not fear,
Jesus, has counted every tear.
To joy your sorrow shall be turned
Into the glory you have earned.

(Written for children: July, 2009).

Tunes: Gift of Love, Tallis' Canon, Church Triumphant, Brookfield.

John 6.28-29
Then said they unto him,
What shall we do,
that we might work the works of God?
Jesus answered and said unto them,
This is the work of God, that ye believe on him whom
he hath sent.

20th June.

CM.

I Have a Little Corner, Lord.

1. I have a little corner, Lord,
Where I can go each day;
And there, I can be anything
My mind would like to play.

2. I like to be a Christian child
And that by heavenly birth.
I like to be a worshipper
Telling our God His worth.

3. I like to be a warrior
Dressed in God's armour
bright.
My Captain is the Lord above;
He'll guard me as I fight.

4. I like to be an athlete keen
To run the race of God.
I like to be a student too
Abiding in His word.

5. I like to be a good shepherd
Caring for God's own sheep.
The wolves and bears, I would
fight off
And cuddle those who weep.

6. I like to be a witness too
Telling of You, dear Lord.
I like to be a comforter
That peace might be restored.

7. All these, O Lord, have
come from You!
How perfect is Your way!
Yet, I would ask for this alone –
In Your blest will to stay.

(Written for Children.).

Tunes: CM: St. Fulbert, Arlington, Beulah, St. Agnes, Tyrone, Belmont, Beatitudo.

2Timothy 2.3
Thou therefore endure hardness, as a good soldier of Jesus Christ .No man that warreth entangleth himself with the affairs of this life; that he may please him who hath chosen him to be a soldier.
And if a man also strive for masteries, yet is he not crowned, except he strive lawfully. The husbandman that laboureth must be first partaker of the fruits.

1Corinthians 924
Know ye not that they which run in a race run all, but one receiveth the prize? So run, that ye may obtain.

21st June.

CMD.

The Sweetest Sound I've Ever Heard.

1. The sweetest sound I've ever heard
Is my dear Saviour's voice.
From a dark pit, it lifted me
And made my heart rejoice.
It set my feet upon a rock;
My path of life made clear.
It put a song into my lips,
Promoting godly fear.

2. The sweetest smell I've ever breathed
Rose from my Saviour's mind.
How fragrant His humility,
So gentle and so kind.
His heart was scented with God's love,
Upon the cross of shame
Where, in His awful agony,
He bore our guilt – our blame.

3. The sweetest sight I've ever seen
Is my dear Saviour's face.
Wounded and scarred by wicked men
It tells of God's good grace.
Yet, in the light of heaven above
I see the Father's name;
For in the face of Jesus Christ
God's glory is a flame.

4. The sweetest touch I've ever felt
Is in my Saviour's hand.
It lifted me from sin and death
And gave me strength to stand.
Secure within its grasp I lie,
Eternal life is mine.
No one shall take me from Him now
His power is divine.

5. The sweetest taste I've ever known
Came from my Saviour's grace.
It filled my soul with tenderness
Within the holy place.
All honour, praise, riches and power
Be to our Lord above.
Come now, adore His precious name!
He's worthy of our love!

Tunes: Jesus is God, No King But Christ, Release, Landas, I Bring My All To Thee.

Psalm 34.8
O taste and see that the LORD is good: blessed is the man that trusteth in him.

22nd June.

76.76D.

Eternal Was the Notion.

1.
Eternal was the notion,
Or so I understand,
To set the worlds in motion
As You, O Lord, had planned.
To put men on this planet
As objects of Your love;
To reach out in Your mercy
And take us up above.

2.
It's through the cross of Jesus
That we belong to You.
Our sin was laid upon Him,
The Faithful and the True.
Your anger was exhausted;
Our judgement on Him fell.
And now, in all His glory,
Of Him, our lips must tell.

3.
Let goodness guard and keep us
As through this world we go.
Let nothing come between us
And harm the joy we know.
Let peace reign in our being
In times of trial and woe.
Let hope be our strong anchor
When grief and sorrow flow.

4.
O Lord, we have discovered
That which we should have
known –
That Jesus loves You dearly,
And sits upon Your throne.
Soon He'll be coming for us,
To carry us on high.
Then we shall be together -
That's why He came to die!

.Tunes: Lymington, Thornbury, Ellacombe, Greenland, Stand Up, Ewing.

Ephesians 2.3-6
Blessed be the God and Father of our Lord Jesus Christ, who hath blessed us with all spiritual blessings in heavenly places in Christ: according as he hath chosen us in him before the foundation of the world, that we should be holy and without blame before him in love: Having predestinated us unto the adoption of children by Jesus Christ to himself, according to the good pleasure of his will, to the praise of the glory of his grace, wherein he hath made us accepted in the beloved.

1Peter 1.20
Who verily was foreordained before the foundation of the world, but was manifest in these last times for you.

23rd June.

98.98.

I've Often Thought of Heaven Above.

1.
I've often thought of heaven above
Where You, O Lord, dwell in Your love.
And one day soon, I'll rise to see
The precious smile that welcomes me.

2.
Yet, while down here, I'll run faith's race
And I'll endure by Your good grace.
You'll strengthen me for every mile.
You'll run with me through time and trial.

3.
I've often dreamed of that cursed cross
Where You once died and suffered loss.
There in Your wounds, I find God's heart;
And through Your blood with Him have part.

4.
While here on earth, I'll serve You, Lord;
To do Your will is my reward.
And when some day, You come for me,
Then I shall prove my destiny.

5.
Angels elect will praise Your name;
All heav'n Your glory will proclaim.
And saints of God, Your worth will tell
For You, O Lord, did all things well.

Tunes: His Wondrous Ways, Church Vigilant.

Mark 7.37
…And were beyond measure astonished, saying, He hath done all things well: he maketh both the deaf to hear, and the dumb to speak.

24th June.

76.76D with refrain.

Lord Jesus, Once a Stranger.

1. Lord Jesus, once a Stranger
In this world that You made.
Your people did not know You.
The Lord as man displayed.
Both hated and rejected,
You were God's only Son.
Emmanuel - God with us,
The Holy, heavenly One.
Lord, look upon the outcasts
And love them as Your own.
Lord, look upon the outcasts
And draw them to Your throne.

2. We see You in the manger,
No room for You down here.
We see Your grief and sorrow,
But few there were to care.
We see You in the garden
In agony and prayer.
We see You on the cross
Where sin You had to bear.
Lord Jesus, bless the outcasts
And cleanse them from all sin.
Lord Jesus, bless the outcasts;
Grant them Your peace within.

3. We know Your tomb is
empty!
The Father's work is done!
We know that You're accepted!
We know the battle's won!
Lord, we are now the outcasts
Without the bounds of men;
For we would stand here for
You
And speak as Your children.
Lord, help us - lowly outcasts,
And hear us when we cry.
Lord, help us - lowly outcasts,
And all our needs supply.

Tunes: Hankey, O House of Many Mansions.

Matthew 8.19-20
And a certain scribe came, and said unto him,
Master, I will follow thee whithersoever thou goest.
And Jesus saith unto him,
The foxes have holes, and the birds of the air have nests;
but the Son of man hath not where to lay his head.

Matthew 25.35
For I was an hungred, and ye gave me meat:
I was thirsty, and ye gave me drink:
I was a stranger, and ye took me in…

25th June.

66.66.

You are the Potentate.

1.
You are the Potentate
Who rules from heaven above.
The only One we know
And have the joy to love.

2.
You are the King of kings!
The Lord of heaven and earth!
Immortal is Your life
And wonderful Your worth.

3.
You dwell in brighter light
Than all suns bound in one.
You are invisible -
And great the work You've done!

4.
You are the Source of life!
You're evermore the Same!
With hearts adoring now
We praise Your holy name!

Tunes: Invitation (Maker), Denby. 66.66: St. Cecilia (Hayne), Quam Dilecta, Moseley.

1Timothy 6.15-16
Which in his times he shall shew,
who is the blessed and only Potentate,
the King of kings, and Lord of lords;
who only hath immortality,
dwelling in the light which no man can approach unto;
whom no man hath seen, nor can see: to whom be honour and power everlasting.
Amen.

26th June.

76.76D with refrain.

There is a New World Coming.

1.
There is a new world coming
Where righteousness shall reign.
There is a new world coming
Where peace shall live again.
There is a new world coming
Where joy shall never cease.
There is a new world coming
Where ages will increase.

When Christ shall come in glory
We'll tell the heav'nly story
When Christ shall come in glory
Both Lord and King, He'll be.

2.
There is a new world coming
Where pain has lost is power
There is a new world coming
When desert lands will flow'r.
There is a new world coming
Where death itself is rare.
There is a new world coming.
Where no lion shall tear.
Refrain:

3.
There is a new world coming
Where cries of woe are stilled.
There is a new world coming
Where fertile fields are tilled.
There is a new world coming
Where suffering is no more.
There is a new world coming
Where we'll praise and adore!
Refrain:

Tunes: Hankey.

Titus 2.14-15
Looking for that blessed hope, and the glorious appearing of the great God and our Saviour Jesus Christ; who gave himself for us, that he might redeem us from all iniquity, and purify unto himself a peculiar people, zealous of good works.

2Timothy 4.1
I charge thee therefore before God, and the Lord Jesus Christ, who shall judge the quick and the dead at his appearing and his kingdom…

2Peter 3.13
Nevertheless we, according to his promise, look for new heavens and a new earth, wherein dwelleth righteousness.

27th June.

77.77.5.

There was Grief and there was Pain.

1.
There was grief and there was pain,
There was death and tears like rain.
There was sorrow and distress
And those woes, we can't address.
Until there was You, Lord.

2.
You came here to bear our sin
On the cross of deepest shame.
In Your wounds, our blame we see
Nailed with You upon the tree.
We now love You, Lord.

3.
Raised with You, we now proclaim
All the wonder of Your name.
Glorified in heaven above
You pour out both light and love.
We will serve You, Lord.

4.
Now there's joy and blessed gain,
Now there's life and hope again.
There is happiness and peace,
Our delight will never cease!
It is found in You, Lord.

Tunes: Wurttemberg.

Isaiah 53.3-4
He is despised and rejected of men; a man of sorrows, and acquainted with grief: and we hid as it were our faces from him; he was despised, and we esteemed him not. Surely he hath borne our griefs, and carried our sorrows: yet we did esteem him stricken, smitten of God, and afflicted.

28th June.

CM.

Father, We Would Not be Ashamed.

1.
Father, we would not be ashamed
To tell of Thy dear Son;
And though we suffer for His name;
Thy will alone be done.

2.
Before the age of Time itself
Our blessing was Thy goal;
And in Thy purpose, by Thy grace,
In Christ, we were made whole.

3.
In Him we see salvation bloom;
Our calling is secure;
Of life and immortality,
He does our souls assure.

4.
The empty grave Thy pow'r declares;
And speaks to hearts Thou'st won.
All praise and glory be to Thee
And to Thy blessèd Son.

Tunes: Westminster (Turle), Beulah, Arlington, St. Agnes.

1John 2.28
And now, little children, abide in him; that, when he shall appear, we may have confidence, and not be ashamed before him at his coming.

1Peter 3.16-17
Yet if any man suffer as a Christian,
let him not be ashamed;
but let him glorify God on this behalf.
For the time is come
that judgment must begin at the house of God…

29th June.

77.77.

When I'm Lonely and Despised.

1. When I'm lonely and despised
With no one to hear my cries;
When there's little love or care,
You'll be there, Lord. You'll be there.

2. When the road of life is long;
And its storms are blowing strong;
When I'm heading for despair;
You'll be there, Lord, You'll be there.

3. When dark forces ambush lay;
And my sin would have its way;
When the devil sets his snare;
You'll be there, Lord. You'll be there.

4. When deep sorrow brings its flood;
And life's trials lead to blood;
When I turn from faith and prayer;
You'll be there, Lord. You'll be there.

5. When I'm weak upon my bed;
And death rears its ugly head;
When I rise to be elsewhere;
You'll be there, Lord. You'll be there.

6. You will never leave my side;
Even when I try to hide.
Ever faithful – ever true;
I can always trust in You!

Tunes: 77.77: Buckland, Nottingham, St. Bees, St. Prisca. 77.77D: St. Edmund Steggall, Benevento, Hollingside, St. George's Windsor.

Proverbs 3.6
In all thy ways acknowledge him, and he shall direct thy paths.

30th June.

CMD.

Father of Lights, We Praise Thy Name.

1.
Father of lights, we praise Thy name,
For all that Thou hast giv'n.
Thy gifts are perfect and divine
And come to us from heav'n.
Yet, too, we see those gifts of grace
That build Thy church down here.
Gifts that encourage and instruct
Delivered without fear.

2.
Thy Spirit Thou hast given too
That we may live in pow'r.
Create in us the moral force
To mark us hour by hour.
The spirit of Thine own great love
Indwells us by Thy grace.
Help us to love as Christ has loved
That all may seek Thy face.

3.
Grant us the pow'r of self-control
To exercise Thy will.
And bless the saints in every way
Thy purpose to fulfil.
Give us grace to suffer, Lord,
As for Thy name we stand.
And may we in Thy calling, Lord,
Soon reach the "Promised Land".

Tunes: Release, Jesus is God, Landas, No King But Christ, Warrior.

James 1.17
Every good gift and every perfect gift is from above, and cometh down from the Father of lights, with whom is no variableness, neither shadow of turning.

1st July.

77.77.

Just Believe and Be Sin Free.

1. Just believe and be sin free;
Just believe – forgiveness see;
Just believe and know God's grace;
Just believe and run faith's race

2. Just believe and peace will flow;
Just believe and in Christ grow.
Just believe the Lord's blest call;
Just believe and strengthen all

3. Just believe and power is yours;
Just believe and open doors.
Just believe and serve today
Just believe and watch and pray

4. Just believe and mountains move;
Just believe and yourselves prove.
Just believe, be pure in heart;
Just believe with Christ have part.

5. Just believe be sanctified;
Just believe with Christ you've died.
Just believe and be made right;
Just believe in faith's great fight

6. Just believe and know God's mind;
Just believe and joy you'll find
Just believe and stand as one;
Just believe God's only Son.

7. Just believe an heir be made;
Just believe and fears will fade.
Just believe and needs are met;
Just believe and cast the net.

8. Just believe and as God give;
Just believe and by faith live.
Just believe - the Spirit gain;
Just believe with Christ to reign.

Tunes: Innocents, Monkland, Confidence (Ouseley), Nottingham, St. Bees, Buckland, Canterbury.

Romans 1.16-17
For I am not ashamed of the gospel of Christ:
for it is the power of God unto salvation to every one that believeth;
to the Jew first, and also to the Greek.
For therein is the righteousness of God revealed from faith to faith:
as it is written,
The just shall live by faith.

2nd July.

66.66.

Soldiers of Christ, Arise!

1. Soldiers of Christ, arise!
The battle has begun.
Leave life's fine ways behind
To please God's only Son.

2. Camp out as soldiers true
And suffer in the fray.
The Lord will fight with you
And keep you day by day.

3. Athletes of Christ, compete!
The race of faith endure.
Follow His faithful word –
The crowning day is sure.

4. Farmers of Christ, toil on!
Labour with sweat and tear.
The fruits are yours to claim
As harvest time draws near.

5. Joiners of Christ, work on!
Cut true the Word of Life.
Be earnest in your toil
Avoiding shame and strife.

6. O, may the Lord be praised,
Whose life pleased God above.
He toiled and suffered here
To claim us in His love.

Tunes: St. Cecilia (Hayne), Holy Guide, Moseley, Ibstone.

Hebrews 12.1
Wherefore seeing we also are compassed about with so great a cloud of witnesses, let us lay aside every weight, and the sin which doth so easily beset us, and let us run with patience the race that is set before us,

3rd July.

88.88.

Lord, Look Upon My Younger Son.

1. Lord, look upon my younger son
And gently bring Him back to Thee.
Reveal Thyself afresh to him;
O, let him from all sin be free.

2. His reas'ning mind has blocked Thy will;
Man's science rules his faith today.
His worldy friends have helped him stray
Oh, lead him back into Thy way.

3. All that is real is found in Thee;
To Thee we owe each living breath.
Without Thee, Lord, we'd only find
Crying and tears with pain and death.

4. He is so young in heart and soul;
Knowing so little of life's pain.
Please, touch him with Thy tender hand;
And show him that this world is vain.

5. Lord, Thou hast seen his caring heart,
Along with gifts Thou didst impart.
Please, let him use these things for Thee
And bring lost souls, Thy grace to see.

6. Lord, Thou dost give and Thou dost take,
Lord, Thou dost heal and Thou dost break.
Grant him the peace and joy to know
That blessings from Thy fountain flow.
(A prayer for a backsliding son).

Tunes: Gift of Love, Tallis' Canon, Federal St., Rimington.

Hebrews 14.4
I will heal their backsliding, I will love them freely: for mine anger is turned away from him.

4th July.

CMD.

Father, I Thank You for the Skills.

1.
Father, I thank You for the skills
That You have given me.
Help me to use them in Your will
That blessing all may see.
And though I suffer in my toil,
I shall not be ashamed.
For in the gospel that I preach
Your Son is always named.

2.
Father, in faith, I bow to You,
Knowing Your will is best.
In love, I'd keep Your faithful word
And know that I am blessed.
And I will ever trust in You
Knowing Your power to keep;
And in that day of days, I'll find
My toil its hire shall reap.

Tunes: Jesus is God, No King But Christ, Landas, Land of Rest, Warrior.

Matthew 25.15
For the kingdom of heaven is as a man travelling into a far country, who called his own servants, and delivered unto them his goods.
And unto one he gave five talents,
to another two,
and to another one;
to every man according to his several ability; and straightway took his journey.
Then he that had received the five talents went and traded with the same, and made them other five talents.
And likewise he that had received two, he also gained other two.
But he that had received one went and digged in the earth, and hid his lord's money.

5th July.

No tune known.

Swish! Clash! Clang! Crash!

1.
Swish! Clash! Clang! Crash!
Faith's battle has begun.
Soldiers of Christ, fight on
Until the vict'ry's won.

2.
Strain! Stretch! Pant! Run!
The marathon's begun.
Athletes of Christ, run on
Until the crown is won.

3.
Dig! Scrape! Plough! Plant!
Faith's tilling has begun.
Farmers of Christ, toil on
Until the harvest's done.

4.
Size! Mark! Score! Saw!
The building has begun.
Joiners of Christ, work on!
The will of God be done.

Tunes: None found.

1Corinthians 3.10-12
According to the grace of God which is given unto me, as a wise masterbuilder, I have laid the foundation, and another buildeth thereon. But let every man take heed how he buildeth thereupon. For other foundation can no man lay than that is laid, which is Jesus Christ. Now if any man build upon this foundation gold, silver, precious stones, wood, hay, stubble; every man's work shall be made manifest: for the day shall declare it, because it shall be revealed by fire; and the fire shall try every man's work of what sort it is.If any man's work abide which he hath built thereupon, he shall receive a reward.

6th July.

75.75D.

Lord, You Taught Us Everything.

1.
Lord, You taught us everything,
Everything we know.
And You're always close to us
Everywhere we go.
You have given everything
That our lives might need.
You're the Source of life and death
True in word and deed.

2.
You are always there for us
When the clouds are grey.
How You love and care for us
Each and every day.
When we're feeling so alone;
When we are depressed;
Then we feel Your warm embrace
And our minds can rest.

3.
Jesus, Lord, we love You so
Our hearts long for You..
We would see Your blessèd face
And Your glory view.
In Your love, Yourself You gave,
When we were undone.
At the cross of Calvary
You have made us one.

4.
You're the Saviour of our souls;
Your love brought us near.
Now the Father's name we know;
What then shall we fear!
Lord, You'll keep us in the way;
Keep us from all strife.
Till that day, we'll be with You
With eternal life.

5.
Father, all praise be to You
And to Your dear Son.
Worshippers will bow to You
Through the work He's done.
May Your name exalted be;
May Your worth be told;
For the wonder of Your will
Blessed us all of old.

Tunes: Guidance.

Matthew 22.
…And they sent out unto him their disciples with the Herodians, saying, Master, we know that thou art true,
and teachest the way of God in truth, neither carest thou for any man: for thou regardest not the person of men.

7^Th July.

87.87D.

Ring, Ye Bells! Ring Out For Freedom!

1.
Ring, ye bells! Ring out for freedom!
Tell the good news without fear.
Chime with joy and adulation,
Freedom's day is drawing near.
Refrain:
Praise the Lord who came from heaven
On a cruel cross to die.
Praise the Father who hath raised Him
And exalted Him on high.

2.
Watch and pray, ye faithful servants,
Listen for His joyful shout.
Lift His banner high above you;
Let His love and power flow out.
Refrain:

3.
Part with Him shall be our portion
When we meet Him in the air.
Look into His face once smitten;
See God's glory shining there.
Refrain:

4.
We His children gather to Him
With the cry of "Liberty!"
'Tis the day of our redemption;
'Tis the day, he sets us free.
Refrain:

5.
We'll be changed into His likeness;
We'll have immortality.
We will worship without hindrance
Free, in Him, we'll always be.
Refrain:

Tunes: Hymn to Joy, Mount of Olives, Love Divine (Stainer), Woodside.

Leviticus 25.8-9
And thou shalt number seven sabbaths of years unto thee, seven times seven years;
and the space of the seven sabbaths of years shall be unto thee forty and nine years.
Then shalt thou cause the trumpet of the jubile to sound on the tenth day of the seventh month, in the day of atonement shall ye make the trumpet sound throughout all your land.

8th July.

86.86.

Give Me the Mind to be Like You.

1.
Give me the mind to be like You
In everything I do.
Lord, make me faithful to your word
And bring honour to You.

2.
Cleanse me from all unrighteousness
From evil teaching too.
Prepare me for Your service, Lord,
Set me apart for You.

3.
To follow You is my desire,
Though suffering will pursue.
Give me the grace to trust You, Lord,
And grow in love for You.

Tunes: Beulah, St. Agnes..

2Timothy 2.19-21
Nevertheless the foundation of God standeth sure, having this seal, The Lord knoweth them that are his.
And, Let every one that nameth the name of Christ depart from iniquity.
But in a great house there are not only vessels of gold and of silver, but also of wood and of earth; and some to honour, and some to dishonour.
If a man therefore purge himself from these, he shall be a vessel unto honour, sanctified, and meet for the master's use, and prepared unto every good work.

1Corinthians 6.11
And such were some of you:
but ye are washed,
but ye are sanctified,
but ye are justified in the name of the Lord Jesus,
and by the Spirit of our God.

9th July.

88.88.Refrain.

Happiness is the Joy in You.

1.
Happiness is the joy in You
A joy beyond the skies so blue
A joy that fills the heart with song
A joy that tells us we belong.

Happiness is love, joy and peace
And by your grace, they'll never cease.
And by your grace, they'll never cease.

2.
Happiness is the peace in You
And flows through every thing You do.
A peace that is not understood
A peace that always works for good.

Happiness is love, joy and peace
And by your grace, they'll never cease.
And by your grace, they'll never cease.

3.
Happiness is the love in You
The love that sin and Satan slew.
The love that gave itself for us;
The love so pure and so precious.

Happiness is love, joy and peace
And by your grace, they'll never cease.
And by your grace, they'll never cease.

Tunes: Solid Rock

Psalm 1.1
Blessed is the man that walketh not in the counsel of the ungodly,
nor standeth in the way of sinners,
nor sitteth in the seat of the scornful.

10th July.

64.64D.

Thy Word is Shining, Lord.

1.
Thy word is shining, Lord,
Upon my way.
Showing the narrow path
In which to stay.
I've walked and wandered
In deep distress.
No purpose did I find -
Only darkness.

2.
I saw Thee on the tree
Bearing my sin.
What kind of love is this
That takes me in?
Love that's stronger than death
Shed blood for me.
Now I am justified -
Perfect in Thee.

3.
My heart is Thine, dear Lord,
As is my soul.
Draw me close to Thy side
Making me whole.
Give me Thy mind, blest Lord,
That all may see
Thy meek humility
Living in me.

4.
Heaven is Thy home, Lord,
The home for me.
There, peace and joy abound -
There, rest I see.
There, love and light astound
As seen in Thee.
Come quickly, blessèd Lord,
With Thee, I'd be.

Tunes: Langport, Bridgewater.

Psalm 119.105-112
NUN.
Thy word is a lamp unto my feet, and a light unto my path. I have sworn, and I will perform it, that I will keep thy righteous judgments. I am afflicted very much: quicken me, O LORD, according unto thy word. Accept, I beseech thee, the freewill offerings of my mouth, O LORD, and teach me thy judgments.
My soul is continually in my hand: yet do I not forget thy law.
The wicked have laid a snare for me: yet I erred not from thy precepts.
Thy testimonies have I taken as an heritage for ever: for they are the rejoicing of my heart.
I have inclined mine heart to perform thy statutes alway, even unto the end.

11th July.

86.86D. Refrain.

You Are the Father's Only Son.

1. You are the Father's only Son,
The Maker of all things.
You are Word of God above,
The Source of all blessings.
You are the Saviour of us all
Who left His home on high.
And here, as man, You suffered much,
For You had come to die.

Glory to You, Lord Jesus,
Set on the throne of God.
Glory to You, blessèd Saviour!

2. You are the Author of all life!
The Lord of heaven and earth!
The good news of salvation sure
Proclaims Your wondrous worth.
You are the First and with the Last,
The God of all we know.
The Alpha and Omega, too,
Revealing God below.

Glory to You, Lord Jesus,
Set on the throne of God.
Glory to You, blessèd Saviour!

3. You are the Chief, the Corner Stone,
Who builds His church with care.
You are the Bright and Morning Star,
The Prophet, Priest and Heir.
You are the True and Living Bread;
By You, we are sustained.
You are the Firstborn from the dead,
The King by God ordained.

Glory to You, Lord Jesus,
Set on the throne of God.
Glory to You, blessèd Saviour!

Tunes: Weinacht.

Hebrews 1.1-4

God, who at sundry times and in divers manners spake in time past unto the fathers by the prophets, hath in these last days spoken unto us by his Son, whom he hath appointed heir of all things, by whom also he made the worlds; who being the brightness of his glory, and the express image of his person, and upholding all things by the word of his power, when he had by himself purged our sins, sat down on the right hand of the Majesty on high; being made so much better than the angels ,,,,

12th July.

66.66.

My Tears, You'll Wipe Away.

1.
My tears, You'll wipe away;
Your strength will hold me fast
My night, You'll turn to day.
Your love about me cast.
You will be in my heart
Wherever I may go.
You will be in my heart
And this I'll always know.

2.
Your kiss, my soul awakes
To love and to obey.
I'm caught in Your embrace
As I kneel down to pray.
You will be in my heart
Wherever I may go.
You will be in my heart
And this I'll always know.

3.
Our unity is firm
Set in the Spirit's power.
Let glory be His seal
And joy a mighty tower.
You will be in my heart
Wherever I may go.
You will be in my heart
And this I'll always know.

Tunes: Invitation (Maker), Denby.

Psalm 56.8 and Revelation 21.4
Thou tellest my wanderings: put thou my tears into thy bottle: are they not in thy book?
And God shall wipe away all tears from their eyes…

13th July.

CM.

Oh, It is Finished!" Wondrous Thought!

1.
Oh, it is finished!" Wondrous thought!
The work has all been done.
There's nothing left for us to do
But trust in God's dear Son.

2.
"O, it is finished!" Christ has died
God's sacrifice for sin;
And now we're reconciled to God
With joy and peace within.

3.
"O, it is finished!" We are saved
From Satan's power and chain.
And justified, we praise the Lord,
From whence comes all our gain.

4.
"O, it is finished!" We are made
The sons of God above.
And through the work of Christ, our Lord,
We know that God is love.

Tunes: Belmont, St. Agnes, Beulah, Nativity, Westminster (Turle).

John 19.28-31

After this, Jesus knowing that all things were now accomplished, that the scripture might be fulfilled, saith, I thirst. Now there was set a vessel full of vinegar: and they filled a spunge with vinegar, and put it upon hyssop, and put it to his mouth. When Jesus therefore had received the vinegar, he said, It is finished: and he bowed his head, and gave up the ghost. The Jews therefore, because it was the preparation, that the bodies should not remain upon the cross on the sabbath day, (for that sabbath day was an high day,) besought Pilate that their legs might be broken, and that they might be taken away.

14th July.

10.10.10.10.

Lord, Hear My Song; Please, Hear My Song Of Love.

1. Lord, hear my song; please, hear my song of love.
When I think of You, God's Son from above -
With joy, my heart is filled and I must tell
Of all the beauty which I know so well.

2. You are adorable in Your own right.
Your beauty exceeds the glory of light.
You are the Christ, of God the Chosen One;
The Daysman from on high who peace has won.

3. You are Eternal Life, the Father's Son.
You are God with us, Head of every one.
You are the Image of our God above.
You are the Judge - the King of light and love.

4. You were the Lamb who for our sins once died;
The Man of Sorrows cruelly crucified.
The Nazarene, rejected here below;
The Only Wise God who all men should know.

5. As our high Priest, You sit upon God's throne,
The Root of David and the living Stone;
You are the Truth – God's gift Unspeakable!
You are the Victor – the invincible!

6. You are most Wonderful in name and deed,
Yahweh who came to this sad earth to bleed.
All riches, power and glory be to You,
Jesus the Lord, who loves us through and through.

Tunes: Toulon, Ellers, Woodlands, Shiplake, Maori, Penetentia.

Psalm 28.7
The LORD is my strength and my shield; my heart trusted in him, and I am helped: therefore my heart greatly rejoiceth; and with my song will I praise him.

15th July.

CM.

The Pow'r of Death is Found in Sin.

1.
The pow'r of death is found in sin,
The devil wields its sword.
But thanks to God who gives us life
In Jesus Christ our Lord.

2.
We find the power of the word
Within our heart and mind.
It led us back to God on high;
Our God- gentle and kind.

3.
We see the power of God's love
Upon the cross of shame.
There Christ has borne our every sin
And taken all the blame.

4.
The power of the blood, we see
Cleansing from all sin.
It makes us fit for heaven above
And gives us peace within.

5.
The power of the Christ, we find
In weakness and defeat.
For trust in Him is all we need
To make our joy complete.

6.
The power of the Spirit too
Acts through us every day.
He shapes us in the mould of Christ
And helps us when we pray.

7.
Look up and see the Lord in power
To this sad world appear.
His glory in that time to come
Removes all doubt and fear.

Tunes: Beulah, Arlington, Christmas Eve, Irish, St. Agnes.

Psalm 21.13
Be thou exalted, LORD, in thine own strength: so will we sing and praise thy power.

Psalm 59.16
But I will sing of thy power; yea, I will sing aloud of thy mercy in the morning: for thou hast been my defence and refuge in the day of my trouble.

16th July.

87.87D.

God, Our Father, We Adore Thee!

God, our Father, we adore Thee!
Worshippers by Christ redeemed.
'Tis His blood that purified us;
'Tis His love that on us beamed.
As Thy children by new birth;
We will trust Thee more each day.
While as sons, we stand before Thee,
Blessed by Thee in every way.

Before Time made its appearance;
Before all the worlds were made;
Thou hadst purposed us for blessing
Through the grace that Christ displayed.
"Abba! Father!" we now call Thee.
As those holy, without blame.
And as heirs by love's adoption
We Thy wondrous name proclaim!

In Thy house of many mansions
Our new home has been prepared.
There, we'll praise and we'll adore Thee;
Where Thy glories are declared;
We will joy in Thy blest presence
There in light no man has seen
We shall rest in love and peace
With Thy Christ eternally.

Tunes: Beecher, Woodside, Shipton, Here is Love, Hymn to Joy, Everton, Deerhurst.

Ephesians 1.3-4
Blessed be the God and Father of our Lord Jesus Christ, who hath blessed us with all spiritual blessings in heavenly places in Christ: according as he hath chosen us in him before the foundation of the world, that we should be holy and without blame before him in love…

17th July.

CM.

Fill Us With Thy Wisdom, Lord.

1.
Fill us with all Thy wisdom, Lord,
To hear and do Thy will.
Then will our lives be well prepared
For times of good and ill.

2.
Make us as wise as serpents, Lord,
As enemies abound.
Help us defeat them with Thy word
And in Thy joy be found.

3.
The scriptures give us wisdom, Lord,
They lead us on to Thee.
By faith salvation is made ours
And gives us victory.

4.
True wisdom makes us fools for Thee
And we suffer each day.
But, Lord, resources found in Thee
Are given when we pray.

5.
To Thee, our Saviour, wise and strong
We bring our note of praise.
All glory, majesty and power,
To Thee, our voices raise.

Tunes: Beulah, Nativity, Westminster (Turle), Pisgah, St. Agnes, Irish.

2Timothy 3.15
And that from a child thou hast known the holy scriptures,
which are able to make thee wise unto salvation through faith
which is in Christ Jesus.

18th July.

76.76.

Greatness and Power and Glory.

1. Greatness and power and glory
Are Thine, O Lord, by right.
All riches and dominion
Tell us of all Thy might.

2. Thy power is found in preaching,
The preaching of the cross!
It brings us to salvation
Through all Thy pain and loss.

3. Death's power kept us captive;
The devil's chain was strong;
But through Thy death and glory
We now to Thee belong.

4. Thy power rests upon us
When weaknesses prevail;
Yet in them, we may glory
For Thy grace will avail.

5. In resurrection power,
We'd live for Thee down here.
We'd trust in Thee completely
And know no doubt or fear.

6. Lord, come in power and glory
As Son of man to reign.
And to this world of sorrow
Bring gladness once again.

Tunes: St. Cecilia (Hayne), Cara, Eden (Boston), Matrimony.

1Chronicles 29.11
Thine, O LORD, is the greatness, and the power, and the glory, and the victory, and the majesty: for all that is in the heaven and in the earth is thine; thine is the kingdom, O LORD, and thou art exalted as head …

19th July.

87.87.

Thank You, Lord, for All Your Goodness.

1. Thank You, Lord, for all Your goodness;
Thank You Lord for life and love;
Thank You, Lord, for every blessing
Poured upon us from above.

2. Thank You, Lord, for food and clothing;
Thank You, Lord, for all that care;
Thank You, Lord, for every moment
That we share with You in prayer.

3. Thank You, Lord, for seeds once planted;
Thank You, Lord, for warmth and rain;
Thank You, Lord, for fruitful produce;
Hence, we praise Your name again.

4. Thank You, Lord, for Your salvation
Brought to us by Your dear Son;
Thank You, Lord, for that great harvest
And the glory, He has won.

Tunes: Gott Wills Machen, Cross of Jesus,

2Thessalonians 1.10-12

When he shall come to be glorified in his saints, and to be admired in all them that believe (because our testimony among you was believed) in that day. Wherefore also we pray always for you, that our God would count you worthy of this calling, and fulfil all the good pleasure of his goodness, and the work of faith with power: that the name of our Lord Jesus Christ may be glorified in you, and ye in him, according to the grace of our God and the Lord Jesus Christ.

Psalm 31. 19

Oh how great is thy goodness, which thou hast laid up for them that fear thee; which thou hast wrought for them that trust in thee before the sons of men!

20th July.

76.76.

We Need Thy Grace, Lord Jesus.

1.
We need Thy grace, Lord Jesus,
The grace that laid aside
Great riches in the Glory
To come and seek Thy bride.

2.
We need Thy cross, Lord Jesus,
The cross where Thou hast died.
There, by Thy God forsaken,
That we might be Thy bride.

3.
We need Thy blood, Lord Jesus,
The blood that justified.
It made us fit for heaven
Where we shall be Thy bride.

4.
We need Thy life, Lord Jesus,
The life that will abide.
It brings us every blessing
As that appointed bride.

5.
We need Thy love, Lord Jesus,
That love so deep and wide.
As Thine own bride, it keeps us
Close to Thy wounded side.

Tunes: Vulpius, Matrimony, Cara.

Acts 15.11
But we believe that through the grace of the Lord Jesus Christ we shall be saved, even as they.

21st July.

CMD.

Fear Not, Ye Suffering Saints of God

1.
Fear not, ye suffering saints of God
The Lord Himself draws near.
Imprisoned for His name and work -
Who bore the nail and spear.
And though death makes a claim on you
Look on to Him above.
The crown of life, He holds for you
With all His grace and love.

2.
Fear not, ye shepherds of His sheep;
Pasture His flock with tears;
For soon the Lord Himself shall come –
With power, He appears!
And He who bore a thorny crown
Will bring His bright reward.
A crown of glory yours shall be,
With blessing on you poured.

3.
Fear not, ye ministers of God,
Jesus will come again.
In majesty, He will ride forth
And you, with Him, will reign.
Yes, those who love that day of days
Will take from His pierc'd hand
A precious crown of righteousness
Just as His God had planned.

4.
Fear not, ye striving souls of Christ,
The Lord will give you rest.
Rejoice in Him - enjoy His peace
Knowing His will is best.
Walk with Him in the narrow way;
Let purity shine through;
A crown that's incorruptible
He has, in heaven, for you.

Tunes: Providence, Jesus is God, Bethlehem, Land of Rest, Minerva, Warrior.

Revelation 1. 17-18
And when I saw him, I fell at his feet as dead. And he laid his right hand upon me, saying unto me, Fear not; I am the first and the last; I am he that liveth, and was dead; and, behold, I am alive for evermore, Amen; and have the keys of hell and of death.

22nd July.

75.75D.

Lord Jesus, Mighty Saviour.

1. Lord Jesus, mighty Saviour,
The church's wondrous Head
The living, You will judge
As You will judge the dead.
When with all glory shining,
And power from Your arm
You will, at Your appearing,
Save all Your own from harm.

2. Until that day of days,
Help us life's race to run
With hope that is enduring
And joy that faith has won.
Then in our Christian conflict
Give us the grace to stand.
Help us resist the devil
And all that he has planned.

3. We'd hear Your word, Lord
Jesus,
Teach us in love that cares.
Reproof, rebuke and comfort,
We'd find its message bears.
So fit us for the service
That You would have us do;
So in that day of blessing
Our crowns, we'll give to You.

4.
The time of our departure
From this sad world of woe,
Draws closer with each moment
As You in wisdom know.
Yet, though we leave in
weakness,
And sorrows mark our brow,
We will be met with glory
As we before You bow.

Tunes: Greenland (Haydn), Passion Chorale, Thornbury, Lymington.

Isaiah 60.16
Thou shalt also suck the milk of the Gentiles, and shalt suck the breast of kings: and thou shalt know that I the LORD am thy Saviour and thy Redeemer, the mighty One of Jacob.

2Peter 3.18
But grow in grace, and in the knowledge of our Lord and Saviour Jesus Christ. To him be glory both now and for ever. Amen.

Acts 5.31
The God of our fathers raised up Jesus, whom ye slew and hanged on a tree. Him hath God exalted with his right hand to be a Prince and a Saviour, for to give repentance to Israel, and forgiveness of sins.

23rd July.

98.98.

Ashamed of Thy Name I Cannot Be.

1.
Ashamed of Thy name, I cannot be,
For there's no other name for me!
Jesus - the gracious Lord who saves!
Jesus – the way to heaven paves!

2.
Ashamed of Thy love, I cannot be
For it's a love poured out on me.
A love that's gentle, humble, kind;
A love that gives me peace of mind.

3.
Ashamed of Thy word, I cannot be
For it's the power that captured me.
In it, Thy beauty I can see
Because Thy Spirit lives in me.

4.
Ashamed of Thy cross, I cannot be
For there Thou gav'st Thyself for me.
Made sin, God's judgement is complete,
And 'tis Thy blood that makes me meet.

5.
Ashamed of Thy life, I cannot be,
For by it my poor soul is free.
And now before Thy throne, I bend
In praise and worship without end.

Tunes: His Wondrous Ways.

Romans 1.16
For I am not ashamed of the gospel of Christ: for it is the power of God unto salvation to every one that believeth; to the Jew first, and also to the Greek.

24th July.

99.99.

There's Nothing To Do! Nothing To Pay!

1. There's nothing to do! Nothing to pay!
Simply to trust Him! Trust Him today!
Come to the Man who died on the tree;
Come to Him quickly, He calleth Thee.

2. By grace we're saved through faith in the Lord!
By blood we're purchased! Kept from the sword!
Come to the Man who died on the tree;
Come to Him quickly, He'll rescue Thee.

3. The work is finished! The price is paid!
Christ bore our judgement! Love was displayed!
Come to the Man who died on the tree;
Come to Him quickly, He'll pardon Thee.

4. His grave is open for all to see
He rose from death, a great victory!
Come to the Man who died on the tree;
Come to Him quickly, He'll set Thee free.

5. Now He is seated high on God's throne
Living and pleading for all His own.
Come to the Man who died on the tree;
Come to Him quickly, He lives for Thee.

Tunes: Bunessan.

Luke 7.41-42
There was a certain creditor which had two debtors: the one owed five hundred pence, and the other fifty. And when they had nothing to pay, he frankly forgave them both. Tell me therefore, which of them will love him most?

Isaiah 52.3
For thus saith the LORD, Ye have sold yourselves for nought; and ye shall be redeemed without money.

25th July.

87.87..

You're my Lord and my Defender.

1.
You're my Lord and my Defender;
You're the power of my soul;
You're the Son of God who loves me;
You're the One who makes me whole.

2.
When all friends desert my chain,
And the wicked do me wrong;
You will stand beside me, Lord;
And Your grace will make me strong.

3.
When I stand up for your name
And the work that you have done;
You will give me words to speak
That lead souls to salvation.

4.
From the lion's mouth, You'll snatch me
That Your word may freely run.
From myself, You will preserve me
And complete the work begun.

5.
May Your Kingdom and Dominion
Spread with every dawning day.
May Your glory shine for ever
And all living own Your sway.

Tunes: St. Andrew (Thorne), Sussex, Cross of Jesus, Stuttgart.

Psalm 59. 16
But I will sing of thy power; yea, I will sing aloud of thy mercy in the morning: for thou hast been my defence and refuge in the day of my trouble.

26th July.

LM.

Peace! Peace Proclaim In Jesus' Name!

1. Peace! Peace proclaim in Jesus' name!
The peace He purchased with His blood
Peace! Peace proclaim in Jesus' name!
The peace that brings us back to God.

2. Peace! Peace proclaim to burdened souls!
The peace that comes through trusting Him.
Peace! Peace proclaim to burdened souls!
The peace without the guilt of sin.

3. Peace! Peace proclaim to suff'ring souls!
The peace that wipes away each tear.
Peace! Peace proclaim to suff'ring souls!
The peace that fills the heart with cheer.

4. Peace! Peace proclaim to fearful souls!
The peace of God who loves us so.
Peace! Peace proclaim to fearful souls!
The peace that strengthens as we go.

5. Peace! Peace proclaim to weary souls!
The peace that gives us hope within.
Peace! Peace proclaim to weary souls!
The peace that keeps our hearts from sin.

6. Peace! Peace proclaim to trusting souls!
The peace to rule our hearts each day.
Peace! Peace proclaim to trusting souls!
The peace that keeps us in His way.

Tunes: Federal St., Tallis' Canon.

Colossians 1.19-20
For it pleased the Father that in him should all fulness dwell; and, having made peace through the blood of his cross, by him to reconcile all things unto himself…

27th July.

CM.

The Earth's Foundations, You Have Laid.

1.
The earth's foundations, You have laid
You measured land and sea.
Your hands have spread the heav'ns above
And, skilfully, made me.

2.
The stars of morning sang their song;
Your sons with gladness cried.
You bound the seas with mighty power
And formed the clouds so wide.

3.
You set the dawning in its place
To light the earth by day.
You opened up the gates of death
And showed the light its way.

4.
You gave the world its life and breath;
The lightning - loud thunder.
You gave the rain to feed the ground;
And we, as men, wonder.

5.
In Plaiedes is Your sweetness found -
Strength at Orion's side;
You time the rise of Mazzaroth;
And all Arcturus guide.

6.
But, Lord, Your love in Christ is found,
Yes, in the Son You gave.
For us He died on Calvary's cross
That He our souls might save.

7.
All praise to the Creator God;
The Lord of heaven and earth.
All glory be to Christ above;
Joy in His work and worth.

Tunes: Beulah, Pisgah, Nativity, Beatitudo, Gerontius, Belmont, Christmas Eve.

Isaiah 40.12
Who hath measured the waters in the hollow of his hand,
and meted out heaven with the span,
and comprehended the dust of the earth in a measure,
and weighed the mountains in scales,
and the hills in a balance?

28th July.

76.76D.

Well, Has the Rain a Father?

1. Well, has the rain a father?
Each drop of dew a heart?
Who gave the ice its being?
Or, to mankind a start?
Refrain:
It is the God of glory
Who lives in heaven above.
Creation tells the story
Of all His pow'r and love.

2. Who counted clouds with wisdom?
And gave the beast its strength?
Who paints the sky of morning
And measures out its length?
Refrain:

3. Who feeds the blackest raven?
Who makes the hinds to calf?
Who gives the ox its wisdom?
Who leads us with His staff?
Refrain:

4. Who gives the peacock feathers?
Who makes the hawk fly high?
Who gave His only Son
To suffer, bleed and die?
Refrain:

Tunes: Greenland, Lymington; Day of Rest, Ewing,

Job 38.28-30
Hath the rain a father? or who hath begotten the drops of dew?
Out of whose womb came the ice? and the hoary frost of heaven, who hath gendered it?
The waters are hid as with a stone,
and the face of the deep is frozen.

29th July.

76.76D.

Beneath the Cross of Jesus.

1. Beneath the cross of Jesus
There is a place for me.
There, peace in all its fullness
With righteousness, I see.
The wounds of my blest Saviour
Are stained by His own blood;
And thorns that crown His brow
Speak of the curse of God.

2. Beneath the cross of Jesus
There is a place for me.
There truth that is unyielding
With God's mercy shall be.
The words of my blest Saviour
Bring comfort to my soul.
And through His pain and anguish
I am, from sin, made whole.

3. Beneath the cross of Jesus
There is a place for me.
There love in its abundance
In His pierced side I see.
When the deep darkness clothes Him,
And God leaves Him alone;
I knew that He must suffer
Before He takes His throne.

4. Beneath the cross of Jesus
There is a place for me.
I look into His face
And there His joy I see.
The cross that He has borne
Has brought blessing to me.
While through this great redemption
His bride, I'll always be.

Tunes: Lymington, Passion Chorale, Thornbury, Greenland (Hadyn).

John 19.23-27

Then the soldiers, when they had crucified Jesus, took his garments, and made four parts, to every soldier a part; and also his coat: now the coat was without seam, woven from the top throughout. They said therefore among themselves, Let us not rend it, but cast lots for it, whose it shall be: that the scripture might be fulfilled, which saith, They parted my raiment among them, and for my vesture they did cast lots. These things therefore the soldiers did. Now there stood by the cross of Jesus his mother, and his mother's sister, Mary the wife of Cleophas, and Mary Magdalene. When Jesus therefore saw his mother, and the disciple standing by, whom he loved, he saith unto his mother, Woman, behold thy son! Then saith he to the disciple, Behold thy mother! And from that hour that disciple took her unto his own home.

30th July.

LM.

Draw me, O Lord, by Cords of Love.

1.
Draw me, O Lord, by cords of love
That I may share Thy joys above.
Hold me most firmly in Thy hand;
Tell me all that Thy will hath planned.

2.
Draw me close to Thy wounded side
That I may love Thee as Thy bride.
Surround me with Thy fond embrace
That I may gaze into Thy face.

3.
Draw me into Thy Father's home
And I shall never from Thee roam.
His name we'll praise with pure delight
And ever dwell in heavenly light.

Tunes: Federal St., Tallis' Canon,

Jeremiah 31.2
Thus saith the LORD, The people which were left of the sword found grace in the wilderness; even Israel, when I went to cause him to rest. The LORD hath appeared of old unto me, saying, Yea, I have loved thee with an everlasting love: therefore with lovingkindness have I drawn thee.

Song 1.2-4
Let him kiss me with the kisses of his mouth:
for thy love is better than wine.
Because of the savour of thy good ointments thy name is as ointment poured forth, therefore do the virgins love thee.
Draw me, we will run after thee: the king hath brought me into his chambers:
we will be glad and rejoice in thee,
we will remember thy love more than wine: the upright love thee.

31st July.

77.77.

Waves of Blessing Surge and Swell.

1.
Waves of blessing surge and swell
Telling souls that all is well;
Christ Salvation's work has done!
Put your trust in God's dear Son.

2.
Rays of blessing brightly shine
Giving light pure and divine.
Telling sinners far and near
Trusting Christ they need not fear.

3.
Flames of blessing leap and glow
That lost souls their sin might know.
They lead on to Christ above
Who gave Himself for them in love.

4.
Winds of blessing softly blow,
In the Spirit's power they go;
Breathing life to those once dead;
Leading them to Christ the Head.

5.
Show'rs of blessing gently fall
Bringing health to one and all.
See each Christian root and grow;
See the living waters flow.

Tunes: St. Bees, Monkland, Buckland, Confidence (Ouseley).

Ezekiel 34.26
And I will make them and the places round about my hill a blessing; and I will cause the shower to come down in his season; there shall be showers of blessing.

1st August.

CMD.

From Every Race and Every Tribe.

1. From every race and every tribe
We are now Yours by grace.
Your blood has ransomed our poor souls
And so we seek Your face.
You made us kings and priests to God
And we with You shall reign.
"Worthy the Lamb!" we cry aloud
As You were for us slain.

2. Let all the heavenly hosts declare
The wonder of Your name.
Wisdom and riches, power and strength
Are Yours, O Lord, to claim.
High honour, glory and blessing
Are crowns upon Your head.
The Lamb who hung upon the tree
Is now our Living Bread.

3. "All praise to God upon the throne
And to the Lamb!" we cry.
"All blessing, honour, glory, power!"
All creatures will reply.
And so to Father and to Son
We lift our voice in song.
For it's by grace, yes, grace alone
That we to You belong.

Tunes: Providence, Jesus is God, No King But Christ, Warrior, Bethlehem, Minerva, Noel, Forest Green, Ellacombe.

Revelation 5.13
And every creature which is in heaven, and on the earth, and under the earth, and such as are in the sea,
and all that are in them, heard I saying, Blessing, and honour, and glory, and power, *be* unto him that sitteth upon the throne, and unto the Lamb for ever and ever.

2nd August.

CMD.

How Pleasant Is Your Praise, Blest Lord.

1.
How pleasant is Your praise, blest Lord,
Our Helper and our Shield.
Upon the strings within our hearts
A new song is revealed.
It praises You for all Your works,
Your goodness and Your grace.
For Your true word, it gives You thanks,
As we Your counsels trace.

2.
And as Your eye upon us falls
Our fears all fly away;
For in Your holy name we trust
And walk in Your own way.
You called us when we were undone!
You keep us by Your side!
And in that bright, eternal day,
You'll love us as Your bride!

Tunes: Providence, Bethlehem, Ellacombe, Warrior.

Revelation 5.6-9

And I beheld, and, lo, in the midst of the throne and of the four beasts, and in the midst of the elders, stood a Lamb as it had been slain, having seven horns and seven eyes, which are the seven Spirits of God sent forth into all the earth. And he came and took the book out of the right hand of him that sat upon the throne.

And when he had taken the book, the four beasts and four and twenty elders fell down before the Lamb, having every one of them harps, and golden vials full of odours, which are the prayers of saints. And they sung a new song, saying,

Thou art worthy to take the book, and to open the seals thereof: for thou wast slain, and hast redeemed us to God by thy blood out of every kindred, and tongue, and people, and nation…

3rd August.

76.76D.

Unto the Cross of Jesus.

.1
Unto the cross of Jesus,
I came in all my sin.
And at the cross of Jesus
I felt my guilt within.
There light shone in His suff'ring
And love bruised His dear face.
My sins were laid upon Him
And now I'm saved by grace.

2.
'Twas at the cross of Jesus
I stood on holy ground.
'Twas at the cross of Jesus
That peace with God, I found.
There truth and mercy promised
A life of joy below.
And faith and hope like flowers
In my glad heart will grow.

3.
'Tis through the cross of Jesus
I bowed to Christ, my Lord.
'Tis through the cross of Jesus
That I claim His reward.
I'll worship Him with gladness.
I'll serve Him day by day.
His blessèd name, I'll treasure
With all I do and say.

Tunes: Lymington, Greenland (Haydn), Aurelia, Thornbury, Passion Chorale, I Love to Hear the Story.

1Corinthians 1.18
For the preaching of the cross is to them that perish foolishness; but unto us which are saved it is the power of God.

4th August.

CM.

I Looked to Jesus Set on High.

1. I looked to Jesus set on high
The Father's pure delight.
I saw the love within His heart
A love that dwelt in light.

2. I looked to Jesus in the crib,
Emmanuel His name.
To save our souls from sin and death
The Son from glory came.

3. I looked to Jesus on this earth,
The perfect, holy Man.
His goodness and His mercy told
Of all redemption's plan.

4. I looked to Jesus on the cross
Tormented by my sin.
My punishment was borne by Him -
I now have peace within.

5. I look to Jesus set on high,
The Saviour shining bright;
And that same love within His heart
Flows forth in all its might.

6.
O blessèd Jesus, Lamb of God,
How wonderful You are!
Worthy of homage and of praise
My Bright and Morning Star!

Tunes: 86.86: Westminster (Turle). . CMD: Bethlehem, Jesus is God.

Acts 7.55
But he, being full of the Holy Ghost, looked up stedfastly into heaven, and saw the glory of God, and Jesus standing on the right hand of God…

5th August.

CMD.

You Came to this Sad Earth Below.

1. You came to this sad earth below
The Father's will to do;
And by the Spirit's pow'r conceived,
Your holiness we view.
Born of a faithful virgin maid,
Your coming was complete.
Your birth by shining angels hailed
Brought shepherds to Your feet.

2. You came to this sad earth below
The Father's will to do.
There in the temple You were found,
And men Your wisdom knew.
The Father's business was Your own,
His word You taught with grace.
And as a lad of tender age,
Your work we love to trace.

3. You came to this sad earth below
The Father's will to do;
And in Your works of goodness here
The Father's heart we view.
Your head was in His bosom laid
From all eternity.
And in His purposes divine
You came to set us free.

4. You came to this sad earth below
The Father's will to do;
And in the garden of the press
We find our peace in You.
For there You gave Yourself to Him
In body, spirit, soul.
Submitting to His holy will
That we might be made whole.

5. You came to this sad earth below
The Father's will to do;
And in the power of the cross
We find that He is true.
Made sin, You bore the wrath of God
And took away our shame.
So now we bless You for Your love
And praise the Father's name.

Tunes: No King But Christ, Jesus is God, Bethlehem, Warrior.

Galatians 4.4
But when the fulness of the time was come, God sent forth his Son, made of a woman, made under the law…

6th August.

CM.

Father Divine, to Thee We Bow.

1.
Father divine, to Thee we bow,
The Source of love and light.
We see the wonder of Thy ways,
Thy glory and Thy might.

2.
'Twas Christ revealed Thee here below
Where sin and death once reigned.
Thy name was by Thy Son declared
And all Thy grace proclaimed!

3.
We boast in all the work Thou'st done
To save our souls from sin.
And sitting at Thy holy feet
We know true peace within.

4.
O righteous Father, for His cross,
So patiently endured,
We praise and bless Thee day by day
And see what love procured.

5.
All glory be to Thee, dear Lord,
Who gav'st Thine only Son.
As those now purged, we sing to Thee -
True worship hath begun.

Tunes: Pisgah, Beulah, Nativity, St. Agnes, Westminster (Turle).

John 14.9
Jesus saith unto him, Have I been so long time with you, and yet hast thou not known me, Philip? he that hath seen me hath seen the Father; and how sayest thou then, Shew us the Father?

7th August.

CM.

Father, We Would Work On In Faith.

Father, we would work on in faith
Thy wonders to proclaim;
And ever active in Thy will
Bring glory to Thy name.
Refrain:
Thou art the God who won our hearts
Through love so vast and free.
Thou art the Source of all our joy;
We gladly worship Thee.

Father, we would toil on in love
Thy nature to reveal!
Then all the service, we perform
Will have the Spirit's seal.
Refrain:

Father, our hope must rest in Thee,
And cheerfully endure
Until that day Thy Son we see
In light that's bright and pure.
Refrain:

Tunes: Release, No King But Christ, Landas, Jesus is God.

Psalm100.1-4
A Psalm of praise. Make a joyful noise unto the LORD, all ye lands. Serve the LORD with gladness: come before his presence with singing. Know ye that the LORD he is God: it is he that hath made us, and not we ourselves; we are his people, and the sheep of his pasture. Enter into his gates with thanksgiving, and into his courts with praise: be thankful unto him, and bless his name.

Psalm 2.11-12
Serve the LORD with fear, and rejoice with trembling. Kiss the Son, lest he be angry, and ye perish from the way, when his wrath is kindled but a little. Blessed are all they that put their trust in him.

8th August.

66.66.

O God, 'Tis Grace Indeed.

1.
O God, 'tis grace indeed
That gave Thy Son to die;
And as those cleansed by blood,
We'll dwell with Him on high.

2.
Nothing we felt or did
Could take away our sin.
No sighs, no prayers, no tears
Could give us peace within.

3.
The work of Christ alone
Upon the cross of shame
Could cleanse away our guilt -
Accepting all our blame.

4.
We'll praise His holy name!
He's worthy of our love.
We'll worship Thy dear Son
In those bright courts above.

Tunes: St. Cecilia (Hayne), Ibstone, Quam Dilecta.

Ephesians 2.4-8
But God, who is rich in mercy, for his great love wherewith he loved us, even when we were dead in sins,
hath quickened us together with Christ, (by grace ye are saved;) and hath raised us up together, and made us sit together in heavenly places in Christ Jesus:
that in the ages to come he might shew the exceeding riches of his grace in his kindness toward us through Christ Jesus.
For by grace are ye saved through faith; and that not of yourselves: it is the gift of God: not of works, lest any man should boast.

9th August.

65.65.

Saviour, Gentle Saviour.

1. Saviour, gentle Saviour,
Come to earth in grace.
Showing God the Father,
With an open face.

2. Saviour, holy Saviour,
Slain upon the tree.
Bearing all sin's judgment
So we might be free.

3. Saviour, loving Saviour,
Risen from the grave.
Seated high in glory,
Thou art strong to save.

4. Saviour, mighty Saviour,
Come into the air.
Call Thy saints up to Thee
All Thy joys to share.

5. Saviour, royal Saviour,
Righteous is Thy reign.
Kings shall bow before Thee
Splendid Thy domain!

6. Saviour, precious Saviour,
Once reproached and tried.
Through eternal ages
We shall be Thy bride.

Tunes: Armentrout, Quietude.

2Timothy 2.26
And the servant of the Lord must not strive; but be gentle unto all men, apt to teach, patient, in meekness instructing those that oppose themselves…

10th August.

CM.

Lord Jesus, We Would Copy Thee,

1.
Lord Jesus, we would copy Thee,
In walk and word this day.
Gladly, we'd live our daily lives
Treading the narrow way.

2.
It was in weakness, we received
That wondrous word of Thine;
And through the joy Thy Spirit brings
We know that it's divine.

3.
May our frail faith be stronger, Lord,
To flow out with Thy word.
May those who see the change in us,
Find love a three-fold cord.

4.
O Lord, from idols we have turned
To serve the living God;
And now we wait for Thee to come
To save from wrath's rough rod.

Tunes: Beulah, St. Agnes, Westminster (Turle), Beatitudo, Belmont.

1Peter 2.21-25

For even hereunto were ye called: because Christ also suffered for us, leaving us an example, that ye should follow his steps: who did no sin, neither was guile found in his mouth: who, when he was reviled, reviled not again; when he suffered, he threatened not; but committed himself to him that judgeth righteously: who his own self bare our sins in his own body on the tree, that we, being dead to sins, should live unto righteousness: by whose stripes ye were healed. For ye were as sheep going astray; but are now returned unto the Shepherd and Bishop of your souls.

11th August.

88.88.

Saviour, Thy Wounds Have Made Me Whole!

1.
Saviour, Thy wounds have
made me whole!
Saviour, Thy wounds have
cleansed my soul!
Your cheeks once plucked by
wicked men
Spring up with life and joy
again.

2.
Saviour, Thy wounds have
made me whole!
Saviour, Thy wounds have
cleansed my soul!
By flinted scourge, Thy back
was peeled
And by Thy stripes from sin,
I'm healed.

3.
Saviour, Thy wounds have
made me whole!
Saviour, Thy wounds have
cleansed my soul!
A crown of thorns has stung
Thy brow!
Beneath God's curse Thou
cam'st to bow!

4.
Saviour, Thy wounds have
made me whole!
Saviour, Thy wounds have
cleansed my soul!
Rough nails have pierced Thy
hands and feet
Shedding the blood that makes
me meet.

5.
Saviour, Thy wounds have
made me whole!
Saviour, Thy wounds have
cleansed my soul!
The blood that flowed from Thy
blest side
Has made me fit to be Thy
bride.

6.
Saviour, Thy wounds have
made me whole!
Saviour, Thy wounds have
cleansed my soul!
The torment of Thy soul within
Has borne the judgement of our
sin.

7.
Saviour, Thy wounds have
made me whole!
Saviour, Thy wounds have
cleansed my soul!
Now I am free to worship Thee,
Rejoicing in my liberty!

Tunes: 88.88: Federal St., Tallis' Canon. 88.88.88.88: Sweet Hour, Stephenson, He leadeth Me, Duane St., Sagina.

12th August.

65.65D.

Jesus, Never Leave Me.

1.
Jesus, never leave me
Stay close by my side.
I am lost and helpless,
You must be my Guide.
Bound in chains of sin
No life left to live.
Breathe on me, blest Lord,
All my sins forgive.

2.
Jesus, never leave me,
Stay close by my side.
I feel love embracing
When, for me, You died.
Your blood has purified,
My soul from every sin;
By Your Spirit's power,
I have peace within.

3.
Jesus, never leave me,
Stay close by my side
When I'm weak and helpless,
When my soul is tried.
Your strength is my fortress,
Wisdom is Your way;
Keep me blessèd Saviour
Safely, day by day.

4.
Jesus, never leave me,
Stay close by my side.
Let me love You dearly
As Your precious bride.
Through eternal ages
I will worship You.
And with eyes of heaven
All Your beauty view.

Tunes: 65.65: Eudoxia, Quietude, Castle Eden, North Coates, German.
11.11.11.11: Ruth (Smith), Evelyns, Look Away to Jesus, Lyndhurst (Vail), Normandy Carol.

Hebrews 13.3-3

Remember them that are in bonds, as bound with them; and them which suffer adversity, as being yourselves also in the body. Marriage is honourable in all, and the bed undefiled: but whoremongers and adulterers God will judge. Let your conversation be without covetousness; and be content with such things as ye have: for he hath said, I will never leave thee, nor forsake thee. So that we may boldly say, The Lord is my helper, and I will not fear what man shall do unto me. Remember them which have the rule over you, who have spoken unto you the word of God: whose faith follow, considering the end of their conversation. Jesus Christ the same yesterday, and to day, and for ever.

13th August.

88.88.

Eternity! Eternity!

1. Eternity! Eternity!
Where will you spend eternity?
The Father's house of light and love
Stands open now in heaven above!

2. Eternity! Eternity!
Where will you spend eternity?
Trust in His own belovèd Son!
Your entrance into rest is won!

3. Eternity! Eternity!
Where will you spend eternity?
The price was paid by God's own Son
And all salvation's work is done!

4. Eternity! Eternity!
Where will you spend eternity?
The blood that made the living way
Trust now in this most favoured day.

5. Eternity! Eternity!
Where will you spend eternity?
The lake of fire with fervent heat
In torment on your head shall beat.

6. Eternity! Eternity!
Where will you spend eternity?
The devil and his angels fear
The judgment, God has made so clear.

7. Eternity! Eternity!
Where will you spend eternity?
Oh, sinner, look to Christ this day;
His heart is showing you the way.

8. Eternity! Eternity!
Where will you spend eternity?
Be loved by Him for evermore
As His eternal bride most pure.

Tunes: Tallis' Canon

Isaiah 57.15 and John 10. 28

For thus saith the high and lofty One that inhabiteth eternity, whose name is Holy; I dwell in the high and holy place, with him also that is of a contrite and humble spirit, to revive the spirit of the humble, and to revive the heart of the contrite ones.

And I give unto them eternal life; and they shall never perish, neither shall any man pluck them out of my hand.

14th August.

76.76.

Only a Prayer to Jesus.

1.
Only a prayer to Jesus
Will make salvation Thine;
Come now, bow down before
Him
Owning His grace divine.

2.
Only a prayer to Jesus
Forgiveness will assure.
Come now, bow down before
Him;
His blood will make Thee pure.

3.
Only a prayer to Jesus
And peace Thy soul shall fill.
Come now, bow down before
Him;
He'll keep thee from all ill.

4.
Only a prayer to Jesus
Will bring thee back to God.
Come now, bow down before
Him
Escaping judgement's rod.

5.
Only a prayer to Jesus
And life eternal's thine.
Come now, bow down before
Him;
Know love better than wine.

6.
Only a prayer to Jesus
Will bring thee joy this day.
Come now, bow down before
Him;
Commit to Him thy way.

Tunes: 76.76: Vulpius, Cara. 76.76D: Webb, Thornbury, Greenland (Haydn), Lymington, Passion Chorale, St. Theodulph, Petition, Aurelia,

Romans 12.10-13
Be kindly affectioned one to another with brotherly love; in honour preferring one another; not slothful in business; fervent in spirit; serving the Lord; rejoicing in hope; patient in tribulation; continuing instant in prayer; distributing to the necessity of saints; given to hospitality.

Ephesians 6.18-20
Praying always with all prayer and supplication in the Spirit, and watching thereunto with all perseverance and supplication for all saints; and for me, that utterance may be given unto me, that I may open my mouth boldly, to make known the mystery of the gospel…

15th August.

11.11D.

So Near to the Saviour.

1.
So near to the Saviour,
Yet what holds you back?
So near to believing;
It's courage you lack!
Oh, come to the Saviour;
He's pleading with you.
Come now to the Saviour
Whose love is so true.

2.
So near to the Saviour
Whose word you have heard.
So near to believing
Now Your heart is stirred.
Oh, come to the Saviour
Who died on the tree.
Come now to the Saviour -
His blood sets us free!

3.
So near to the Saviour,
But fears fill your mind.
So near to believing
The Lord who is kind.
Oh, come to the Saviour,
Be cleansed from all sin!
Come now to the Saviour,
Let new life begin!

4.
So near to the Saviour,
But faith is required.
So near to believing
In the grace supplied.
Oh, come to the Saviour
Before it's too late.
Come now to the Saviour,
Enter heaven's gate.

Tunes: 11.11D: Evelyns, Ruth (Smith). 65.65: Eudoxia, North Coates, Quietude, Castle Eden.

Matthew 11.27-30
All things are delivered unto me of my Father: and no man knoweth the Son, but the Father; neither knoweth any man the Father, save the Son, and he to whomsoever the Son will reveal him. Come unto me, all ye that labour and are heavy laden, and I will give you rest. Take my yoke upon you, and learn of me; for I am meek and lowly in heart: and ye shall find rest unto your souls. For my yoke is easy, and my burden is light.

Luke 14.16- 17
Then said he unto him, A certain man made a great supper, and bade many: and sent his servant at supper time to say to them that were bidden, Come; for all things are now ready.

16th August.

87.87.

Look Upon the Cross of Jesus.

1.
Look upon the cross of Jesus
When bowed down beneath
your sin.
Look upon the precious blood
That can give you peace within.

2.
Look upon the cross of Jesus
See the wounds that make you
whole.
In His agony and anguish
See the cleansing of your soul.

3.
Look upon the cross of Jesus
Where He bore God's wrath for
you
Look into its deepest darkness
Where God's blessing you will
view.

4.
Look upon the cross of Jesus
Where the world was crucified.
Turn from all its fads and
fashions
Knowing Christ is glorified.

5.
Look upon the cross of Jesus
Where salvation is assured.
For the joy that lay before Him
He sin's judgement has
endured.

6.
Look upon the cross of Jesus
See the wisdom of God's plan.
Through the pain and all the
suffering
There is hope for ruined man.

Tunes: 87.87: Gott Wills Machen, Cross of Jesus, Sussex, Hyfrydol.
87.87D: here is Love, Hymn to Joy, Shipton, Beecher, Woodside.

Matthew 27.31-37

And after that they had mocked him, they took the robe off from him, and put his own raiment on him, and led him away to crucify him. And as they came out, they found a man of Cyrene, Simon by name: him they compelled to bear his cross. And when they were come unto a place called Golgotha, that is to say, a place of a skull, they gave him vinegar to drink mingled with gall: and when he had tasted thereof, he would not drink. 35 And they crucified him, and parted his garments, casting lots: that it might be fulfilled which was spoken by the prophet, They parted my garments among them, and upon my vesture did they cast lots. And sitting down they watched him there…

17th August,

85.85D.

Majesty and Strength, Lord Jesus.

1.
Majesty and strength, Lord Jesus,
Both to You belong;
You're the Lion come of Judah;
You're our joy and song.
Kings will bow to you, Lord Jesus,
All will give You praise,
For Your wisdom and Your judgement
Shall their souls amaze.

2.
Glory, riches and dominion
All to You belong.
You're the little Lamb in heaven!
You have done no wrong!
Son of man, we see You slaughtered,
Standing by God's throne.
You are worthy, blessèd Saviour,
Precious Corner-stone.

3.
Root of David, now we see You
Crowned as Man above.
You're the Lord of earth and heaven,
Clothed in light and love.
You're most worthy of the honour
God has given You.
You are worthy of the homage
That is justly due.

Tunes: Sinclair.

Revelation 5.5
And one of the elders saith unto me, Weep not: behold, the Lion of the tribe of Juda, the Root of David, hath prevailed to open the book, and to loose the seven seals thereof.

18th August.

85.85.

We Would Be Like Thee, Lord Jesus.

1. We would be like Thee, Lord Jesus,
Like Thee day by day.
May Thy truth and deep compassion
Mark us in the way.

2. We would follow Thee, Lord Jesus,
Walking in truth and love.
Giving ourselves in Thy service
Till with Thee above.

3. We would do Thy will, Lord Jesus,
Show us what to do.
Give us strength and holy boldness
Till Thy face we view.

4. We would love Thee more, Lord Jesus,
Love Thee unto death.
May Thy grace and power protect me
Till my dying breath.

Tunes: Cairnbrook.

1Peter 1. 7-11
That the trial of your faith, being much more precious than of gold that perisheth, though it be tried with fire,
might be found unto praise and honour and glory at the appearing of Jesus Christ:
whom having not seen, ye love; in whom, though now ye see him not, yet believing, ye rejoice with joy unspeakable and full of glory:
receiving the end of your faith, even the salvation of your souls.
Of which salvation the prophets have enquired and searched diligently, who prophesied of the grace that should come unto you:
searching what, or what manner of time the Spirit of Christ which was in them did signify,
when it testified before-hand the sufferings of Christ, and the glory that should follow.

19th August.

87.87.

Father, We, Thy Children, Praise Thee.

1.
Father, we, Thy children, praise Thee
For Thy wisdom, grace and love.
How we thank Thee for the blessings
Through Thy Son in heaven above.

2.
Thou didst choose us in the Saviour
E'en before the world was made.
Thou didst mark us off for Jesus
With a hope that shall not fade.

3.
Thou art for us, blessèd Father,
Keep us in Thy Son's dear name.
Thou gav'st Him to bear our judgement
With deep sorrow, grief and shame.

4.
We adore Thee, God and Father,
For Thou art both love and light;
Thou hast brought us full redemption;
Freed us from this world's dark night.

Tunes: 87.87: Sussex, St. Andrew (Thorne), Gott Will's Machen, Cross of Jesus. 87.87D: Hymn to Joy, Here is Love, Mount of Olives, Shipton, Beecher, Deerhurst, Bishopgarth.

Romans 8.15-17

For ye have not received the spirit of bondage again to fear; but ye have received the Spirit of adoption, whereby we cry, Abba, Father. The Spirit itself beareth witness with our spirit, that we are the children of God: And if children, then heirs; heirs of God, and joint-heirs with Christ; if so be that we suffer with him, that we may be also glorified together.

20th August.

65.65.

Pray For Us, Lord Jesus.

1.
Pray for us, Lord Jesus,
Pray for us today.
Bring the Father's blessing
In a special way.

2.
Pray for us, Lord Jesus,
There is much to fear;
Heavy burdens press us;
Bring Thy Father near.

3.
Pray for us, Lord Jesus,
When we're weak and ill.
May Thy healing power
Be the Father's will.

4.
Pray for us, Lord Jesus,
As we work for Thee.
May Thy Father help us
More like Thee to be.

5.
Pray for us, Lord Jesus,
Keep us in God's way.
May Thy Father's mercy
Rest on us today.

6.
Pray for us, Lord Jesus,
Fruit for God to bear.
May Thy Father shield us
By His loving care.

Tunes: 65.65: Eudoxia, Quietude, Castle Eden, North Coates, German.
11.11.11.11: Ruth (Smith), Evelyns, Look Away to Jesus, Lyndhurst (Vail), Normandy Carol.

Romans 8.26-27

Likewise the Spirit also helpeth our infirmities: for we know not what we should pray for as we ought: but the Spirit itself maketh intercession for us with groanings which cannot be uttered. And he that searcheth the hearts knoweth what is the mind of the Spirit, because he maketh intercession for the saints according to the will of God.

Romans 8.34

Who is he that condemneth? It is Christ that died, yea rather, that is risen again, who is even at the right hand of God, who also maketh intercession for us.

21st August.

77.77.

Look to Jesus on the Tree.

1. Look to Jesus on the tree;
There He dies for you and me.
There His God has made Him sin
That we might have peace within.

2. Look to Jesus on the tree;
See the blood that sets you free.
See Him suffer grief and pain
So that we might live again.

3. Look to Jesus on the tree,
Cursed by God for you and me.
From Him every blessing flows;
Gone our fears and gone our woes.

4. Look to Jesus on the tree
Wounded there for you and me.
See the nails in hands and feet;
Know your healing is complete.

5. Look to Jesus on the tree;
As the serpent raised was He.
Look to Him and you will live!
All your sin will God forgive.

6. Look to Jesus on the tree;
See God's love for you and me.
Praise Him for a work well done!
Praise Him for His only Son!

Tunes: 77.77: St. Bees, Nottingham, 77.77D: St. Edmund Steggall.

Matthew 27.46
And about the ninth hour Jesus cried with a loud voice, saying, Eli, Eli, lama sabachthani? that is to say, My God, my God, why hast thou forsaken me?

22nd August.

CMD.

Rejoice in Prayer for All the Saints.

1.
Rejoice in prayer for all the saints
Joy in their Christ-like growth;
Rejoice in love and in one mind;
Come, let's rejoice in both.
Joy in the Spirit's unity,
Guarding that bond of peace;
Rejoice that Christ has gone on high
Where praise shall never cease.

2.
Rejoice in those who as lights shine
In this dark world of sin.
Rejoice in fellowship divine
And God's Spirit within.
Rejoice in His almighty power
That brings the dead to life.
Rejoice in those who pledge their lives
To serve in days of strife.

3.
Rejoice in sacrificial love
That gives its all each day.
Joy in the Lord who gave Himself!
Rejoice in Him we pray!
Rejoice in weakness and defeat;
Rejoice when all is well.
Rejoice in grief and sorrow too;
In them God's purpose tell.

4.
Rejoice in all the Father gives
To His belovèd Son.
Rejoice in all the majesty
That He, the Victor, won!
Rejoice that Christ shall come again
That we with Him might be.
Rejoice in that bright home above;
Rejoice eternally!

Tunes: No King But Christ, None But Christ, Bethlehem, Cleansing Fountain, Alman, All Saints, Landas, Ellacombe, Forest Green, Spes Coelestis, Warrior.

Philippians 2.15-16
That ye may be blameless and harmless,
the sons of God, without rebuke,
in the midst of a crooked and perverse nation, among whom ye shine as lights in the world;
holding forth the word of life; that I may rejoice in the day of Christ, that I have not run in vain, neither laboured in vain.

23rd August.

65.65.

Tell Me of God's Mercy.

1. Tell me of God's mercy,
His wisdom and love;
Tell me of His glory
In the heavens above.

2. Tell me of His power,
Of His works of old;
Tell me of His blessings
As the times unfold.

3. Tell me of the Saviour
Sent to be made sin.
Tell me of the manger
And the Lord within.

4. Tell me of His blest life
Tried by pain and grief.
Tell me of His cross
Borne for my relief.

5. Tell me of the Spirit
Sent from heav'n on high;
Tell me of His witness
And all-knowing eye.

6. Tell me of His leading
Of His quick'ning power;
Tell me of His teaching
Each and every hour.

7. Father, we would praise Thee
For Thy lovely Son;
And we turn to thank Thee
For salvation won.

8. For Thy Spirit given
We bless Thee below;
With hearts tuned in worship
We like Christ would grow.

Tunes: North Coates, Armentrout, Quietude, Castle Eden.

Psalm 6.1-4

To the chief Musician on Neginoth upon Sheminith, A Psalm of David. O LORD, rebuke me not in thine anger, neither chasten me in thy hot displeasure. Have mercy upon me, O LORD; for I am weak: O LORD, heal me; for my bones are vexed. My soul is also sore vexed: but thou, O LORD, how long? Return, O LORD, deliver my soul: oh save me for thy mercies' sake.

Psalm 26.7

I will wash mine hands in innocency: so will I compass thine altar, O LORD: that I may publish with the voice of thanksgiving, and tell of all thy wondrous works. LORD, I have loved the habitation of thy house, and the place where thine honour dwelleth.

24th August.

88.88.

O Come, Ye People Lost in Sin.

1.
O come, ye people lost in sin,
Turn from the way that you walk in;
For 'tis a path that leads to Hell
With sorrows that no man can tell.

2.
There is a way that leads to God,
And sets you free from judgement's rod.
It brings you first to Calv'ry's tree
Where Christ was slain for you and me.

3.
He is the Door that we pass through
That our poor souls be born anew.
Faith in His blood will cleanse sin's stain
And through His loss will come our gain.

4.
Soon Heaven's gate will open wide
As Jesus takes us for His bride.
He'll bring us to that place prepared
Where all His joy with us is shared.

Tunes: Winchester New, Tallis' Canon, Federal St., Gift of Love, Abends, Brookfield, Deep Harmony.

John10.7-11
Then said Jesus unto them again, Verily, verily, I say unto you, I am the door of the sheep. All that ever came before me are thieves and robbers: but the sheep did not hear them.
I am the door: by me if any man enter in, he shall be saved, and shall go in and out, and find pasture. The thief cometh not, but for to steal, and to kill, and to destroy: I am come that they might have life, and that they might have it more abundantly. I am the good shepherd: the good shepherd giveth his life for the sheep.

25th August.

10.10.10.10.

Tell Me of Jesus, the Story of Love.

1.
Tell me of Jesus, the story of love;
Tell of my Saviour sent from heav'n above;
Tell of the baby in Bethlehem's stall;
Speak of "God with us" - He is Lord of all.

2.
Tell me of God's Son come to this sad earth;
Tell of His beauty - speak of all His worth.
Tell of His wonders - speak well of His grace;
Tell of the glory seen in His dear face.

3.
Tell me of His cross, the thorns and the spear;
Tell me of suff'ring that removes all fear.
Tell me of judgement poured on His blest head;
Speak of the torment He took in my stead.

4.
Tell me of Jesus raised up from the dead;
Tell me of my Lord, now the church's Head.
Tell me of splendour, majesty and light;
Speak of my Saviour in that glory bright.

Tunes: Eventide, Skara, New Year's Day, Penitentia, Toulon.

Acts 2.22-27

Ye men of Israel, hear these words; Jesus of Nazareth, a man approved of God among you by miracles and wonders and signs, which God did by him in the midst of you, as ye yourselves also know: him, being delivered by the determinate counsel and foreknowledge of God, ye have taken, and by wicked hands have crucified and slain: whom God hath raised up, having loosed the pains of death: because it was not possible that he should be holden of it. For David speaketh concerning him, I foresaw the Lord always before my face, for he is on my right hand, that I should not be moved…

26th August.

88.88D.

"There is No God!" the Sinner Cries.

1. "There is no God!" the sinner cries.
"No God to fill my heart with sighs.
There is no God to judge my sin;
I'll please myself with joy within."
"There is no God!" the rich man cries
I'll eat! I'll drink! "Merry, I'll rise!"
My harvests are both rich and vast
And through this life of mine they'll last!"

2. "There is a God!" all nature cries!
His name is written in the skies.
The stars declare that He is light
His strength is in a mountain's height.
A lily tells His glory bright;
A bird His wisdom in its flight.
His face is found in hail and snow;
His voice is heard where rivers flow.

3 "There is a God!" the Bible cries.
It is the book that makes you wise.
It tells of Jesus and His love;
It shows He came from God above.
It speaks of all the Father's planned
And of the grace in which we stand!
All glory be to God on high
The God on Whom we all rely.

Tunes: Duane St., Stephenson, Sagina, He Leadeth Me, Maryland, Sweet Hour.

Psalm 53.1
To the chief Musician upon Mahalath, Maschil, A Psalm of David. The fool hath said in his heart, There is no God. Corrupt are they, and have done abominable iniquity: there is none that doeth good.

27th August.

65.65D

Jesus, Never Leave Me.

1.
Jesus, never leave me
Stay close by my side.
I am lost and helpless,
You must be my Guide.
Bound in chains of sin
No life left to live.
Breathe on me, blest Lord,
All my sins forgive.

2.
Jesus, never leave me,
Stay close by my side.
I feel love embracing
When, for me, You died.
Your blood has now purged
My soul from all sin;
By Your Spirit's power,
I have peace within.

3.
Jesus, never leave me,
Stay close by my side
When I'm weak and helpless,
When my soul is tried.
Your strength is my fortress,
Wisdom is Your way;
Keep me blessèd Saviour
Safely, day by day.

4.
Jesus, never leave me,
Stay close by my side.
Let me love You dearly
As Your precious bride.
Through eternal ages
I will worship You.
And with eyes of heaven
All Your beauty view.

Tunes: 65.65: Eudoxia, Quietude, Castle Eden, North Coates, German.
11.11.11.11: Ruth (Smith), Evelyns, Look Away to Jesus, Lyndhurst (Vail), Normandy Carol.

Psalm 18.1-3
To the chief Musician, A Psalm of David, the servant of the LORD, who spake unto the LORD the words of this song in the day that the LORD delivered him from the hand of all his enemies, and from the hand of Saul: And he said, I will love thee, O LORD, my strength.
The LORD is my rock, and my fortress, and my deliverer; my God, my strength, in whom I will trust; my buckler, and the horn of my salvation, and my high tower.
I will call upon the LORD, who is worthy to be praised: so shall I be saved from mine enemies.

28th August.

77.77.

The Origin of Species, Lord.

1.
The origin of species, Lord,
Lies in the power of Thy word.
All things have come from Thy blest hand
Who blessing for creation planned.

2.
We see the grass, the herb and tree
All bearing witness unto Thee.
After their kind, their seed is found
As they spring from the fertile ground.

3.
All creatures of land, air and sea
Are shaped with forms that come from Thee.
After their kind their young are knit
Within the code that Thou didst fit.

4.
Creator of the heavens and earth,
Thou art the Source of our new birth.
Into Thy kingdom, we have come
That, through the death of Thy dear Son.

5.
We are a new creation, Lord,
Formed by Thy Spirit and Thy word.
In Christ, the old has passed away,
And 'tis Thy works we'd do today.

6.
One day, we'll see Thee face to face,
And marvel at Thy wondrous grace.
Then we shall all be like Thee, Lord,
And worship Thee with one accord.

Tunes: Gift of Love, Abends, Winchester (New), Tallis' Canon.

Isaiah 45.18
For thus saith the LORD that created the heavens; God himself that formed the earth and made it; he hath established it, he created it not in vain, he formed it to be inhabited: I am the LORD; and there is none else.

29th August.

CMD.

'Twas Unto Death, You Loved Us, Lord.

1.
'Twas unto death, You loved Us, Lord;
A death of shame and loss.
A death where wrath was poured on You!
The death of Calv'ry's cross!
As fragrance sweet Your off'ring rose
Up to Your God on high.
The wonder of Your sacrifice
To Him has brought us nigh.

2.
You brought us life and endless joy!
You brought us grace and peace!
You brought us rest and righteousness!
Your praise will never cease!
Help us to love as You have loved;
Help us ourselves to give!
Help us proclaim Your precious name
Prompting lost souls to live!

Tunes: No King But Christ, Landas, Land of Rest, Bethlehem, Jesus is God, Warrior, Tyrol, I Bring My All To Thee, Forest Green, Euphemia, Release.

Philippians 2.5-11
Let this mind be in you, which was also in Christ Jesus: who, being in the form of God, thought it not robbery to be equal with God: but made himself of no reputation, and took upon him the form of a servant, and was made in the likeness of men: and being found in fashion as a man, he humbled himself, and became obedient unto death, even the death of the cross. Wherefore God also hath highly exalted him, and given him a name which is above every name: that at the name of Jesus every knee should bow, of things in heaven, and things in earth, and things under the earth; And that every tongue should confess that Jesus Christ is Lord, to the glory of God the Father.

30th August.

77.77D.

Cleansed By Blood! 'Tis Christ I See...

1.
Cleansed by blood! 'Tis Christ I see
In His death at Calvary.
Bought by blood, I look above
Where He sits in light and love.
Refrain:
Depths of mercy flowed for me!
And His blood has set me free!
Depths of mercy, flowed for me!
Yes! His blood has set me free!

2.
"Sheltered!" cries the word of God;
Christ has borne the wrath and rod!
See Him now in heav'nly light,
With His glory shining bright
Refrain:

3.
Saved from sin by God's own Son;
See the work that He has done!
Praise His name for evermore!
At His feet your worship pour!
Refrain:

Tunes: Mount of Olives, Here is Love, Cassell, Hymn to Joy.

1John 1.6-9
If we say that we have fellowship with him, and walk in darkness, we lie, and do not the truth: but if we walk in the light, as he is in the light, we have fellowship one with another,
and the blood of Jesus Christ his Son cleanseth us from all sin.
If we say that we have no sin, we deceive ourselves, and the truth is not in us. If we confess our sins, he is faithful and just to forgive us our sins, and to cleanse us from all unrighteousness.

31st August.

77.77D.

Jesus Calls You From the Labour.

1.
Jesus calls you from the labour
Sin inflicts upon your head.
From such burdens, Jesus calls you;
He removes all fear and dread.
"Come now, take my yoke upon you;
Come and learn blest things from me.
Come and feel my hand is gentle;
Come and learn humility."

2.
"Take my yoke upon your shoulder;
Work with me, my burdens share.
Find my yoke is good and gracious;
Find my load is light to bear."
Come and you will find refreshment;
Come and find rest for your soul.
Come and find deep joy in sorrow;
Find His blood will make you whole.

Tunes: Here is Love, Shipton, Deerhurst, Hymn of Joy, Woodside, Beecher, Mount of Olives.

Matthew 11.27-29
All things are delivered unto me of my Father: and no man knoweth the Son, but the Father; neither knoweth any man the Father, save the Son, and he to whomsoever the Son will reveal him. Come unto me, all ye that labour and are heavy laden, and I will give you rest. Take my yoke upon you, and learn of me; for I am meek and lowly in heart: and ye shall find rest unto your souls.

2Corinthians 6.14
Be ye not unequally yoked together with unbelievers: for what fellowship hath righteousness with unrighteousness? and what communion hath light with darkness?

1st September.

85.85.

Are You Standing? Are You Standing...

1.
Are you standing? Are you standing
Where the fire has been?
Are you free from sin and judgement
With God's peace within?

2.
Are you standing? Are you standing
Where the cross once stood?
Do you see the wrath and torment
My dear Lord withstood?

3.
Are you standing? Are you standing
In His suffering love?
Will you spend eternal ages
With Him up above?

4.
Are you standing? Are you standing
By the Bridegroom's side?
Will your faith and righteousness
Clothe you as His bride?

Tunes: 85.85: Cairnbrook. 85.85D: Sinclair.

Romans 5.2
Therefore being justified by faith, we have peace with God through our Lord Jesus Christ: by whom also we have access by faith into this grace wherein we stand, and rejoice in hope of the glory of God.

1Corinthians.1-2
Moreover, brethren, I declare unto you the gospel which I preached unto you, which also ye have received, and wherein ye stand; by which also ye are saved, if ye keep in memory what I preached unto you, unless ye have believed in vain.

2nd September.

76.76D.

Glory to Thee, Blest Father.

1.
Glory to Thee, blest Father,
The God of light and love,
Immortal and eternal
In those bright courts above.
Glory to Thee, blest Father,
The God who sent His Son
To die for this world's sinners
Both ruined and undone.

2.
Glory to Thee, blest Father,
Who planned His pathway here.
'Twas lived in lonely vigil;
'Twas lived with godly fear.
Glory to Thee, blest Father,
The God revealed below;
Yes, Thine own Son declared Thee
That we Thy will might know.

3.
Glory to Thee, blest Father,
The God who takes our part.
No one can e'er defeat us
Shielded within Thine heart.
Glory to Thee, blest Father,
Thou art the God all-wise.
Thou crown'st Thy Son with gladness –
His is the name we prize.

Tunes: Lymington, Greenland, St. Edith, St. Theodulph, Thornbury.

John 4.23
But the hour cometh, and now is, when the true worshippers shall worship the Father in spirit and in truth: for the Father seeketh such to worship him.

3rd September.

CMD.

My Love, We Part, But Not For Long.

1. My love, we part, but not for long
For hope fills us with joy!
The coming of the Lord draws near;
His presence, we'll enjoy.
We'll meet again in heav'n above
And join to sing His praise.
We'll bow before His majesty
And happy anthems raise.

2. We'll sing in tune with perfect pitch;
We'll sing in harmony;
We'll sing with grace within our hearts;
Perfect the melody.
We'll sing, conducted by our Lord,
Who led our song below.
We'll sing with harps that sound God's worth
And love, to Him, will flow.

Tunes: Jesus is God, Bethlehem, Forest Green, Landas, No King But Christ.

Psalm 31.23-24
O love the LORD, all ye his saints: for the LORD preserveth the faithful, and plentifully rewardeth the proud doer. Be of good courage, and he shall strengthen your heart, all ye that hope in the LORD.

2Thessalonians 2.16-17
Now our Lord Jesus Christ himself, and God, even our Father, which hath loved us, and hath given us everlasting consolation and good hope through grace, comfort your hearts, and stablish you in every good word and work.

Titus 2.13
Looking for that blessed hope, and the glorious appearing of the great God and our Saviour Jesus Christ…

4th September.

CMD.

Behold, What Kind of Love is This!

1.
Behold, what kind of love is this
That on our souls is poured!
A love that brought us back to God
A love that is assured.
It gives us all the right to be
Children of light this day.
It has the pow'r to keep our feet
Within the narrow way.

2.
Behold, the measure of God's love;
The love that gave His Son.
It sent Him to this world below
That our souls might be won.
It led Him on to Calv'ry's tree
The work of God to do.
He bled, and died to give us peace
And cleanse us through and through.

3.
Behold, the fullness of God's love
That binds us to His Son.
The love that blesses us each day;
The love that makes us one.
Father, we thank Thee for the love
That set Christ on Thy throne.
Father, we bless Thy holy name
For all Thy love has done!

Tunes: No King But Christ, Bethlehem, Forest Green, Jesus is God.

1John 3.1
Behold, what manner of love the Father hath bestowed upon us, that we should be called the sons of God: therefore the world knoweth us not, because it knew him not.

5th September.

76.76D.

Lord, Gathered Round Thy Table.

1. Lord, gathered round Thy table,
We would remember Thee -
Beneath Thy love's bold banner
We'd think of Calvary.
Blest Lord, Thyself Thou gavest,
Up to the darkest night.
There, to a cross, men nailed Thee
Controlled by hate and spite.

2. Lord, gathered round Thy table,
We would remember Thee -
The holy Lamb of God,
Made sin to set us free.
Blest Lord, Thyself Thou gavest
Up to Thy Father's will.
Now that His work is finished,
His peace our hearts can fill.

3. Lord, gathered round Thy table,
We would remember Thee -
The righteous Son of God
Who died upon the tree.
Blest Lord, Thyself Thou gavest,
To save our souls from sin.
The blood that Thou hast shed
Has made us pure within.

4. Lord, gathered round Thy table,
We would remember Thee -
The gentle Son of man,
In light and love, we see.
There, on the cross Thou gavest
Thyself, to gain a bride.
Now, as Thy church, we love Thee,
And worship at Thy side.

Tunes: Thornbury, Wolvercote, Ewing, Day of Rest, Greenland, Lymington, Passion Chorale, Penlan.

1Corinthians 10.15-17 and 20-21
I speak as to wise men; judge ye what I say. The cup of blessing which we bless, is it not the communion of the blood of Christ? The bread which we break, is it not the communion of the body of Christ? For we being many are one bread, and one body: for we are all partakers of that one bread...But I say, that the things which the Gentiles sacrifice, they sacrifice to devils, and not to God: and I would not that ye should have fellowship with devils. Ye cannot drink the cup of the Lord, and the cup of devils: ye cannot be partakers of the Lord's table, and of the table of devils.

6th September.

LM.

Come, See the Work our God has Done.

1.
Come! See the work our God has done
All through the death of His dear Son.
By blood, He cleanses from all sin!
By blood, He gives us peace within!

2.
By blood, He draws us to His side!
By blood, He's made us His Son's bride!
By blood, we're clothed in righteousness!
By blood, we're saved from sin's distress!

3.
We know the world is crucified!
We know in love the Saviour died!
We know that Satan's power is drained!
We know eternal life is gained!

4.
The Lord our God is for us now;
Before His holy feet, we bow.
We bless Him for His only Son!
We praise Him for the work well done.

5.
To Heaven's gates, He leads us on;
He is our strength! He is our song!
Yes, soon, we'll be with Christ above
In all the fullness of God's love!

Tunes: Gift of Love, Winchester New, Federal St., Abends, Mozart, Duke St., Brookfield, Deep Harmony.

Ephesians 2.13
But now in Christ Jesus ye who sometimes were far off are made nigh by the blood of Christ.

7th September.

76.76D.

Father, We See Thy Glory.

1. Father, we see Thy glory
In Jesus' face of love.
All mercy, grace and kindness
Dwells in Thee up above.
We see that love forbearing!
We feel Thy goodness here!
Thy truth always sustains us!
Whom then have we to fear?

2. Father, by Thee begotten,
We joy before Thy throne;
The Son whom Thou hast given
Has made us all Thine own.
We love Thee for Thy wisdom,
Thy majesty and might!
We praise Thee for the power
That brought us to the Light!

Tunes: Lymington, Greenland (Hadyn), Thornbury, Webb, St. Edith.

Exodus 33.22-23

And it shall come to pass, while my glory passeth by, that I will put thee in a clift of the rock, and will cover thee with my hand while I pass by: And I will take away mine hand, and thou shalt see my back parts: but my face shall not be seen.

Exodus 34.5-8

And the LORD descended in the cloud, and stood with him there, and proclaimed the name of the LORD. And the LORD passed by before him, and proclaimed, The LORD, The LORD God, merciful and gracious, longsuffering, and abundant in goodness and truth, keeping mercy for thousands, forgiving iniquity and transgression and sin, and that will by no means clear the guilty; visiting the iniquity of the fathers upon the children, and upon the children's children, unto the third and to the fourth generation. And Moses made haste, and bowed his head toward the earth, and worshipped.

8th September.

11.11.11.11.

Come, Jesus Is Waiting, Is Waiting For You!

Come, Jesus is waiting, is waiting for you!
Come, sinner, come to Him, there's nothing to do.
He paid for salvation on Calvary's tree
Where once He was offered for you and for me.

Come, Jesus is waiting, is waiting for you!
Trust Him, sinner, trust Him, there's nothing to do.
His blood was poured out upon Calvary's cross
That life you might gain through His suff'ring and loss.

Come, Jesus is waiting, is waiting for you!
Pray, sinner, pray to Him, there's nothing to do.
Your works have no merit! Your tears cannot save!
'Tis Christ who has triumphed o'er death and the grave!

Come, Jesus is waiting, is waiting for you!
Come, sinner, come to Him, there's nothing to do.
All things are now ready, the work has been done;
Your joy is assured through the grief of God's Son.

Come, Jesus is waiting, is waiting for you;
Cast yourself upon Him, He's faithful and true.
Then in new creation, these words come to you,
"In love, you may serve me! There's plenty to do!"

Tunes: Cradle Song, St. Denio, Lyndhurst (Vail), Merry Christmas, Normandy Carol, Resignation, Ruth (Smith),

Matthew 16.24-26
Then said Jesus unto his disciples,
If any man will come after me, let him deny himself, and take up his cross, and follow me.
For whosoever will save his life shall lose it:
and whosoever will lose his life for my sake shall find it. For what is a man profited, if he shall gain the whole world, and lose his own soul? or what shall a man give in exchange for his soul?

9th September.

CM.

Lord, You're Our Everlasting Song.

.1.
Lord, You're our everlasting song,
The joy of heaven and earth.
Eternal is your matchless grace
And glorious Your worth.

2.
Lord, You're our strength for evermore;
A strong and mighty tower.
All enemies You will put down,
And blessings on us shower.

3.
Lord, You're our Rock, our refuge too;
Most perfect are Your ways.
You'll guard and keep us through the storm
And through eternal days.

4.
All praise and glory be to You
Upon Your throne above.
Accept the gift we to You bring -
Ourselves, with all our love.

Tunes: Westminster (Turle), Winchester (Old), Tallis' Ordinal.

2Samuel 22.2-4

And he said, The LORD is my rock, and my fortress, and my deliverer; the God of my rock; in him will I trust: he is my shield, and the horn of my salvation, my high tower, and my refuge, my saviour; thou savest me from violence. I will call on the LORD, who is worthy to be praised: so shall I be saved from mine enemies.

Psalm 62.7

In God is my salvation and my glory: the rock of my strength, and my refuge, is in God.

10th September.

76.76.

Love Made Him an Apostle.

1. Love made Him an Apostle
Sent from His Father's side.
Love brought Him to the manger;
The Saviour, God supplied.

2. Love took Him to the Baptist
Where Jordan's waters flowed.
Love led Him to the desert
Where He, God's truth has showed.

3. Love led Him to the leper,
The blind, the lame, the poor;
Love made Him the Good Shepherd,
The Dayspring and the Door.

4. Love led Him to the garden
In deepest agony.
Love bound Him to the altar -
His blood now sets us free.

5. Love wrapped Him in fine linen
And laid Him in the tomb.
Love covered Him with spices
A costly, sweet perfume.

6. Love raised Him up in glory
And set Him at God's side.
Loves brings Him back as Victor
To claim, by right, His bride.

Tunes: 76.76: Cara, Vulpius. 76.76D: Lymington, Thornbury, Ewing, Greenland, Passion Chorale, St. Edith, Aurelia, Wolvercote.

John 15.9
As the Father hath loved me, so have I loved you: continue ye in my love.

11th September

88.88D.

Father, It's In Your Son We See.

Father, it's in Your Son we see:
A heart of deep humility;
A nature holy and divine;
A purpose of faithful design.
A spirit that's both meek and kind;
A life that's harmless there we find
A servant to Thy will most true;
He is the man that pleases You.

Tunes: He Leadeth Me, Duane St., Stephenson, Sweet Hour, Hayes, Sagina, Nazareth,

Isaiah 42.1-8

Behold my servant, whom I uphold; mine elect, in whom my soul delighteth; I have put my spirit upon him: he shall bring forth judgment to the Gentiles.He shall not cry, nor lift up, nor cause his voice to be heard in the street. A bruised reed shall he not break, and the smoking flax shall he not quench: he shall bring forth judgment unto truth. He shall not fail nor be discouraged, till he have set judgment in the earth: and the isles shall wait for his law. Thus saith God the LORD, he that created the heavens, and stretched them out; he that spread forth the earth, and that which cometh out of it; he that giveth breath unto the people upon it, and spirit to them that walk therein: I the LORD have called thee in righteousness, and will hold thine hand, and will keep thee, and give thee for a covenant of the people, for a light of the Gentiles; to open the blind eyes, to bring out the prisoners from the prison, and them that sit in darkness out of the prison house.I am the LORD: that is my name: and my glory will I not give to another, neither my praise to graven images.

Hebrews 7.24-26

But this man, because he continueth ever, hath an unchangeable priesthood. Wherefore he is able also to save them to the uttermost that come unto God by him, seeing he ever liveth to make intercession for them. For such an high priest became us, who is holy, harmless, undefiled, separate from sinners, and made higher than the heavens…

12th September.

77.77.

Grace is Free! Christ Died for Me!

1.
Grace is free! Christ died for me!
Now I'll live eternally!
Grace is free! It enfolds me;
Now the Father's love I see.

2.
Grace is free! It pardoned me;
Sins dismissed at Calvary!
Grace is free! I'm justified
By the blood of Him who died.

3.
Grace is free! My fears all gone!
Vanquished by God's only Son!
Grace is free! My tears are dried
For my Lord is glorified!

4.
Grace is free! Satan destroyed!
Now God's mercy is deployed.
Grace is free! The world is slain!
God's Spirit it cannot drain.

5.
Grace is free! Infirmity
Finds the pow'r of Christ in me.
Grace is free! O praise His name!
All God's blessings we can claim!

Tunes: Buckland, Confidence (Ouseley), St. Bees, Monkland, Innocents.

Isaiah 55. 7
Let the wicked forsake his way, and the unrighteous man his thoughts: and let him return unto the LORD, and he will have mercy upon him; and to our God, for he will abundantly pardon.

13th September.

CM.

Seek Out the LORD and You Shall Live.

1. Seek out the LORD and you shall live
Yes, live for evermore.
Trust in Him, the Almighty God,
His holy name adore.

2. He set the dawning in its place
To light the earth by day.
He opened up the gates of death
And showed the light its way.

3. In Pleaides is His sweetness found -
Strength at Orion's side;
He times the rise of Mazzaroth;
And shall Arcturus guide.

4. Come, turn from evil, embrace good;
Let justice have its way.
Then know the presence of the LORD
And His grace every day.

5. Your offerings, He can't accept
While tainted by your sin.
Trust in the Christ who gave Himself
And you'll find peace within.

6. Look on to see the glory bright
That fills Immanuel's land.
Then you will reign with Christ your king
Just as the LORD had planned.

Tunes: CM: Beulah, Pisgah, Nativity, Beatitudo, Gerontius, Belmont.CMD: No King But Christ, Bethlehem, Ellacombe.

Job 38.31
Canst thou bind the sweet influences of Pleiades, or loose the bands of Orion?

14th September.

CM.

Without the Son There is no Life!

1. Without the Son, there is no life!
The Spirit's word is true.
For He, the lowly Jesus here
Has been made sin for you.

2. Without the Son, there is no life!
Heaven's gates are closed to you.
You must believe on Christ alone
To be one of the few.

3. Without the Son, there is no life!
You're dead in all your sin.
But He is risen from the grave
To make you right within.

4. Without the Son, there is no life!
Hell's gates are open wide!
But as He lives for you on high
He'll bring you to His side.

5. Without the Son, there is no life!
Satan has gripped your heart!
But Christ has bruised the serpent's head
And quenched the devil's dart!

6. So trust the Son! Take hold on life!
From sin and death be free!
For he who has the Son has life –
And lives eternally!

Tunes: CM: St. Agnes, Beulah, Beatitudo, Westminster (Turle). CMD: No King But Christ, Bethlehem, Tyrol, Warrior.

John 1.4
In him was life; and the life was the light of men.

15th September.

85.85.

Jesus, Lord, Made of a Woman.

1. Jesus, Lord, made of a woman;
Perfect man below.
Holy thing of Bethlehem
We Thy worth, now know.

2. Jesus, Lord, made like Thy brethren
In all things but sin.
Thou hast Satan's power destroyed;
Hope we have within.

3. Jesus, Lord, made seed of David,
Thou shalt rule as king.
Righteousness shall be Thy sceptre;
Peace and joy Thy wing.

4. Jesus, Lord, made under law,
Love and light, Thou art.
All is found complete in Thee;
Pure and just in heart.

5. Jesus, Lord, made sin for us,
Lowly Lamb of God.
Made a curse on Calv'ry's tree;
Suff'ring judgement's rod.

6. Jesus, Lord, made poor for us
In humility.
Thou a servant's form didst take
That we might be free.

Tunes: Sinclair, Cairnbrook.

John 7.42
Hath not the scripture said,
That Christ cometh of the seed of David,
and out of the town of Bethlehem, where David was?

16th September.

CMD.

Lord Jesus, Thou Hast Glorified.

1.
Lord Jesus, Thou hast glorified
The Father here on earth.
His holy name Thou hast declared
With all its precious worth.
The Father's work by Thee was done
With suffering, shame and loss;
And bound by love to Him above
Thou hast endured the cross.

2.
Lord Jesus, Thou hast kept Thine own
In Thy blest way below.
The word of truth Thou'st given them
That they Thy will might know.
Thou'st sent them forth into the world
As Thou wast sent before.
Thou wilt with them Thy glory share
In heaven, evermore.

Tunes: Release, No King But Christ, Jesus is God, Bethlehem, Tyrol, Landas, Warrior.

John 17.1-6

These words spake Jesus, and lifted up his eyes to heaven, and said, Father, the hour is come; glorify thy Son, that thy Son also may glorify thee: as thou hast given him power over all flesh, that he should give eternal life to as many as thou hast given him. And this is life eternal, that they might know thee the only true God, and Jesus Christ, whom thou hast sent. I have glorified thee on the earth: I have finished the work which thou gavest me to do. And now, O Father, glorify thou me with thine own self with the glory which I had with thee before the world was. I have manifested thy name unto the men which thou gavest me out of the world: thine they were, and thou gavest them me; and they have kept thy word.

17th September.

76.76.

Jesus, Almighty Saviour.

1. Jesus, Almighty Saviour,
How free You are to give!
Yourself You gave on Calv'ry
That we for God might live!

2. You gave us living water,
Eternal life, we claim.
It was that Holy Spirit
Sent in Your precious name.

3. You gave us peace for ever
Deep down our souls within.
Your blood for ever cleanses
Our hearts from every sin.

4. The True Bread you have given
To feed us in the way.
The Bread of God the Father,
Who keeps us day by day.

5. You gave a new commandment
That we should love like You.
It is the boldest witness
This world can ever view.

6. All praise is yours, dear Saviour,
Our lives are yours to rule.
So in your Spirit's power
Our hearts with Your love fuel.

Tunes: 76.76: Cara, Matrimony. 76.76D: Greenland, Lymington, Thornbury, Passion Chorale, Ewing, Ahnfelt, St. Edith, St. Theodulph.

John 13. 34
A new commandment I give unto you, That ye love one another; as I have loved you, that ye also love one another.

18th September.

10.10.10.10.

Mighty to Save! Mighty to save!

1. Mighty to Save! Mighty to save!
Jesus the Saviour is mighty to save!
'Tis He who suffered on Calv'ry's tree
Who dwells in Heaven!
Where He lives for Thee!

2. Mighty to Save! Mighty to save!
Jesus the Saviour is mighty to save!
He who has humbled Himself on the tree;
Sits at God's right hand -
The Lord of Glory!

3. Mighty to Save! Mighty to save!
Jesus the Saviour is mighty to save!
He was accursed on Calv'ry's tree;
Now blessed on God's throne
And ruling for Thee.

4. Mighty to Save! Mighty to save!
Jesus the Saviour is mighty to save!
He who once prayed - nailed to a tree,
Lives as the High Priest
Who's praying for Thee.

5. Mighty to Save! Mighty to save!
Jesus the Saviour is mighty to save!
He has gained vict'ry over the grave.
Soon He'll come for Thee;
He's mighty to save!

Tunes: Glory to Jesus.

Hebrews 7.24-25
But this man, because he continueth ever, hath an unchangeable priesthood. Wherefore he is able also to save them to the uttermost…

19th September.

CMD.

There is a Better World, We Know.

1.
There is a better world, we know
Where sin can find no place.
Pure music fills its atmosphere;
With love in every space.
No tears are there to stain saint's eyes;
There is no pain to trace.
But joy in all its fullness flows
From God, in all His grace.

2.
Sorrow and suffering fret no more;
They're banished from the scene!
The Saviour is its Lamp of Light
And shines with peace supreme.
Now Death has gone, we see life reign
Throughout eternal days.
So lift your hearts to God above
And give Him all your praise.

Tunes: No King But Christ, Providence, Bethlehem, Minerva, Jesus is God.

Revelation 21.3-5
And I heard a great voice out of heaven saying, Behold, the tabernacle of God is with men, and he will dwell with them, and they shall be his people, and God himself shall be with them, and be their God. And God shall wipe away all tears from their eyes; and there shall be no more death, neither sorrow, nor crying, neither shall there be any more pain: for the former things are passed away. And he that sat upon the throne said, Behold, I make all things new. And he said unto me, Write: for these words are true and faithful.

Revelation 21.23
And the city had no need of the sun, neither of the moon, to shine in it: for the glory of God did lighten it, and the Lamb is the light thereof.

20th September.

88.88D.

How Vast and Wondrous was the Love.

1. How vast and wondrous was the love,
That brought my Saviour from above.
The love of God, so full and free!
The love revealed at Calvary!
See the crude crown forced on His head
Speaking of both earth's curse and dread.
See His dear face so badly bruised
Showing that men can't be excused.

2. See His bare back both ripped and torn;
The back that had men's burdens borne.
See iron nails struck through His hands;
The Servant does as God commands.
See the two feet that walked God's way,
Stained with His blood upon that day.
See the spear thrust into His side,
Tell out His love for His dear bride.

3. Oh, hear His cry of agony
As there He was made sin for thee.
Fathom the judgement - feel the loss
As He hung high upon the cross.
Then hear His cry of victory
As the just Saviour died for thee.
Now by His blood to God draw near;
Trust in His love and know no fear.

Tunes: Sweet Hour, Stephenson, He Leadeth Me.

Song 8.6-7

Set me as a seal upon thine heart, as a seal upon thine arm: for love is strong as death; jealousy is cruel as the grave: the coals thereof are coals of fire, which hath a most vehement flame. Many waters cannot quench love, neither can the floods drown it; if a man would give all the substance of his house for love, it would utterly be contemned.

21st September.

87.87D.

When the Shout of Jesus Calls Us.

1.
When the shout of Jesus calls us
To arise and with Him be.
Will you fly up to His presence?
Will you all His glory see?
When the "angel's voice" commands us
To be free of death's dark dust.
Will your body change for ever?
Will you be both wise and just?

2.
When the trump of God is sounded
Telling us to leave this earth;
Will you see the face of Jesus?
Will you know His precious worth?
"Come, Lord Jesus! Come from heaven!
Take Thine own with Thee to be.
Fill them with Thy pow'r and glory
Love them all eternally."

Tunes: Woodside, Beecher, Hymn to Joy, Mount of Olives, Here is Love, Shipton.

1Thessalonians 4.15-18
For this we say unto you by the word of the Lord,
that we which are alive and remain unto the coming of the Lord shall not prevent them which are asleep.
For the Lord himself shall descend from heaven with a shout,
with the voice of the archangel,
and with the trump of God:
and the dead in Christ shall rise first: then we which are alive and remain shall be caught up together with them in the clouds,
to meet the Lord in the air:
and so shall we ever be with the Lord.
Wherefore comfort one another with these words.

22nd September.

77.77.

Grace Divine, So Full and Free.

1. Grace divine, so full and free,
Found its source at Calvary.
There my Saviour for me died;
For my sin was crucified!

2. Grace divine, so full and free,
Is the grace that found out me.
Bound by sin, I had no life;
'Cept that filled with hate and strife!

3. Grace divine, so full and free,
Has poured God's love on me,.
Jesus died on Calvary's cross;
Mine the gain through His great loss!

4. Grace divine, so full and free;
Is the power of God for me.
By blood washed from every sin,
His Spirit now dwells within!

5. Grace divine, so full and free
Is the will of God in me.
In afflictions, I rejoice;
To His praise, I lend my voice!

6. Grace divine, so full and free,
Into Heaven carries me.
Soon my Lord shall come again,
Then in glory grace shall reign!

Tunes: 77.77: St. Bees, Monkland, Confidence (Ouseley). 77.77D: St. Edmund Steggall, Hollingside, Benevento.

Romans 3.24
Being justified freely by his grace through the redemption that is in Christ Jesus…

23rd September.

77.77.

Boundless Mercy Flows From Heaven.

1.
Boundless mercy flows from heaven
Where Christ's blood now pleads for thee.
Come and thou shalt be forgiven
For God's love is full and free.

2.
Boundless mercy flows from heaven
Flooding us with all we need.
Filling us with loving kindness
Fitting us for every deed.

3.
Boundless mercy flows from heaven;
'Tis the blood that justifies;
Makes us fit for heaven's glory
Where God's wonders fill our eyes.

Tunes: Sussex, Gott Wills Machen, Rathbun, Cross of Jesus,

Psalm 25.1-10
A Psalm of David.
Unto thee, O LORD, do I lift up my soul.
O my God, I trust in thee: let me not be ashamed, let not mine enemies triumph over me.
Yea, let none that wait on thee be ashamed: let them be ashamed which transgress without cause. Shew me thy ways, O LORD; teach me thy paths. Lead me in thy truth, and teach me: for thou art the God of my salvation; on thee do I wait all the day. Remember, O LORD, thy tender mercies and thy lovingkindnesses; for they have been ever of old. Remember not the sins of my youth, nor my transgressions: according to thy mercy remember thou me for thy goodness' sake, O LORD. Good and upright is the LORD: therefore will he teach sinners in the way. The meek will he guide in judgment: and the meek will he teach his way. All the paths of the LORD are mercy and truth unto such as keep his covenant and his testimonies.

24th September.

76.76D.

Before the World's Foundation.

1.
Before the world's foundation
You saw us in our
sin.
You chose us for salvation
And now we're cleansed
within.
You lifted us from darkness
You brought us into light.
And now, we hope for glory
In heaven pure and bright.

2.
We lay under Your judgement
When you called us to
live.
You showered us with blessing
That we might learn to give.
You washed us with pure water;
Your word has cleansed our
way.
You poured Your oil upon us;
Your Spirit now has sway.

3.
You clothed us with rich
garments
Of righteousness and love.
You moulded us with kindness
To be like Christ above.
You crowned our head with
goodness;
Your glory decked our brow.
Your beauty rested on us
And we are perfect now.

4.
All glory, blessèd Father;
All glory be to You.
For through our sin and
weakness
A bride You came to view.
Your Son will joy for ever,
Delighting in our
love;
As we Your children worship
Yourself in heaven above.

Tunes: Lymington, Greenland (Haydn), Passion Chorale, St. Edith, Thornbury.

1Peter 1.18-20

Forasmuch as ye know that ye were not redeemed with corruptible things, as silver and gold, from your vain conversation received by tradition from your fathers; but with the precious blood of Christ, as of a lamb without blemish and without spot: who verily was foreordained before the foundation of the world, but was manifest in these last times for you, Who by him do believe in God, that raised him up from the dead, and gave him glory; that your faith and hope might be in God.

25th September.

99.99.

Saved Without Money.

1.
Saved without money;
Christ was the price.
Saved without labour;
Faith will suffice.
Saved by the blood
Shed on Calvary.
Saved both for time
And eternity.

2.
Saved for God's purpose;
Saved by His love!
Saved for His pleasure
And joy above.
Saved as His people
His name to praise.
Saved every moment
Of earth's long days.

3.
Saved as a bride
For God's only Son,
Saved to reign with Him
Through work He's done.
Saved to be children,
Children of light.
Saved for God's glory
Pure, white and bright.

Tunes: Adelaide, St. Cecilia (Sewall).

Revelation 21.2
And I John saw the holy city, new Jerusalem, coming down from God out of heaven, prepared as a bride adorned for her husband.

26th September.

77.77D.

What a Bundle of Blessings.

1.
What a bundle of blessing
Thou hast laid on us, dear Lord.
Blessing of goodness and life;
Blessing that Thy grace had stored.
Loved with love that never fails;
Chosen and foreknown by Thee;
Called in Time to heav'n above;
Saved by blood shed on the tree.

2.
Destined for life evermore;
Moulded like Thyself to be.
For Thy glory as Firstborn
We're redeemed and we're set free.
Blessed by the Father of love,
To His presence drawn by Thee;
Now with hearts righteous and pure,
Thee, we'll praise eternally.

Tunes: St. Edmund Steggall, Madrid (Carr), Hollingside, New St. Andrew, St. George's (Windsor).

1Samuel 25.29
Yet a man is risen to pursue thee, and to seek thy soul:
but the soul of my lord shall be bound in the bundle of life with the LORD thy God;
and the souls of thine enemies, them shall he sling out, as out of the middle of a sling.

Ephesians 1.3-4
Blessed be the God and Father of our Lord Jesus Christ, who hath blessed us with all spiritual blessings in heavenly places in Christ: according as he hath chosen us in him before the foundation of the world, that we should be holy and without blame before him in love…

27th September.

CM.

We See Thy Mighty Pow'r, O God.

1. We see Thy mighty pow'r, O God,
That made the earth and skies.
Nature itself proclaims Thy worth
Presenting Thee "All-wise!"

2. We see Thy wondrous love, O God,
In Thy dear Son once giv'n.
He has Himself proclaimed Thy worth
As by Thy Spirit driv'n.

3. We see Him hanging on the tree,
A sacrifice for sin;
And through the precious blood, He shed,
He's made us pure within!

4. We see Thy great delight, O God,
In raising Him again.
He sits as Lord in glory bright
Free from all grief and pain.

5. We see Thy holiness, O God,
Reflected in His face.
And in the heavens high above
We'll soon sing of His grace.

6. We see Thee glorified, O God,
By all He's said and done.
And when we stand at His blest side
All shall adore Thy Son.

Tunes: St. Agnes, Irish, Westminster (Turle), Belmont, Nativity.

Romans 6.4
Therefore we are buried with him by baptism into death: that like as Christ was raised up from the dead by the glory of the Father, even so we also should walk in newness of life.

28th September.

87.87D.

Hear the Voice of Love and Mercy.

1.
Hear the voice of love and mercy
Sounding forth from Calv'ry's tree
Where the Saviour dies in torment;
Where the Saviour dies for me.
"It is finished!" Voice of triumph!
Rings the air with all its might.
Gone for ever is Death's darkness
Chased away by Life's pure light.

2.
Hear the voice of peace and pardon
From the Saviour on the tree.
From the curse and depths of torture
His poor soul is now set free.
"It is finished!" Voice of triumph!
All salvation's work is done.
Trust in Christ and find forgiveness!
Taste the joy of God's dear Son!

Tunes: Shipton, Mount of Olives, Woodside, Beecher, Hymn to Joy, Here is Love.

Ephesians 2.4-10

But God, who is rich in mercy, for his great love wherewith he loved us, even when we were dead in sins, hath quickened us together with Christ, (by grace ye are saved;)
and hath raised us up together, and made us sit together in heavenly places in Christ Jesus:
that in the ages to come he might shew the exceeding riches of his grace in his kindness toward us through Christ Jesus.
For by grace are ye saved through faith; and that not of yourselves: it is the gift of God: not of works, lest any man should boast.
For we are his workmanship,
created in Christ Jesus unto good works, which God hath before ordained that we should walk in them.

29th September.

CM.

I'm Cast Upon You, Gracious Lord.

1. I'm cast upon You, precious Lord,
For all I am and do.
I'm cast upon You from that day
I placed my trust in You.

2. I'm cast upon You, gracious Lord,
Blest Saviour of mankind.
I'm cast upon the precious blood
That gives me peace of mind.

3. I'm cast upon You, righteous Lord,
For You are over all.
I'm cast upon the love and pow'r
That keeps me lest I fall.

4. I'm cast upon You, holy Lord,
The Servant to the cross.
I'm cast upon the blessings, Lord,
That flow out from Your loss.

5. I'm cast upon You, faithful Lord,
For all my earthly need.
I'm cast upon You for the life
That is from judgement freed.

6. I'm cast upon You, precious Lord,
In every thought and prayer.
Cast me in Your own likeness, Lord,
With beauty pure and rare.

Tunes: St. Agnes, Westminster (Turle), Beulah, St. Edmund (Hoyte),
Winchester (Old), Irish, Pisgah.

Psalm 55.22
Cast thy burden upon the LORD, and he shall sustain thee: he shall never suffer the righteous to be moved.

30th September.

76.76D.

O Lord, the Day is Over.

1.
O Lord, the day is over
A day of heavy toil.
A day in which Your presence
The wheels of life did oil.
In prayer, we knelt before You,
And read Your precious word,
We went out in Your goodness
With our blest hearts assured.

2.
You gave us grace and wisdom
For every working hour.
You gave us all we needed
By Your almighty power.
You knew our every weakness
And kept us in Your hand;
You knew each word of witness
As by You, it was planned.

3.
O Lord, we've sinned against
You,
In word and thought and deed.
But through Your cross, Lord
Jesus,
You have our spirits freed.
Your chastening hand, Lord
Jesus,
Now paves the way of grace.
Oh, may we learn most humbly
Until we see Your face.

4.
Now may Your wings enclose
us
As we our rest would take.
Guard us in love and mercy
Till with the dawn we
wake.
Refreshed by sleep so precious
Help us to serve You here
Until the day of glory
When there's no pain or tear.

Tunes: Lymington, Mountain, Greenland, Thornbury, Ahnfelt, Aurelia, Day of Rest, Passion Chorale, St. Edith, St. Theodulph, Wolvercote.

James 4.13-15
Go to now, ye that say, To day or to morrow we will go into such a city, and continue there a year, and buy and sell, and get gain:
whereas ye know not what shall be on the morrow.
For what is your life? It is even a vapour, that appeareth for a little time, and then vanisheth away.
For that ye ought to say, If the Lord will, we shall live, and do this, or that.

1st October.

CM.

Sound Out the Song of Love Divine!

1. Sound out the song of love divine!
See God in human form!
A manger for a crib was His,
A baby loved and warm.

2. Sound out the song of love divine!
For Christ walked here below.
He bore our griefs and sorrows then
That we God's name might know.

3. Sound out the song of love divine!
For Christ hung on a tree.
And there accursed by God and man
He was made sin for me.

4. Sound out the song of love divine!
His grave is empty now.
So cleansed and justified by blood
At His blest feet we bow.

5. Sound out the song of love divine!
Our Lord is glorified!
He lives our Great High Priest on high
And shall be satisfied.

6. Sound out the song of love divine!
Our Lord is soon to come.
He'll take us to Him as His bride
And then we'll know God's Son.

Tunes: Beulah, Westminster (Turle), Christmas Eve, Nativity, St. Agnes,

Isaiah 53.4
Surely he hath borne our griefs, and carried our sorrows: yet we did esteem him stricken, smitten of God, and afflicted.

2nd October.

CM.

Through Christ Alone, We're Saved from Sin.

1.
Through Christ alone, we're saved from sin;
His blood has met our need.
Through Him who died upon the tree
We're ransomed, cleansed and freed!

2.
With Christ alone, we'll walk in love
While in this world of woe.
Then with His joy, His grace, and peace
Our hearts will overflow.

3.
For Christ alone, we'll toil on earth
To win souls lost in sin.
While with the saints, we'd seek to share
The blessings found in Him.

4.
By Christ alone, we'll fight the fight;
Satan will have no place.
And when faith's battle is complete
We'll see our Captain's face.

5.
In Christ alone, our hope is found;
A hope of life above -
Where there's no sorrow! No more pain!
We'll dwell with Him in love!

Tunes: Beulah, St. Fulbert, I Do Believe, Pisgah, Arlington, Belmont, Beatitudo.

Mark 16. 20
And they went forth, and preached every where, the Lord working with them, and confirming the word with signs following. Amen.

3rd October.

CM.

The Trumpet of Salvation Sounds.

1. The trumpet of salvation sounds
With notes of grace and peace.
It echoes over land and sea!
Its work shall never cease.

2. The trumpet of salvation sounds
Telling of God as man.
In Jesus Christ upon this earth
Lay God's eternal plan.

3. The trumpet of salvation sounds
As Christ for us has died.
His blood now cleanses every sin
And we are justified.

4. The trumpet of salvation sounds
Of Christ the risen Lord.
The empty grave now testifies
That life is our reward.

5. The trumpet of salvation sounds
As Christ is glorified.
He lives as our High Priest above
And shall our footsteps guide.

6. The trumpet of salvation sounds
And tells that Christ is near.
And when He shouts to call us home
We'll fly to Him - so dear.

Tunes: Nativity, Campmeeting, Barrow, Beulah, Brecon, Arlington.

1Corinthians 15.52
…In a moment, in the twinkling of an eye, at the last trump: for the trumpet shall sound, and the dead shall be raised incorruptible, and we shall be changed.

4th October.

66.66.

"You Must Be Born Again!"

1.
"You must be born again!"
There is no other way.
The works of "righteousness" you do
Are filthy rags this day.

2.
"You must be born again!"
The word of Christ is sure.
You cannot know the heav'nly way
Until you are made pure.

3.
"You must be born again!"
That by the Spirit's power.
The water of the word will cleanse
Your soul this very hour.

4.
"You must be born again!"
A child of God to be.
O come and put your faith in Christ!
Be saved eternally!

Tunes: Energy, Cambridge (Harrison), Carlisle, Lake Enon, St. Ethelwald, St. Michael, Trentham, Soldiers of Christ, Boylston.

John 3.
Nicodemus saith unto him, How can a man be born when he is old? can he enter the second time into his mother's womb, and be born? Jesus answered, Verily, verily, I say unto thee, Except a man be born of water and of the Spirit, he cannot enter into the kingdom of God. That which is born of the flesh is flesh; and that which is born of the Spirit is spirit. Marvel not that I said unto thee, Ye must be born again.

5th October.

CM.

You Crown the Year With Goodness, Lord.

1. You crown the year with goodness, Lord,
The corn waves in the field.
The pastures, clothed with flocks, are white
And trees their fruit must yield.

2. The barley, oil and wine, we see
Drawn from the fertile ground.
While in the cotton, flax and silk
Our garments are well found.

3. We bring the firstfruits to You, Lord,
To feed the lowly poor.
We know Your eye is on them, Lord,
Supply them from Your store.

4. There is a harvest still to come;
The harvest from Your word.
For all who hear and trust in You
Shall reap a great reward.

5. Eternal life is theirs to claim;
Along with joy and peace.
And through the blood that Christ has shed
Their blessings must increase.

Tunes: St. Fulbert, Beulah, Christmas Eve, St. Agnes, Westminster (Turle), St. Edmund (Hoyte).

Psalm 65.11-13
Thou crownest the year with thy goodness; and thy paths drop fatness.
They drop upon the pastures of the wilderness: and the little hills rejoice on every side.
The pastures are clothed with flocks; the valleys also are covered over with corn; they shout for joy, they also sing.

6th October.

CMD.

Lord, in this Water I Recall.

1. Lord, in this water, I recall
That dreadful agony
When Thou didst hang upon the tree
To bear all sin for me.
'Twas there God's wrath was freely poured
Upon Thy holy soul.
'Twas there that love shone out with power
In blood that makes me whole.

2. Lord, in this water, I recall
Salvation's work is done.
'Tis now I own Thee as "My Lord" -
God's own Belovèd Son.
Soon into death, I will descend,
A death of loss and shame;
But I shall live to serve Thee, Lord,
And prove Thy precious name.

3. Lord, in this water, I recall
A tomb now robbed of death.
And from its depths, I'll rise to praise
With every living breath.
Newness of life, I claim, dear Lord,
A life lived out with Thee.
Oh, keep me faithful to Thy word
Until Thy face I see.

Tunes: No King But Christ, Bethlehem, Ellacombe, Jesus is God.

Romans 6.3-4
Know ye not, that so many of us as were baptized into Jesus Christ were baptized into his death?
Therefore we are buried with him by baptism into death: that like as Christ was raised up from the dead by the glory of the Father, even so we also should walk in newness of life.

7th October.

88.88D.

Lord Jesus, We Have Died With Thee.

1.
Lord Jesus, we have died with Thee;
Our sins were nailed to Calv'ry's tree.
Buried in Thy dark grave, we lay;
Till we arose in glorious day.
Firstfruits in resurrection, Thou,
With crowns of glory on Thy brow.
Thy name is set all names above
And we are blessed in all Thy love.

2.
In new creation, we now stand
As those redeemed by God's good hand;
And, Lord, we'd serve Thee here below
Thy name to tell! Thy love to show.
Lord, take us home to be with Thee
Then these poor bodies will be free!
Changed in a moment – like Thine own -
To honour Thee upon the throne.

Tunes: Duane St., He Leadeth Me, Sweet Hour.

1Corinthians 15. 20-23
But now is Christ risen from the dead, and become the firstfruits of them that slept. For since by man came death, by man came also the resurrection of the dead. For as in Adam all die, even so in Christ shall all be made alive. But every man in his own order: Christ the firstfruits; afterward they that are Christ's at his coming.

Revelation 14.4
These are they which were not defiled with women; for they are virgins. These are they which follow the Lamb whithersoever he goeth. These were redeemed from among men, being the firstfruits unto God and to the Lamb.

8th October.

88.88.88.

Lord, Thou Wast Once a Guest Divine.

1. Lord, Thou wast once a Guest divine
Who changed pure water into wine.
The master of the feast proclaimed
That no such wine on earth was named.
This brought Thee glory as God's Son,
And showed by Thee His work was done.

2. Lord, now a Guest, we find Thee here
Where two souls would Thy dear voice hear.
United they would seek to be
In holy wedlock - blessed by Thee!
Oh, grant them all Thy grace to know
And as their Guide before them go.

3. Lord, as a Guest, they ask Thee in
So that they might be free from sin.
Oh, may they find Thy peace within
As they, with Thee, new lives begin.
Grant them the love that never fails
And guard them when the storm prevails.

4. Lord, as the Bridegroom loves His bride
Thy love to us shall all provide.
And when we see Thee in the air
We'll rise with joy to meet Thee there.
Then we shall see Thee face to face
And know the riches of Thy grace.

Tunes: 88.88.88: Sussex Carol. 88.88.88.88: (Repeating last two lines of each verse). Solid Rock, Sweet Hour, He Leadeth Me, Stephenson,

John 2.10
...And saith unto him, Every man at the beginning doth set forth good wine; and when men have well drunk, then that which is worse: but thou hast kept the good wine until now.

9th October.

CMD.

Father, Allow My Soul to Rise.

1. Father, allow my soul to rise
In light that bathes the sun;
Help me, this day, to walk with Thee
As Thy belovèd one.
Oh, keep my conscious crystal clear;
Help me Thy will to do;
Please, guard my mind from wicked thoughts;
And let my tongue be true.

2. Oh, take the gifts Thou gavest me
And furnish them with love;
Grant me the wisdom and the power
To lead lost souls above.
May Thy dear saints receive from me
A blessing in this day.
And may Thy Son in me be seen
In all I do and say.

3. All praise and glory be to Thee
And to Thy precious Son.
I bless Thee for the wondrous works
That Thou through Him hast done.
Father, I love Thee for His cross
Borne patiently for me.
I love Thee for the worth I find
Residing, Lord, in Thee.

Tunes: Jesus is God, No King But Christ, Bethlehem, Land of Rest, Landas, Forest Green, Minerva, Release.

Romans 12. 5-6
So we, being many, are one body in Christ, and every one members one of another. Having then gifts differing according to the grace that is given to us, whether prophecy, let us prophesy according to the proportion of faith…

10th October.

88.88.88.

New Every Morning is the Love.

1.
New every morning is the love
That flows from Thee in heav'n above.
It's poured in kindness on our head
And with Thy kisses it is shed.
O Lord, Thy faithfulness is sure!
Our every blessing is secure!

2.
O Lord, we hope in Thee each day
To keep us in the narrow way.
Thou art the portion of our soul!
Thou by Thy grace hast made us whole!
O Lord, Thy faithfulness is sure!
Our every blessing is secure!

3.
In righteousness, we are now Thine;
Saved by Thy judgment, just, divine.
To Thee in mercy, we're Thy bride
And loving-kindness Thou'lt provide.
O Lord, Thy faithfulness is sure!
Our every blessing is secure!

Tunes: Melita, St. Catherine, St. Petersburgh.

Lamentations 3.22-26
It is of the LORD'S mercies that we are not consumed, because his compassions fail not.
They are new every morning: great is thy faithfulness.
The LORD is my portion, saith my soul; therefore will I hope in him.
The LORD is good unto them that wait for him, to the soul that seeketh him.
It is good that a man should both hope and quietly wait for the salvation of the LORD.

11th October.

CMD.

We Have a Great High Priest Above.

1. We have a great High Priest above,
And Jesus is His name.
He is the Lord of heaven and earth
Who, once, to this world came.
As Man He walked a lowly path
Forever doing good.
He sorrowed, suffered, bled and died
And Satan's wiles withstood.

2. Then raised by God to glory bright,
His work as Son well done,
He sat upon the Father's throne
The holy, harmless One.
He bears our burdens, grants us grace,
From that pure mercy seat.
For, by His blood, we can draw near
In fellowship complete.

3. In all points tested such as we,
No sin in Him was found!
In every thing He gave God praise!
His teaching was profound!
His sympathy is clear to see;
His hand supports us here.
His prayers for us in heaven abound
And He is always near.

Tunes: Providence, Landas, No King But Christ, Bethlehem, Fair Haven, Jesus is God..

Romans 3.25
(Christ Jesus) Whom God hath set forth to be a propitiation through faith in his blood, to declare his righteousness for the remission of sins that are past, through the forbearance of God…

12th October.

CM.

Immortal God, Invisible

1.
Immortal God, invisible
To our terrestrial eyes;
Eternal King most powerful,
So merciful and wise.

2.
Thy wondrous works declare
Thy name
Thy light - Thy holiness;
Thine everlasting love and
peace
Thy beauteous worth express

3.
Thy justice stands like
mountains firm,
Righteous in every act;
While judgement that surrounds
Thy throne
Is faithful and exact.

4.
Thou gav'st Thine only Son to
die
Upon the accursed tree;
'Tis through His precious blood
poured out
That we now worship Thee.

5.
O God, Thy victory is seen
In Christ seated on high;
Thy righteousness and peace
abound
With truth and mercy nigh.

6.
Father of glory, grant to us,
Through Thy long-suffering
grace,
That Christ in our poor hearts
may dwell
Until we see His face

7.
Father of lights, Thou changest
not,
Thou'rt evermore the Same;
We praise Thee for Thy perfect
gifts
As we revere Thy name.

Tune: Irish, Crimond.

1Timothy 1.17
Now unto the King eternal, immortal, invisible, the only wise God, be honour and glory for ever and ever. Amen.

Romans 1.14-15
In whom we have redemption through his blood, even the forgiveness of sins…

13th October.

CM.

Another Year is Rising, Lord.

1.
Another year is rising, Lord,
A year that's planned by Thee.
Another year in Thy blest will
Where blessing we will see.

2.
Another year to walk with Thee
Along the pilgrim way.
Another year to talk with Thee
As we would watch and pray.

3.
Another year of witness, Lord,
To lead lost souls to Thee.
Another year of teaching, Lord,
That saints, Thy love might see.

4.
Another year of warfare, Lord,,
As we resist the foe.
Another year to stand with Thee
And in Thy strength to grow.

5.
Another year of working too
That men Thy grace might know.
Another year of worship, Lord,
As we our love would show.

Tunes: Westminster (Turle), Pisgah, Winchester (Old), Nativity, Beulah,

Psalm 90.10
The days of our years are threescore years and ten; and if by reason of strength they be fourscore years, yet is their strength labour and sorrow; for it is soon cut off, and we fly away.

14th October.

CMD.

Father, we Thank Thee for the Gift.

1.
Father, we thank Thee for the Gift
That every gift contains.
We thank Thee for Thy precious Son
Who every gift sustains.
We bless Thee for Thy ceaseless care
And all Thy loving grace.
We thank Thee for that future hope
When we shall see His face.

2.
Thou art the Fount of every good
And perfect gift we know.
Thou art the Saviour God above
From whom all blessings flow.
Yes, all thy mercies are revealed
In needs met here below;
And by the token of this "meal"
Thy bounteous heart, we know.

3.
Thus we would praise Thee, glorious Lord
And joy in Thee, the Same.
In worship, we most humbly bow
For worthy is Thy name!
All riches, strength and power are Thine!
All majesty and might!
Wisdom and blessing crown Thy brow
While clothed, Thou art, in light!

Tunes: Release, No King But Christ, Jesus is God, Landas, Bethlehem, Ellacombe.

Romans 8. 2
He that spared not his own Son, but delivered him up for us all, how shall he not with him also freely give us all things?

15th October.

87.87.

Every Day with God my Saviour.

1.
Every day with God my Saviour,
I would walk the narrow way.
Every day, He'll lead and guide me;
All His love and grace display.

2.
Every day with God my Saviour,
I would seek to hear His voice.
Every day, He'd teach me wisdom
And in Him, I would rejoice.

3.
Every day with God my Saviour,
I would seek His power to know.
Every day, I'd work on with Him;
In His service, I would go.

4.
Every day with God my Saviour,
I would fight in Faith's good fight.
Every day, He'll guard and keep me
As I, steadfast, stand for right.

5.
Every day with God my Saviour,
I would seek His glory here.
Every day, I'd praise and worship;
In His presence, show no fear.

Tunes: Gott Wills Machen, Galilee, St. Andrew (Thorne), St. Oswald, Stuttgart, Cross of Jesus, Adoration (Doane).

Psalm 145.2
Every day will I bless thee; and I will praise thy name for ever and ever.

16th October.

88.88D.

Lord, At Our Table Take Thy Place.

Lord, at our table take Thy place
And may we speak of all Thy grace.
Please, let Thy fellowship abide
With all that love hath well supplied.
And for this food, we thank Thee, Lord.
Forever be Thy name adored!
Bless those who serve us faithfully
And care for this small family.

Tunes: Duane St., Sweet Hour.

Psalm 118.1-9
O give thanks unto the LORD; for he is good: because his mercy endureth for ever.
Let Israel now say, that his mercy endureth for ever.
Let the house of Aaron now say, that his mercy endureth for ever.
Let them now that fear the LORD say, that his mercy endureth for ever.
I called upon the LORD in distress: the LORD answered me, and set me in a large place.
The LORD is on my side; I will not fear: what can man do unto me?
The LORD taketh my part with them that help me: therefore shall I see my desire upon them that hate me.
It is better to trust in the LORD than to put confidence in man.
It is better to trust in the LORD than to put confidence in princes.

Psalm 78.20-25
Behold, he smote the rock, that the waters gushed out, and the streams overflowed;
can he give bread also?
can he provide flesh for his people?
Therefore the LORD heard this, and was wroth: so a fire was kindled against Jacob, and anger also came up against Israel; because they believed not in God, and trusted not in his salvation: though he had commanded the clouds from above, and opened the doors of heaven, and had rained down manna upon them to eat, and had given them of the corn of heaven. Man did eat angels' food: he sent them meat to the full.

17th October.

76.76D.

Lord Jesus, You Have Been Here.

1. Lord Jesus, You have been here
Before a lonely grave;
And with Your mighty power
A friend You came to save.
You wept with tears of sorrow!
You groaned with pity too!
Your tender heart was bleeding
With love faithful and true!

2. Lord Jesus, You have lain here,
A Victim crucified.
The Prince of life and glory
Who for our sins once died.
In heaven's light, we see You,
Now seated on the throne!
Our Saviour and Redeemer,
Our Head and Living Stone.

3. We hear those words of triumph,
"Oh, death where is your sting!"
Blest Son of God, eternal,
Your resurrection bring!
Your shout will be victorious
And joy our souls shall fill;
For we'll rise up to meet You
According to Your will.

Tunes: Lymington, Thornbury, St. Edith, Greenland (Haydn), St. Theodulph, Passion Chorale, Webb.

Hebrews 4.15
For we have not an high priest
which cannot be touched with
the feeling of our infirmities;
but was in all points tempted like as we are,
yet without sin.

18th October.

SM.

The Lamb Will be the Light.

1.
The Lamb will be the light
In that most glorious day
When God is pleased with men to dwell
And be their God alway.

2.
But first the Lord must come
To take us all above.
Then raised or changed His saints shall rest
For ever in His love.

3.
O Lord, our eyes would see
Thy glory even now.
We'd in Thy presence praise Thy name;
In holy worship bow.

4.
Thou, Thou art worthy, Lord,
All blessing to receive;
For Thou didst die to slay our sin
And all Thine own retrieve.

Tunes: Lake Enon, Cambridge (Harrison), Energy, Sandys2, Holyrood.

Revelation 21.22-24
And I saw no temple therein: for the Lord God Almighty and the Lamb are the temple of it.
And the city had no need of the sun, neither of the moon, to shine in it: for the glory of God did lighten it, and the Lamb is the light thereof.
And the nations of them which are saved shall walk in the light of it: and the kings of the earth do bring their glory and honour into it.

19th October.

CMD.

Father, 'Tis Where Thy People Meet.

1.
Father, 'tis where Thy people meet
On Thee their love to pour.
There, at the blood-stained mercy seat,
Is blessing evermore.
We bow before Thee, precious Lord,
With souls that know no fear.
We lift our hands with one accord
In prayers that Thou wilt hear.

2.
Father, we flee to Thee for aid
When trials bring us down.
Oh, may Thy grace our hearts pervade
That we might win the crown.
Let Satan's darts by faith be crushed;
Let Satan's wiles be turned;
Let Satan's lying tongue be hushed
And evil be discerned.

3.
Father, we plead for all Thine own,
The poor and the oppressed.
To Thee their every need is known;
With peace may they be blessed.
We think of those who stumble, Lord,
Whose lives are torn by sin.
Oh, may they turn with one accord
And find Thy joy within.

4.
Father, we cry for those who rule
In this most evil day.
Oh, may they see Thy law a tool
And gladly own Thy sway.
Oh, let all Christian souls stand firm!
Revive our hearts, blest Lord.
Oh, may our words Thy truth confirm
And strike a saving chord.

Tunes: Bethlehem, No King But Christ, Landas, Fair Haven, Land of Rest, Minerva, Providence, Ellacombe, Jesus is God.

Revelation 3.11
Behold, I come quickly: hold that fast which thou hast, that no man take thy crown.

20th October.

CM.

Lord Jesus, to Thy Holy Name.

1. Lord Jesus, to Thy holy name
With happy hearts we meet;
Along with saints of heavenly light,
Come to the mercy-seat.

2. 'Tis there we find Thy blood, dear Lord,
The blood that washed us clean.
'Tis in that blood we find God's grace
And all His blessings glean.

3. And so we come to Him in prayer
Through all Thy love has done.
For Thee we bless Him, precious Lord,
His own Belovèd Son.

4. 'Tis here we would our souls lay bare!
'Tis here His name would praise!
'Tis here our thanks would rise to Him
And all our needs would raise.

5. Lord Jesus, send our prayers above
Empowered by Thy name.
And in the fullness of Thy love,
Prove 'thence comes all our gain.

Tunes: Westminster (Turle), Beulah, St. Agnes, Arlington, Abends, Beatitudo.

Leviticus 16.13

And he shall put the incense upon the fire before the LORD, that the cloud of the incense may cover the mercy seat that is upon the testimony, that he die not:

and he shall take of the blood of the bullock, and sprinkle it with his finger upon the mercy seat eastward; and before the mercy seat shall he sprinkle of the blood with his finger seven times.

21st October.

76.76D.

Thy Face We Seek, Blest Father.

1.
Thy face we seek, blest Father,
In Christ's most precious name.
This privilege of glory
We're pleased, on earth, to claim.
And as Thy children, Father,
We to Thy throne draw near
Where we may speak with boldness
And bring each need and tear.

2.
Thy face we seek, blest Father,
Through our High Priest above.
We come to Thee in worship
Feebly expressing love.
Made priests, we bow before Thee,
And gladly intercede
For all who choose to serve Thee;
And those in greatest need.

3.
We seek Thy face, blest Father,
And bring before Thee now
The fatherless and widow -
To them Thy grace endow.
Stir up Thy deep compassion
For those who are oppressed,
And see those heavy-laden -
By Thee, they must be blessed.

4.
Thy face we seek, blest Father,
According to Thy will.
And by Thy Spirit prompted
Let prayer the heavens fill.
The cries that rise before Thee,
Must move Thy holy arm;
For Thou, the perfect Father,
Can do Thine own no harm.

Tunes: St. Edith, Lymington, Wolvercote, Passion Chorale, Greenland (Hadyn), Thornbury, Aurelia,

1Samuel 16.8-11
Give thanks unto the LORD, call upon his name, make known his deeds among the people.
Sing unto him, sing psalms unto him, talk ye of all his wondrous works.
Glory ye in his holy name: let the heart of them rejoice that seek the LORD. Seek the LORD and his strength, seek his face continually.
Remember his marvellous works that he hath done, his wonders, and the judgments of his mouth;
O ye seed of Israel his servant, ye children of Jacob, his chosen ones.

22nd October.

CMD.

Lord Jesus, As You Faced the Foe.

1. Lord Jesus, as You faced the foe,
In God Your trust was found.
His will was Your delight to do;
Yet, by it You were bound.
"The battle is the Lord's!" You cried
As lines of war were drawn.
Gethsemane, in darkness veiled,
With agony was torn

2. Lord Jesus, as You faced the foe,
In God Your strength was found.
By wicked hands abused and flayed
And in Your weakness crowned:
"The battle is the Lord's!" You cried
As to the cross You came.
Bleak Calvary, in darkness veiled,
Brought You the curse and shame

3. Lord Jesus, as You faced the foe,
In God Your hope was found;
And, by Your blood shed on the tree,
The "man of strength" was bound.
"The battle is the Lord's!" You cried -
Salvation's work complete.
The empty tomb with light was filled
And great was Death's defeat!

Tunes: Bethlehem, Jesus is God, Warrior, Ellacombe.

Hebrews2.14-16

Forasmuch then as the children are partakers of flesh and blood, he also himself likewise took part of the same; that through death he might destroy him that had the power of death, that is, the devil; and deliver them who through fear of death were all their lifetime subject to bondage. For verily he took not on him the nature of angels; but he took on him the seed of Abraham.

23rd October.

10.10.10.10.

Eternal God, Before Thy Face We Fall.

1. Eternal God, before Thy face we fall,
Thou art our light, our life, our joy, our all.
Afflicted or oppressed, to Thee we flee
We have no sanctuary, Lord, but Thee!

2. Under Thy wings, we dwell with peace assured;
We are by everlasting arms secured.
In Thee both hope and rest, we gladly see;
We have no sanctuary, Lord, but Thee!

3. Our Rock for evermore, Thou art the Same!
Our strength is found in Thy most precious name!
When troubles mount like billows in the sea;
We have no sanctuary, Lord, but Thee!

4. Thou art our Saviour, seen in majesty!
Through Thy blest grace, we are made sons to Thee!
And by the love poured out at Calvary!
Our sanctuary, Lord, is found in Thee.

Tunes: Penitentia, Eventide, Ellers, Toulon, Woodland.

Ezekiel 11.15-17

Son of man, thy brethren, even thy brethren, the men of thy kindred, and all the house of Israel wholly, are they unto whom the inhabitants of Jerusalem have said,
Get you far from the LORD: unto us is this land given in possession.
Therefore say, Thus saith the Lord GOD;
Although I have cast them far off among the heathen, and although I have scattered them among the countries, yet will I be to them as a little sanctuary in the countries where they shall come.
Therefore say,
Thus saith the Lord GOD; I will even gather you from the people, and assemble you out of the countries where ye have been scattered, and I will give you the land of Israel.

24th October.

LM.

O Father, in Thy Courts Above

1.
O Father, in Thy courts above
Stands our High Priest in all His love.
He brings our names before Thee there
And pleads our cause in perfect prayer.

2.
He was the Man of Sorrows here –
He felt our pain and knew our fear.
Compassion moved His tender hand
Doing all well at Thy command.

3.
He shared our weakness, felt our woe!
He lived a life divine below.
Upon His heart, our names He bore!
His power is ours for evermore!

4.
To suffer, bleed and die, He came,
Yet, He is God, the Lord the Same!
He lives for us in heav'nly light
And keeps our souls for glory bright.

5.
Father, we thank Thee for Thy Son –
For all the blessing, He has won!
And as we come before Thy face,
We'd praise and worship by His grace.

Tunes: Gift of Love, Deep Harmony, Duke St., Tallis' Canon, Abschied, Abends.

2Corinthians 9. 15
Thanks be unto God for his unspeakable gift.

25th October.

66.66D.

For Me to Live is Christ.

1. For me to live is Christ,
I joy His saints to see.
To die is greater gain
For with Him, I would be.
Faintly, I see His face
As in the shade of night.
His beauty, I will see
In heaven's purest light.

2. For me to live is Christ,
To serve Him faithfully!
To die is greater gain,
When Jesus calls for me.
My earthly tent, I'll leave
And soar to Him above.
He'll take me in His arms –
The fond embrace of love.

3. For me to live is Christ,
His name to glorify!
To die is greater gain -
To live beyond the sky!
He'll draw me to His side;
And keep me till that day
When I shall be His bride
Complete in every way.

Tunes: 12.12.12.12: Corbet, Lausanne, The Blessed Home. 66.66D: Invitation, Denby,

Galatians 2.20
I am crucified with Christ: nevertheless I live; yet not I, but Christ liveth in me:
and the life which I now live in the flesh I live by the faith of the Son of God, who loved me, and gave himself for me.

26th October.

CMD.

Father, Your Eye is Keen to See.

1. Father, Your eye is keen to see
All that we find to do;
It keeps us in the narrow way
For we are loved by You.
The fatherless find help and joy
In grace that from You pours.
The widow in her deep distress
Can trust with faith that soars.

2. Father, Your ear is open too;
Our prayers to You are known.
You answer them most faithfully
From Your most gracious throne.
To You, we cry in Jesus' name,
For those with greater need.
For those still bound in chains of sin
We, with our tears, would plead.

3. Father, Your arm will never tire,
It gently, draws us near.
It shields us from the evil one
And takes away all fear.
Outstretched in love, we see it save
A people for Your own.
While by its blest, redeeming power
We may draw near Your throne.

4. Father, Your love will never fail!
It bears us up each day.
It calms the mighty storms of life
And keeps us in the way.
When sorrow floods our life with grief
And when our footsteps stray.
It brings us comfort, joy and strength
And makes us watch and pray.

Tunes: No King But Christ, Warrior, Ellacombe, Jesus is God, Forest Green, Bethlehem, Landas.

Matthew 6.6-8

But thou, when thou prayest, enter into thy closet, and when thou hast shut thy door, pray to thy Father which is in secret; and thy Father which seeth in secret shall reward thee openly. But when ye pray, use not vain repetitions, as the heathen do: for they think that they shall be heard for their much speaking. Be not ye therefore like unto them: for your Father knoweth what things ye have need of, before ye ask him.

27th October.

77.77D.

See the Serpent Lifted High.

1.
See the serpent lifted high -
See the Saviour come to die.
See the snake upon the pole -
See God's judgement on Christ roll.
See the brass from which it's made -
See God's righteousness displayed.

2.
"Look and live!" is God's command –
Look and live and by faith stand!
Look and live and be sin-free!
Look and live eternally!
Look and live! God's blessing know.
Look and live! His glory show.

Tunes: Dix, Toplady, Spanish Hymn, Redhead (Petra), Heathlands.

Numbers 21.6-9
Therefore the people came to Moses, and said,
We have sinned,
for we have spoken against the LORD, and against thee; pray unto the LORD, that he take away the serpents from us.
And Moses prayed for the people.
And the LORD said unto Moses, Make thee a fiery serpent, and set it upon a pole: and it shall come to pass, that every one that is bitten, when he looketh upon it, shall live.
And Moses made a serpent of brass, and put it upon a pole,
and it came to pass, that if a serpent had bitten any man, when he beheld the serpent of brass, he lived.

John 3.14-15
And as Moses lifted up the serpent in the wilderness, even so must the Son of man be lifted up:
that whosoever believeth in him should not perish,
but have eternal life.

28th October.

LM.

Father, We're Saved By Grace Alone.

1. Father, we're saved by grace alone
And now approach Your glorious throne.
We pray that, in Your might and will,
You shall Your purposes fulfil.

2. Let Christ descend into the air
That we may in His blessing share.
Like His, oh, let our bodies be
Shining in light and majesty.

3. With Him in the high heavens above
We'll see the wonders of His love.
And, at His Judgement Seat, we'll see
How He assesses righteously.

4. Father, we'd see Him as the Lamb;
The One who'd suffered as a man.
And in His beauty dressed, we'd stand
For the blest marriage You had planned.

5. Then we would see Him as the King;
Of all His power and glory sing.
Then Israel shall Messiah see
And weep with deep humility.

6. In love and light, Your Son shall reign;
Your peace and joy mark His domain.
Then He'll return the world to You;
So "All in All" Yourself, we'll view.

7. Hades and Death are then destroyed
In blazing fires that You deployed.
'Tis then we'll see Your glory bright
In a new universe of light.

Tunes: Winchester (New), Federal St., Gift of Love, Church Triumphant, Pentecost, Rachel, Duke St., St. Crispin, Tallis' Canon.

Romans 14. 10
But why dost thou judge thy brother? or why dost thou set at nought thy brother? for we shall all stand before the judgment seat of Christ.
For it is written, As I live, saith the Lord, every knee shall bow to me, and every tongue shall confess to God.

29th October.

75.75.

After Thee, Lord, I Would Run.

1. After Thee, Lord, I would run;
Drawn by love divine.
After Thee, and Thee alone
True and living Vine.

2. After Thee, Lord, I would run
In faith's race down here.
After Thee, and Thee alone,
Saviour, pure and dear.

3. After Thee, Lord, I would run
In temptation's hour.
After Thee, and Thee alone,
God of might and power.

4. After Thee, Lord, I would run
When the way is hard.
After Thee, and Thee alone,
My Shepherd and Guard.

5. After Thee, Lord, I would run
When in conflict here.
After Thee, and Thee alone,
The King who'll appear.

6. After Thee, Lord, I would run
Till the course is done.
After Thee, and Thee alone,
God's belovèd Son!

Tunes: 75.75D: Guidance, Fisherman's Wharf. 75.75: Bruce.

Hebrews 12.1
Wherefore seeing we also are compassed about with so great a cloud of witnesses, let us lay aside every weight, and the sin which doth so easily beset us, and let us run with patience the race that is set before us…

30th October.

66.66.

Your Love Won't Let Me Go.

1. Your love won't let me go;
It keeps me day by day.
It's love that cannot fail
And leads me in Your way.
Mercy is its delight
And peace is in its song.
It boasts in what is right
And knows no strife or wrong.

2. Your love won't let me go;
It keeps me by Your side.
It brings me to Your throne
Forgiveness to provide.
Kindness is in its power
And hope fills up its flow.
Its patience is well known;
Its lowliness, I know.

3. Your love won't let me go;
It gave Your only Son.
Your love won't let me go
E'en when Your work is done.
Your love won't let me go
In that blest home above.
Your love won't let me go;
Always I'll dwell in love.

Tunes: 12.12.12.12: Corbet, Lausanne. 66.66D: Invitation, Denby.

Song 2.4-6
He brought me to the banqueting house, and his banner over me was love.
Stay me with flagons, comfort me with apples:
for I am sick of love.
His left hand is under my head,
and his right hand doth embrace me.

31st October.

LM.

I Saw the Symbol of Your Cross.

1. I saw the symbol of Your cross;
I knew it spoke of shame and loss.
I also saw this world as dross;
Yet, doubting still, I passed You by.

2. I knew Your Father sent You here
To win our hearts and draw us near;
I also saw His word was clear;
Yet, doubting still, I passed You by.

3. I knew Your Spirit worked in men;
I'd seen His pow'r time and again.
I may believe, I can't tell when;
So, doubting still, I passed You by.

4. Then in the stillness of the night,
I heard a voice that brought me light.
It came from You, in heaven's height;
And, in love, said, "I won't pass by."

Tunes: Gift of Love, Abends, Federal St., Duke St., Deep Harmony, Rachel.

Luke 24.15-20

And it came to pass, that, while they communed together and reasoned, Jesus himself drew near, and went with them. But their eyes were holden that they should not know him.

And he said unto them, What manner of communications are these that ye have one to another, as ye walk, and are sad? And the one of them, whose name was Cleopas, answering said unto him, Art thou only a stranger in Jerusalem, and hast not known the things which are come to pass there in these days? And he said unto them, What things? And they said unto him, Concerning Jesus of Nazareth, which was a prophet mighty in deed and word before God and all the people: and how the chief priests and our rulers delivered him to be condemned to death, and have crucified him.

1st November.

87.87D.

Look, Ye Saints, the Sight is Wondrous.

1.
Look, ye saints, the sight is wondrous,
'Tis the banner of the cross.
Lifted by our Lord in heaven;
He who suffered shame and loss.

Refrain:
Gather to Him in His glory!
Gather to His precious name!
Gather to the Son who loves us!
Evermore, He is the Same!

2.
See the standard raised triumphant;
See "Forgiveness" 'broidered there.
See sin's curse is passed for ever;
See the Saviour bright and fair.
Refrain:

3.
Scarlet is the holy emblem
Telling us of cleansing blood.
Blue the background in its beauty
Telling us, we're fit for God.
Refrain:

4.
Praise the Saviour, all who know Him!
Praise His righteous worth above!
Praise Him for His power and wisdom!
Praise Him for the cross of love!
Refrain:

Tunes: Mount of Olives, Shipton, Beecher, Cassell, Woodside, Deerhurst, Here is Love, Hyfrydol, Hymn to Joy, Theodoret.

2nd November.

77.77D.

Lead Us, Saviour, in the Way

1.
Lead us, Saviour, in the way
Till Your love's dazzling display;
May Your tenderness preside
As You walk close by our side.
May You only be our Guide
That we may in peace reside;
Then we'll know whate'er the test
It is always for our best.

2
Lead us, Saviour, to the well
Where love's waters rise and swell -
Life eternal drinking deep
E'er our time to fall asleep.
Here by faith, in You, we dwell!
Knowing You do all things well!
Hence, we have Your full support,
As those whom Your blood has bought.

3
Lead us, Saviour, to the pool
Where Your joy and kindness rule;
In our sickness and our health
May we know Your mercy's wealth.
Cheer the rugged path we tread;
Feed us with Your living bread;
And please cleanse us in the way –
Living in this evil day.

4
Lead us, Saviour, to that home -
Never more this earth to roam -
To the Father's house above
Which is marked by peace and love.
In that day of perfect rest,
We shall all be fully blessed;
Then our song shall gladly be
"Precious Lord, You're so lovely!"

Tunes: St. Georges Windsor, Mendelssohn, St. Edmund Steggall,

Genesis 28.15-16

And, behold, I am with thee, and will keep thee in all places whither thou goest, and will bring thee again into this land; for I will not leave thee, until I have done that which I have spoken to thee of. And Jacob awaked out of his sleep, and he said, Surely the LORD is in this place; and I knew it not.

3rd November.

65.65D.

Wash my Feet, Lord Jesus.

1.
Wash my feet, Lord Jesus,
By Thy word each day.
Help me know the power
By Thy side to stay.
Let Thy love surround me;
With it fill my heart.
Draw me closer to Thee.
Never from me part.

2.
Wash my feet, Lord Jesus;
Teach me how to pray.
Grant me strength and kindness
To walk in Thy way.
May I be a servant
To Thy saints down here.
Help me through Thy teaching
To remove all fear.

Tunes: 65.65: North Coates, Quietude, Armentrout, Eudoxia.
11.11.11.11: Ruth (Smith), Evelyns, Happy Fac

John 13.3
Jesus knowing that the Father had given all things into his hands, and that he was come from God, and went to God; he riseth from supper, and laid aside his garments; and took a towel, and girded himself. After that he poureth water into a bason, and began to wash the disciples' feet, and to wipe them with the towel wherewith he was girded.
Then cometh he to Simon Peter: and Peter saith unto him, Lord, dost thou wash my feet?
Jesus answered and said unto him, What I do thou knowest not now; but thou shalt know hereafter.
Peter saith unto him, Thou shalt never wash my feet. Jesus answered him, If I wash thee not, thou hast no part with me. Simon Peter saith unto him, Lord, not my feet only, but also my hands and my head.

4th November.

SM.

"Jesus the Christ is Lord!"

1. "Jesus the Christ is Lord!"
Come, sing it out today.
The Saviour who came down to earth
In manhood holds all sway.

2. "Jesus the Christ is Lord!"
Let all things now agree.
The Christ who sits upon God's throne
Is He who sets souls free.

3. "Jesus the Christ is Lord!"
To God all glory be.
'Tis Yahweh who is over all;
So let us bend the knee.

4. "Jesus the Christ is Lord!"
The Father speaks the word.
The Son who gave Himself for us
Is worshipped and adored.

Tunes: Cambridge, Energy, Lake Enon, Sandy, Soldiers of Christ, St. Ethelwald.

Acts 2.36
Therefore let all the house of Israel know assuredly,
that God hath made that same Jesus,
whom ye have crucified,
both Lord and Christ.

Acts 10.36
The word which God sent unto the children of Israel, preaching peace by Jesus Christ: (he is Lord of all:)

Philippians 2.11
And that every tongue should confess that Jesus Christ is Lord, to the glory of God the Father.

5th November.

66.66D.

Would You Believe God's Word?

1.
Would you believe God's
word?
Then count the cost today!
Would you accept its terms
And walk the narrow way?
Faith in the living God
Leads to a life of love;
Love means a life of trust
In Jesus Christ above.

2.
Would you believe God's
word?
Then count the cost today!
Would you accept its terms
And walk the narrow way?
Faith in the living God
Gives you a race to run.
The course is rough and steep
To reach God's blessèd Son!

3.
Would you believe God's
word?
Then count the cost today!
Would you accept its terms
And walk the narrow way?
Faith in the living God
Leads you to serve Him here.
His work is hard to do
And bears no earthly cheer..

4.
Would you believe God's
word?
Then count the cost today!
Would you accept its terms
And walk the narrow way?
Faith in the living God
Commissions you for war.
The fight is fierce and long;
And hardship you'll endure.

5.
Would you believe God's
word?
Then count the cost today!
Would you accept its terms
And walk the narrow way?
Faith in the living God
Requires you watch and pray.
And when you stand for Him
Mind the things you say.

Tunes:66.66D: Invitation, Denby. 12.12.12.12: Corbet, Lausanne

Philippians 3.7-8

But what things were gain to me, those I counted loss for Christ. Yea doubtless, and I count all things but loss for the excellency of the knowledge of Christ Jesus my Lord: for whom I have suffered the loss of all things, and do count them but dung, that I may win Christ…

6th November.

77.77.

Rise up, Christian! Onward Go!

1.
Rise up, Christian! Onward go!
Though in sorrow, fear and woe.
Fight the fight though weakened so;
Take God's strength and face the foe.

2.
Rise up, Christian! Onward go!
Let God's truth with judgement flow!
Let his righteousness shine bright!
Let your life be filled with light!

3.
Rise up Christian! Onward go!
Christ's assurance you will know.
Let the Spirit wield His sword.
Let the battle be endured.

4.
Rise up, Christian! Onward go!
God's salvation you must show!
Fight with faith that makes you free!
Fight and live eternally!

Tunes: Monkland, Innocents, Confidence (Ousely), Evelyn (Ashford), St. Bees, St. Prisca.

Ephesians 5.13-17
But all things that are reproved are made manifest by the light: for whatsoever doth make manifest is light.
Wherefore he saith, Awake thou that sleepest, and arise from the dead, and Christ shall give thee light. See then that ye walk circumspectly, not as fools, but as wise,
Redeeming the time, because the days are evil. Wherefore be ye not unwise, but understanding what the will of the Lord is.

7th November.

88.86.

‘Tis in My Prayer, Father, I’d See.

1. ‘Tis in my prayer, Father, I’d see
A heart that truly worships Thee;
And from the treasures of Thy love
I’d know that I am free.

2. ‘Tis in my prayer, Father, I’d see
Thanksgiving rise with joy to Thee;
And from the treasures of Thy love
I’d know Thy care for me.

3. ‘Tis in my prayer, Father, I’d see
My many sins declared to Thee;
And from the treasures of Thy love
Forgiveness there for me.

4. ‘Tis in my prayer, Father, I’d see
The needs of souls made clear to Thee;
And from the treasure of Thy love
Abundant grace I’d see.

5. ‘Tis in my prayer, Father, I’d see
My burdens cast upon Thy care;
And from the treasure of Thy love
Thou wilt my sorrows share.

6. ‘Tis in my prayer, Father, I’d see
My Priest and Advocate on high;
And from the treasure of Thy love
Thou wilt our needs supply.

Tunes: Misericordia, Saffron Walden.

Matthew 6.9
After this manner therefore pray ye: Our Father which art in heaven, Hallowed be thy name. Thy kingdom come. Thy will be done in earth, as it is in heaven. Give us this day our daily bread…

8th November.

87.87.

Onward Press Through Rolling Billows.

1.
Onward press through rolling billows;
Trust the Lord of heav'n and earth.
Onward press through waves of terror;
Sing God's praise and know His worth.

2.
Onward press though foes surround you
The Lord's arm will see you through.
Onward press though Satan hinders;
The Almighty will keep you.

3.
Onward press through deepest sorrow;
Feel the touch of God above.
Onward press though pain oppress you;
Know the tenderness of love.

4.
Onward press when sin attacks you;
Find your refuge in the Lord.
Onward press through fear and weakness;
Of God's wisdom be assured.

Tunes: Sussex, Gott Will's Machen, Rathbun, Oxford (Stainer).

Exodus 40. 34-37
Then a cloud covered the tent of the congregation, and the glory of the LORD filled the tabernacle.
And Moses was not able to enter into the tent of the congregation, because the cloud abode thereon, and the glory of the LORD filled the tabernacle.
And when the cloud was taken up from over the tabernacle, the children of Israel went onward in all their journeys:
But if the cloud were not taken up, then they journeyed not till the day that it was taken up.

9th November.

76.76D.

A Man's Enthroned in Glory.

1.
A Man's enthroned in glory,
A kind and righteous Man;
He's finished all the work
Found in His Father's plan.
He saved my soul from sin
By dying on a tree.
He sits at God's right hand -
The Priest who prays for me.

2.
A Man's enthroned in glory,
A good and gentle Man.
He glorifies His Father
As only God's Son can.
He is the Lord of Hosts!
The King of Glory, He!
My Captain and my Saviour
Who lives in heav'n for me!

3.
A Man's enthroned in glory,
A meek and lowly Man.
He is the First and Last!
God's only begotten!
He's Alpha and Omega
Of God, the A to Z.
The End and the Beginning
By all God's counsels led.

4.
A Man's enthroned in glory,
A pure and gracious Man.
He is my Lord – my Master!
He's Yea and He's Amen!
He is my Advocate
And pleads my cause above!
He is my All in All
Because of His great love!

Tunes: Ewing, Thornbury, Greenland (Haydn), Lymington, Ellacombe, Passion Chorale, St. Theodulph.

Revelation 22.13-17
I am Alpha and Omega, the beginning and the end, the first and the last.
Blessed are they that do his commandments, that they may have right to the tree of life, and may enter in through the gates into the city.
For without are dogs, and sorcerers, and whoremongers, and murderers, and idolaters, and whosoever loveth and maketh a lie.
I Jesus have sent mine angel to testify unto you these things in the churches.
I am the root and the offspring of David, and the bright and morning star.
And the Spirit and the bride say,
Come. And let him that heareth say, Come. And let him that is athirst come. And whosoever will, let him take the water of life freely.

10th November.

55.55.

Come with Joyful Song.

1. Come with joyful song;
Come and praise the Lord!
Lift your hand and heart;
Praise with one accord!

2. Come with joyful song;
Come, the Saviour praise!
Bless Him for the cross,
And His worth and ways.

3. Come with joyful song;
Come, your Captain praise.
Stand like men, be strong!
His bright banner raise.

4. Come with joyful song;
Come and praise your King!
Bow to His blest name;
Praise Him as you sing!

5. Come with joyful song;
Praise the God of love!
Give your lives an off'ring;
Dwell with Him above.

Tunes: Ernstein, Quietude, Castle Eden, Newland (Armstrong).

Psalm 66.1-4
To the chief Musician, A Song or Psalm.
Make a joyful noise unto God, all ye lands:
Sing forth the honour of his name: make his praise glorious.
Say unto God, How terrible art thou in thy works! through the greatness of thy power shall thine enemies submit themselves unto thee.
All the earth shall worship thee, and shall sing unto thee; they shall sing to thy name.
Selah.

11th November.

66.66D.

What Kind of Love is This?

Questions:
1. What kind of love is this
That made us sons of God?
What kind of love is this
That saved from judgment's rod?
What kind of love is this
That gave a Son most dear?
What kind of love is this
That takes away all fear?

Answers:
2. It is the Father's love
That made us sons of God!
It is the Father's love
That saved from judgment's rod!
It is the Father's love
That gave a Son most dear!
It is the Father's love
That takes away all fear!

Questions:
3. What kind of love is this
That brings us to God's throne?
What kind of love is this
That makes us all His own?
What kind of love is this
That hears us when we cry?
What kind of love is this
That comforts when we sigh?

Answers:
4. It is the Father's love
That brings us to God's throne!
It is the Father's love
That makes us all His own!
It is the Father's love
That hears us when we cry!
It is the Father's love
That comforts when we sigh!

Questions:
5. What kind of love is this
That made us saints in light?
What kind of love is this
That leads to Glory bright?
What kind of love is this
That casts us in Christ's mould?
What kind of love is this
That realms of joy unfold?

Answers:
6. It is the Father's love
That made us saints in light!
It is the Father's love
That leads to Glory bright!
It is the Father's love
That casts us in Christ's mould!
It is the Father's love
That realms of joy unfold!

Tunes: Webb, Lymington, Thornbury, Greenland, Passion Chorale, Mountain.

12th November.

85.85.

Father, Lead Us Through this Desert.

1.
Father, lead us through this desert;
Keep us by Thy hand.
May Thy words of help and comfort
Tell us what is planned.

2.
There may be a storm that's rising
To break on our head.
There may be a drought pursuing
Filling us with dread.

3.
Be our Refuge in the tempest;
Keep us safe – secure!
From the stricken Rock now fill us
And our souls assure.

4.
Father, may the hidden Manna
Feed us in the way;
May our spirits know Thy joy
In that eternal day.

Tunes: Cairnbrook.

Revelation 2.17
He that hath an ear, let him hear what the Spirit saith unto the churches; To him that overcometh will I give to eat of the hidden manna, and will give him a white stone, and in the stone a new name written, which no man knoweth saving he that receiveth it.

Exodus 17.6
Behold, I will stand before thee there upon the rock in Horeb; and thou shalt smite the rock, and there shall come water out of it, that the people may drink. And Moses did so in the sight of the elders of Israel.

13th November.

77.77.

Pilgrims of the Lord Above.

1. Pilgrims of the Lord above
As we journey, sing of love.
Sing the worth of Him who died!
Praise the Lord now glorified!

2. Children of the Lord on high,
We shall see Him by and by!
He shall come into the air;
When he calls, we'll meet Him there!

3. Saints of God the Lord has blessed,
On Christ's bosom we may rest.
There His love will all fears still;
He will keep us from all ill.

4. Strangers for our Lord below,
In His wisdom, we must go.
More like Jesus may we be
That His beauty all may see.

5. Envoys of our Lord while here,
Let us to His word adhere.
Let His purposes be known
Till we bow before His throne.

6. Fools for our Lord on this earth,
We may suffer for His worth.
Yet, in glory we'll be found
And as kings and priests abound.

Tunes: St. Bees, Monkland, Buckland, Evelyn (Ashford), St. Prisca, Nottingham, Innocents.

1Corinthians 4. 10
We are fools for Christ's sake, but ye are wise in Christ; we are weak, but ye are strong; ye are honourable, but we are despised.

14th November.

76.76D.

Death on the Cross, Lord Jesus.

1. Death on the cross, Lord Jesus,
Speaks of obedience rare!
God's curse and our sin's judgement
Were there for Thee to bear!
Blood from Thy cross, Lord Jesus,
Tells us of peace procured!
A peace with God Thy Father
Through all Thou hast endured!

2. Preaching Thy cross, Lord Jesus,
The power of God proclaims!
It saves us from all danger
And righteousness exclaims!
Shame from Thy cross, Lord Jesus,
Falls on the faithful here!
But seeing Thee in Glory,
Nothing have they to fear!

3. The foes of Thy cross, Saviour,
Have no real joy within!
They shun Thy precious blood
To die in all their sin!
But we are blessed, Lord Jesus,
Through all the work Thou'st done!
We bow our hearts before Thee
And praise Thee as God's Son!

Tunes: 76.76D: Webb, Ewing, Lymington, St. Edith, Passion Chorale, Greenland, Thornbury, Wolvercote.

Philippians 3.18
For many walk, of whom I have told you often, and now tell you even weeping,
that they are the enemies of the cross of Christ:
Whose end is destruction, whose God is their belly, and whose glory is in their shame, who mind earthly things.

15th November.

CMD.

Father, How Precious are the Thoughts.

1.
Father, how precious are the thoughts
You have towards Your own.
And every action that You take
Is centred in Your Son.
Your purposes in Him are planned;
For us You seek the best.
So, blessèd Father, in Your love
Our souls have found their rest.

2.
Father, how precious are the thoughts
You have towards Your own.
You care for us as children, Lord,
As those drawn to Your Son.
So when the storms of life assail,
We'll shelter 'neath Your wing;
And, in the fierceness of the blast
Of your great love, we'll sing.

3.
Father, how precious are the thoughts
You have towards Your own.
And though the hopes of earth should fail,
We'll glory in Your Son.
'Tis love that brings us joy while here;
It carries sorrow too;
'Tis love that brings the toughest times;
'Tis love that comes from You.

4.
Father, how precious are the thoughts
You have towards Your own.
So let us all with boldness fall
Before Your royal throne.
We'll love You for Your wondrous worth
And praise for all You've done.
We'll thank You for the love and grace
That's found in Your dear Son.

Tunes: Jesus is God, Forest green, No King But Christ, Bethlehem, Release, Ishpeming, Landas.

Psalm 133.14-18
I will praise thee; for I am fearfully and wonderfully made: marvellous are thy works; and that my soul knoweth right well… How precious also are thy thoughts unto me, O God! how great is the sum of them! If I should count them, they are more in number than the sand: when I awake, I am still with thee.

16th November.

88.88D.

Dear Saints, the Road is Rough and Long.

1.
Dear Saints, the road is rough and long;
Smooth it with hope; cheer it with song.
In rank and file, march on as one
Until the war is fought and done.
With shield on arm and sword in hand
Let's face the foe in his own land.
And when the devil's darts are gone
We'll know the joy of God's dear Son.

2.
In heaven, rest is found sublime
So let's not fear the toil of time.
When trouble strikes with all its force;
The Lord will keep us on His course.
So hush your groans and sing instead
For Christ now lives who once was dead.
Lift up your voice to praise His name
Knowing His love remains the same.

Tunes: Stephenson, Sagina, Sweet Hour, We saw Thee Not, Redemption Ground, Harding.

The line: "Smooth it with hope; cheer it with song" is taken from the hymn "Our Rest is in heaven" by Henry Lyte, 1793-1847.

1Samuel 17.45-46
Then said David to the Philistine,
Thou comest to me with a sword, and with a spear, and with a shield: but I come to thee in the name of the LORD of hosts, the God of the armies of Israel, whom thou hast defied.
This day will the LORD deliver thee into mine hand; and I will smite thee, and take thine head from thee; and I will give the carcases of the host of the Philistines this day unto the fowls of the air, and to the wild beasts of the earth; that all the earth may know that there is a God in Israel.

17th November.

10.10.10.10.

Blessed with all Blessings in the Heav'ns Above.

1.
Blessed with all blessings in the heav'ns above.
Blessed in abundance through the Father's love.
Blessed by the Saviour who died for our sin;
Blessed by the Spirit who's working within.

2.
Chosen by God e'er this world was begun,
Chosen in Christ, His own beloved Son.
Chosen as vessels His blest name to bear;
Chosen, His glory and virtue to share.

3.
Joint-heirs with Christ as we stand for Him here;
Heirs of salvation with nothing to fear;
Heirs of the kingdom ruled in righteousness;
Heirs by His promise and His faithfulness.

4.
Children of God who seek both peace and rest;
Children of faith by which we are so blessed;
Children of light found working in the day.
Children of truth walking the narrow way;

5.
Sons by adoption - saved by His good grace;
Sons crying, "Father!" when they seek His face;
Sons - holy, harmless, shining in His sight;
Sons of the Father who leads them in light.

Tunes: Woodlands, Penetentia, Skara, Toulon.

Acts 9.15-16
...Go thy way: for he is a chosen vessel unto me, to bear my name before the Gentiles, and kings, and the children of Israel: For I will shew him how great things he must suffer for my name's sake.

18th November.

10.10.10.10.

Put on Your Armour, Children of the Day.

1.
Put on your armour, children of the day.
"Hope in salvation!" let your helmet say.
Let your light shine from the breastplate of love
Till in the Glory with your Lord above.

2.
The shield of faith take up to watch and pray!
Thread on your belt and truth shall be your stay!
Sandals of peace shall mark you in the way!
The Spirit's sword defend you in the fray!

3.
Quit you like men! Stand in this evil day!
Let righteousness keep Satan's force at bay!
Look to your Captain in the heavens on high!
He will command you! Guide you with His eye!

Tunes: Woodlands, Penetentia, Skara, Toulon.

Ephesians 6.10-16

Finally, my brethren, be strong in the Lord, and in the power of his might.
Put on the whole armour of God, that ye may be able to stand against the wiles of the devil.
For we wrestle not against flesh and blood, but against principalities, against powers, against the rulers of the darkness of this world, against spiritual wickedness in high places.
Wherefore take unto you the whole armour of God, that ye may be able to withstand in the evil day, and having done all, to stand.
Stand therefore, having your loins girt about with truth, and having on the breastplate of righteousness; and your feet shod with the preparation of the gospel of peace;
above all, taking the shield of faith, wherewith ye shall be able to quench all the fiery darts of the wicked.

19th November.

CM.

Dear Christian, When the Way is Rough.

1. Dear Christian, when the way is rough
And blocked by landslides too;
Then seek the guidance of the Lord
And He will see you through.

2, Dear Christian, when the lion roars
Your spirit to subdue;
Then seek the power of your Lord
And He will see you through.

3. Christian, when sin in ambush waits
To set its seal on you.
Then seek the face of your dear Lord
And He will see you through.

4. Dear Christian, when the world attacks
And would your soul pursue;
Then seek the wisdom of your Lord
And He will see you through.

5. Dear Christian, when the floods of life
Drown you in sorrows too;
Then seek the comfort of the Lord
And He will see you through.

6. Dear Christian, when the journey ends
And Christ shall fill your view;
Then you will know it was His grace -
The grace that saw you through.

Tunes: CM: Beulah, Pisgah, Beatitudo, Westminster (Turle). CMD: No King But Christ, Release, Jesus is God.

Romans 8.18
For I reckon that the sufferings of this present time are not worthy to be compared with the glory which shall be revealed in us.

20th November.

11.10.11.10.

Lord, You are Able to Keep Us from Falling.

1.
Lord, you are able to keep us from falling;
Able to bring us before you with joy.
Present us faultless in heavenly glory
Where praise and worship our hearts will employ.

2.
To you our Saviour and God only wise
Be riches, glory, dominion and power.
To you, the Maker of heaven and earth,
Be all our love in this and every hour.

Tunes: 11.10.11.10: Epiphany (Thrupps), Perfect Love (Sandringham), Hold Thou my Hand. 11.10.11.10D: Be Thou Exalted.

Jude 1.1-2
Jude, the servant of Jesus Christ, and brother of James, to them that are sanctified by God the Father,
and preserved in Jesus Christ, and called:
Mercy unto you, and peace, and love, be multiplied.

Jude 1.20-25
But ye, beloved, building up yourselves on your most holy faith, praying in the Holy Ghost,
keep yourselves in the love of God, looking for the mercy of our Lord Jesus Christ unto eternal life.
And of some have compassion, making a difference:
And others save with fear, pulling them out of the fire; hating even the garment spotted by the flesh.
Now unto him that is able to keep you from falling,
and to present you faultless before the presence of his glory with exceeding joy,
To the only wise God our Saviour, be glory and majesty,
dominion and power, both now and ever. Amen.

21st November.

87.87.

Sow the Seed in Faithful Witness.

1.
Sow the seed in faithful witness
To the Christ who for Thee died.
Sow the seed until the harvest
When we shall be glorified.

2.
Sow the seed in every furrow;
Mark the ground on which it falls.
Sow the seed in rain or sunshine;
Know it is the Lord who calls.

3.
Sow the seed Christ's love displaying
That the world might see His face.
Sow the seed with tears and sorrow;
Let the cross reveal God's grace.

4.
Many plant and many water;
Many work and know no rest;
Yet 'tis prayer that has the power
By which tender plants are blessed.

Tunes: St. Andrew (Thorne), Galilee, Sussex, St. Oswald, Stuttgart, Day By Day, Gott Will's Machen, Rathbun.

John 4.34
Jesus saith unto them, My meat is to do the will of him that sent me, and to finish his work. Say not ye, There are yet four months, and then cometh harvest? behold, I say unto you, Lift up your eyes, and look on the fields; for they are white already to harvest. And he that reapeth receiveth wages, and gathereth fruit unto life eternal: that both he that soweth and he that reapeth may rejoice together. And herein is that saying true, One soweth, and another reapeth.

22nd November.

12.12.12.12D.

Mem'ries Prompted by Your Blest Words Upon a Page.

1.
Mem'ries prompted by Your blest words upon a page;
Mem'ries that thread through the fine fabric of my mind
Mem'ries embroidered with a love matured with age
Mem'ries bordered by the heart of One so kind.

I'm happy to adore! To make You wholly mine!
I'm happy to remember Your love more than wine.
I'm happy to serve You, my Master and my King!
To You my heart and mind I would most gladly bring!

2.
Mem'ries that were once pierced by suffering and grief;
Mem'ries that lifted You next to a dying thief.
Mem'ries stained by the blood from Your head, hands and feet
Mem'ries where the dark threads of death and judgement meet.

I'm happy to adore! To make You wholly mine!
I'm happy to remember Your love more than wine.
I'm happy to serve You, my Master and my King!
To You my heart and mind I would most gladly bring!

3.
Mem'ries once torn by all the terror of the grave!
Mem'ries now patched by power - the power of life divine!
Mem'ries that are displayed in One mighty to save!
Mem'ries that fill out all my Saviour's own design.

I'm happy to adore! To make You wholly mine!
I'm happy to remember Your love more than wine.
I'm happy to serve You, my Master and my King!
To You my heart and mind I would most gladly bring!

Tunes: 12.12.12.12: Corbet, Lausanne, Harvington. 66.66D: Invitation, Denby.

23rd November.

66.66D.

Love is as Strong as Death.

Refrain:
Love is as strong as death
That rivers cannot quench
Jealousy is a cruel grave
It cannot from you wrench.
Love can't be bought with gold
Nor drowned by mighty floods.
Jealousy is a coal of fire
That tests out love's new buds.

I lie upon my bed
My heart is beating fast -
Each beat a word from my Beloved
Now drumming through my head
Then at the glass I stand
My heart is beating fast -
Each beat a step of my Beloved
Approaching without fear.

I run towards the key
My heart is beating fast -
Each beat a kiss for my Beloved
Who gave His life for me.
I stand in gardens fair
My heart is beating fast -
Each beat a stroke of my Beloved
Running through my hair.
Refrain:

Tunes: Diademata, Nearer Home.

Song 5.4-5
My beloved put in his hand by the hole of the door, and my bowels were moved for him. I rose up to open to my beloved; and my hands dropped with myrrh, and my fingers with sweet smelling myrrh, upon the handles of the lock.

24th November.

CMD.

Jerusalem! Jerusalem!

1.
Jerusalem! Jerusalem!
The city set on high.
'Twas for the beauty of your face
Our Saviour came to die.
Your holiness is seen throughout;
Your glory gleams with light.
Your streets are paved with purest gold
Your walls are garnished bright.

2.
Jerusalem! Jerusalem!
The city of the KIng.
Redeemed by His most precious blood
Your gates with praises ring.
Your pearls tell us of truth divine;
And gems with blessing shine;
The bride of Christ in His worth dressed;
How wondrous your design!

Tunes: Jesus is God, Bethlehem, Landas.

Psalm 48.1-8
A Song and Psalm for the sons of Korah.
Great is the LORD, and greatly to be praised in the city of our God, in the mountain of his holiness.
Beautiful for situation, the joy of the whole earth, is mount Zion, on the sides of the north, the city of the great King. God is known in her palaces for a refuge.
For, lo, the kings were assembled, they passed by together.
They saw it, and so they marvelled; they were troubled, and hasted away.
Fear took hold upon them there, and pain, as of a woman in travail.
Thou breakest the ships of Tarshish with an east wind.
As we have heard, so have we seen in the city of the LORD of hosts, in the city of our God: God will establish it for ever. Selah. We have thought of thy lovingkindness, O God, in the midst of thy temple.

25th November.

CMD.

Lord Jesus, For a Little While.

1. Lord Jesus, for a little while,
You walked this earth below
Where many sick and suffering
Came Your blest worth to know.
'Twas from Your Father, You were sent
Our sinful souls to save.
And though accurs'd on Calvary,
You rose up from the grave.

2. You were the Man who knew no sin;
No sin was found in You.
But righteousness and truth prevailed
Proving You faithful too.
And now You sit in heaven above
Upon the Father's throne.
The Son of God, in majesty,
We worship as Your own.

3. Lord Jesus, in a little while,
We'll meet you in the air.
'Tis there, we'll see You face to face
And in Your glory share.
The judgement seat will our work try
And set Your servants free.
Then at the Marriage of the Lamb
Your loving bride, we'll be.

Tunes: Release, Jesus is God, Minerva, No King But Christ, Warrior, Bethlehem, Landas, Forest Green.

2Corinthians 5.21
For he hath made him to be sin for us, who knew no sin; that we might be made the righteousness of God in him.

26th November.

CM.

All Things Above the Skies are Bright.

1. All things above the skies are bright,
No shadow mars the scene;
Bathed in the light of holiness,
There rest is most serene.

2. All things above the skies are pure,
Sin cannot have its way.
The Lamb who did the cross endure
Holds everlasting sway.

3. All things above the skies are calm
And peace the whole pervades.
There righteousness in glory shines
With joy that never fades.

4. All things above the skies are marked
By worship and by praise.
And to our God and His dear Son
Our anthems we shall raise.

5. All things above the skies are blessed
By God's eternal hand.
The love that gave His Son to die
Now floods Emmanuel's land.

6. All things above the skies are Christ's
(As He is Son and Heir);
And 'tis our joy to be with Him
And in His glory share.

Tunes: Winchester (Old), Nativity, Horsley, Beulah, Pisgah, St. Edmund (Hoyte),

Ephesians 4.10
...He that descended is the same also that ascended up far above all heavens, that he might fill all things.

27th November.

88.88D.

We'll Sing of the Mansion on High.

1. We'll sing of the mansion on high;
The house of the Father above.
We'll sing of the place that is ours
Prepared by the Son of His love.
We'll tell of its freedom from sin,
From death, sorrow, clamour and pain.
We'll tell of its peace and delight;
Yes! Over and over again!

2. We'll sing of the Father on high
By whom we are mightily blessed.
We'll sing of His mercy and grace
And enter His glorious rest.
We'll tell of His wisdom at length -
His glory, dominion and might.
We'll tell of His honour and worth
His riches, His love and His light!

3. We'll sing of the Son who once came
The will of His Father to do.
We'll sing of His death on the tree
Where suff'ring unfathomed we view.
We'll tell of His coming again –
The shout of His triumph and joy.
We'll tell of His beauty and grace,
While worship our hearts will employ.

Tune: Green Fields.

John 14.1-3

Let not your heart be troubled: ye believe in God, believe also in me. In my Father's house are many mansions: if it were not so, I would have told you. I go to prepare a place for you. And if I go and prepare a place for you, I will come again, and receive you unto myself; that where I am, there ye may be also.

28th November.

76.76D.

Show Me Thy Hands, Dear Saviour.

1.
Show me Thy hands, dear
Saviour;
The hands that made the stars.
Show me the wounds, dear
Saviour,
The nail prints - whitened scars.
Then shall my heart be
humbled;
My spirit filled with awe.
Then I shall bow before Thee
And my soul shall adore.

2.
Show me Thy feet, Lord Jesus,
The feet that marked Thy way.
Show me the wounds, dear
Saviour,
The suff'ring of that day.
Then shall my heart be
humbled;
My spirit filled with awe.
Then I shall bow before
Thee
And my soul shall adore.

3.
Show me Thy side, dear
Saviour,
The side torn by a spear.
Show me the wound, dear
Saviour,
I'd see Thy love appear.
Then shall my heart be
humbled;
My spirit filled with awe.
Then I shall bow before Thee
And my soul shall adore.

4.
Show me Thy heart, dear
Saviour,
The heart that wrath endured.
Show me the wounds, dear
Saviour,
That life for me procured.
Then shall my heart be
humbled;
My spirit filled with awe.
Then I shall bow before Thee
Adoring evermore.

Tunes: Ewing, Lymington, Thornbury, St. Theodulph, Wolvercote, Gerhardt, Passion Chorale, Greenland

John 20.26-28

And after eight days again his disciples were within, and Thomas with them: then came Jesus, the doors being shut, and stood in the midst, and said, Peace be unto you. Then saith he to Thomas, Reach hither thy finger, and behold my hands; and reach hither thy hand, and thrust it into my side: and be not faithless, but believing. And Thomas answered and said unto him, My Lord and my God.

29th November.

85.85.

Hallelujah! Hallelujah!

1. Hallelujah! See your Saviour
In a manger born.
See the Dayspring from on high
Bring the light of dawn.
Hallelujah! Hallelujah!
Come ye, praise the Lord!
Hallelujah! Hallelujah!
His name be adored!

2. Hallelujah! See your Maker
Bringing joy and peace.
See His wisdom and His power;
His praise must increase!
Hallelujah! Hallelujah!
Come ye, praise the Lord!
Hallelujah! Hallelujah!
His name be adored!

3. Hallelujah! See Christ Jesus,
God's beloved Son!
See the Alpha and Omega
And the work He's done!
Hallelujah! Hallelujah!
Come ye, praise the Lord!
Hallelujah! Hallelujah!
His name be adored!

4. Hallelujah! See your Shepherd
Die upon a cross.
See the Author of Salvation
Suffer shame and loss.
Hallelujah! Hallelujah!
Come ye, praise the Lord!
Hallelujah! Hallelujah!
His name be adored!

5. Hallelujah! Praise the Lord
Now at God's right hand.
See the brightness of His glory
In Immanuel's Land.
Hallelujah! Hallelujah!
Come ye, praise the Lord!
Hallelujah! Hallelujah!
His name be adored!

Tunes: Cairnbrook, Sinclair.

Revelation 19.4-7

And the four and twenty elders and the four beasts fell down and worshipped God that sat on the throne, saying, Amen; Alleluia. And a voice came out of the throne, saying, Praise our God, all ye his servants, and ye that fear him, both small and great. And I heard as it were the voice of a great multitude, and as the voice of many waters, and as the voice of mighty thunderings, saying, Alleluia: for the Lord God omnipotent reigneth. Let us be glad and rejoice, and give honour to him: for the marriage of the Lamb is come, and his wife hath made herself ready.

30th November.

76.76D.

We See You Clothed in Glory.

1.
We see You clothed in glory,
The Son of God most high.
We see You in the
manger,
The Saviour come to die.
We lift our hearts in worship
And ask the reason why.
"I came because I loved
you,"
Was Your tender reply.

2.
We see Your life of suff'ring;
We see Your works of grace;
We see Your sinless service
And Your gentle embrace.
We lift our hearts in worship
And ask the reason why.
"I toiled because I loved you,"
Was Your tender reply.

3.
We see You in the garden
In depths of agony.
We see You whipped and
mocked
By men in cruelty.
We lift our hearts in worship
And ask the reason why.
"I grieved because I loved
you,"
Was Your tender reply.

4.
We see You on the cross,
Great David's greater Son.
There cursed by God above,
Salvation's work was done.
We lift our hearts in worship
And ask the reason why.
"I died because I loved you,"
Was Your tender reply.

Tunes: Ewing, Greenland, Passion Chorale, St. Edith.

Galatians 2.20
I am crucified with Christ: nevertheless I live; yet not I, but Christ liveth in me: and the life which I now live in the flesh I live by the faith of the Son of God, who loved me, and gave himself for me.

Ephesians 5.1-2 and Ephesians 5.25
Be ye therefore followers of God, as dear children; and walk in love, as Christ also hath loved us, and hath given himself for us an offering and a sacrifice to God for a sweetsmelling savour…
Husbands, love your wives, even as Christ also loved the church, and gave himself for it;

1st December.

CM.

O Lord, Your People Know Your Name.

1.
O Lord, Your people know Your name,
They hear You say "I'm He";
And in the heights of heaven above
Yahweh the Same we see.

2.
The fearful sailors heard You, Lord,
In all their deep distress:
"'Tis I," You said; be not afraid."
For You had come to bless.

3.
The sad disciples saw You, Lord;
Beheld Your hands and feet.
"'Tis I," You said, "Be not afraid."
And took some food to eat.

4.
O Lord, the keys of death and hell
Are Yours by right to use.
"Fear not, I am the First and Last,"
You say to those You choose.

5.
So when we're fearful, sad and weak,
Please come to us and say,
"'Tis I, Your Lord. Be not afraid
For by Your side, I'll stay."

Tunes: St. Fulbert, Beulah, Horsley, Pisgah, St. Agnes.

Matthew 14.26-27
And when the disciples saw him walking on the sea, they were troubled, saying, It is a spirit; and they cried out for fear. But straightway Jesus spake unto them, saying, Be of good cheer; it is I; be not afraid.

2nd December.

CM.

Lord Jesus, We Your Love Recall.

1. Lord Jesus, we Your love recall,
A love so full and free.
A love that brought You to this world
To die on Calv'ry's tree.

2. Lord Jesus, we Your birth recall,
In Bethl'em's manger bare.
We see a babe of David's line -
One who was God lay there.

3. Lord Jesus, we Your life recall,
The good works that You've done.
Your miracles and power too
Revealing God's dear Son.

4. Lord Jesus, we Your death recall -
Nailed to a cross of shame.
There all our sins on You were laid!
All praise to Your blest name!

5. Lord Jesus, we Your tomb recall,
Dark death within its breast.
But You are raised, Lord Jesus Christ!
And in You we can rest.

6. All praise to You, Lord Jesus Christ,
For all that You have done.
We gladly bow before You now
As worshippers You've won!

Tunes: Westminster (Turle), St. Agnes, Winchester (Old), St. Fulbert, Beulah, Nativity, Pisgah.

Luke 22.19 And he took bread, and gave thanks, and brake it, and gave unto them, saying, This is my body which is given for you: this do in remembrance of me.

3rd December.

87.87D.

Washed in Blood that's Wonder-Working.

Washed in blood that's wonder-working;
Cleansed from sin and all its might;
Reconciled, with all forgiven;
Justified, made fit for light.
Peace with God we have with promise;
Set apart to His blest name;
We can come into His presence;
All His virtues to proclaim.

Tunes: Mount of Olives, Woodside, Beecher, Deerhurst, Shipton, Here is Love, Hymn to Joy,

Colossians 1.20-22
And, having made peace through the blood of his cross, by him to reconcile all things unto himself; by him, I say, whether they be things in earth, or things in heaven. And you, that were sometime alienated and enemies in your mind by wicked works, yet now hath he reconciled in the body of his flesh through death, to present you holy and unblameable and unreproveable in his sight:

Revelation 1. 5
And from Jesus Christ, who is the faithful witness, and the first begotten of the dead, and the prince of the kings of the earth. Unto him that loved us, and washed us from our sins in his own blood, and hath made us kings and priests unto God and his Father; to him be glory and dominion for ever and ever. Amen.

Ephesians 2.13
But now in Christ Jesus ye who sometimes were far off are made nigh by the blood of Christ.

Romans 5.9
Much more then, being now justified by his blood, we shall be saved from wrath through him. For if, when we were enemies, we were reconciled to God by the death of his Son, much more, being reconciled, we shall be saved by his life.

4th December.

88.84.

O Lord, Your Death has Won our Love.

1.
O Lord, Your death has won our love
And cleansed our souls for heaven above.
Help us the living God to serve
Until You come.

2.
Lord, we're the hope of those who cared;
The joy of those the gospel shared.
Help us to tell of You, God's Son,
Until You come.

3.
Lord, let Your love in us abound,
In us may holy hearts be found.
Give us the strength sin's power to shun
Until You come.

4.
Lord, You shall come to take us home,
Never again from You to roam.
May this blest hope remain wholesome
Until You come.

5.
Lord, sanctify us by Your grace
Protect us in Faith's rugged race
Oh, with what joy we'll see Your face
When You have come.

Tunes: Almsgiving, Oldbridge, In Memoriam (Maker), Redcliff.

Revelation 2.25-26
But that which ye have already hold fast till I come. And he that overcometh, and keepeth my works unto the end, to him will I give power over the nations…

5th December.

87.87D.

Father, We as Children Bless Thee.

1. Father, we as children bless Thee
Born by water and by blood.
Those who are redeemed by Jesus!
Those washed in the crimson flood!
At Thy throne, we bow before Thee,
Knowing love that cost Thee dear.
At Thy throne, we shall adore Thee,
Pleading boldly without fear.

2. Father, we are called in Jesus;
He, Thine own belovèd Son.
In Thy purpose Thou hast freed us
In the victory He has won.
Blessed with every gift of goodness,
Blessed in Christ, the Holy One!
Blessed with life in heavenly glory!
How wondrous Thy salvation!

3. Father, by Thee we were chosen
'Ere this world was first begun.
Appointed to be like Jesus
Through the work He has done.
'Twas through grace that Thou didst find us
In a gutter full of sin.
In Thy love Thou now hast drawn us
And hast breathed new life within.

4. Father, through the changing seasons
Thou shalt ever be the Same.
We adore Thee, blessèd Father,
Love Thy mercy and Thy name.
May we live our lives before Thee
In Thy service without blame.
And as sons by pure adoption,
All Thy tenderness proclaim.

Tunes: Here is Love, Hymn to Joy, Shipton, Woodside.

John 1.11-13
He came unto his own, and his own received him not. but as many as received him, to them gave he power to become the sons of God, even to them that believe on his name: which were born, not of blood, nor of the will of the flesh, nor of the will of man, but of God.

6th December.

88.88D.

Lord, Once my Life was Such a Bore.

1.
Lord, once my life was such a bore;
The daily round a constant chore!
I always thought it should mean more
But sin had ripped me to the core.
Your love has brightened all my days!
Your blood has cleansed my sinful ways!
God's word Your beauty now displays
And 'tis Your name I'll ever praise!

2.
The blessing of Your cross is peace!
The joy it brings will never cease!
My love for You, Lord, must increase!
Until that day of sweet release!
Your love has brightened all my days!
Your blood has cleansed my sinful ways!
God's word Your beauty now displays!
And 'tis Your name, I'll ever praise!

Tunes: Sweet Hour, Stephenson, Duane St..

Psalm 100.1-5
A Psalm of praise.
Make a joyful noise unto the LORD, all ye lands.
Serve the LORD with gladness:
come before his presence with singing.
Know ye that the LORD he is God:
it is he that hath made us, and not we ourselves;
we are his people, and the sheep of his pasture.
Enter into his gates with thanksgiving,
and into his courts with praise:
be thankful unto him, and bless his name.
For the LORD is good; his mercy is everlasting;
and his truth endureth to all generations.

7th December.

CMD.

Rise Up, Ye Saints, Before the Day.

1.
Rise up, ye saints, before the day;
The Morning Star appears!
It's seen through darkest skies above
And takes away all fears.
Brightly it shines before the dawn
To lead us all away.
Yes, soon its cry shall lift our souls
Beyond this planet's sway.

2.
It is the Christ, the Lord of all
Who calls us up above!
The focus of God's purposes
Completed through His love.
Yes, He has kept us through the night
And brought us into day.
And we shall dwell in Glory's light
And His sweet face survey.

Tunes: Warrior, No King But Christ, Release, Jesus is God, Bethlehem.

Genesis 1.16
And God made two great lights; the greater light to rule the day, and the lesser light to rule the night: he made the stars also.

Numbers 24.17
I shall see him, but not now: I shall behold him, but not nigh: there shall come a Star out of Jacob, and a Sceptre shall rise out of Israel, and shall smite the corners of Moab, and destroy all the children of Sheth.

Revelation 22.16
I Jesus have sent mine angel to testify unto you these things in the churches. I am the root and the offspring of David, and the bright and morning star.

8th December.

76.76D.

You Look to Those, Blest Father.

1. You look to those, blest Father,
Who seek to do Your will;
Who joy Your name to honour;
Who have passed through the mill.
Their hearts are contrite, Father,
Their spirits brought so low;
Yet, now by grace they're strengthened
To worship You below.

2. Eternity's Your dwelling!
You're high and lifted up!
You're merciful and holy!
Compassion fills Your cup!
You sent Your Son to save us!
For us, He had to die!
But now in heaven He's seated;
His blood has brought us nigh.

3. O Father, we adore You;
We praise Your lovely name.
We all bow down before You
As purged and without blame!
Your Son, we wave before You,
The Firstborn from the dead!
And own with hearts subjected
He is our Lord and Head.

Tunes: Thornbury, Greenland, Ellacombe, Lymington,

Isaiah 57.15
For thus saith the high and lofty One that inhabiteth eternity, whose name is Holy; I dwell in the high and holy place, with him also that is of a contrite and humble spirit, to revive the spirit of the humble, and to revive the heart of the contrite ones.

9th December.

76.76D.

You are the God of Wisdom!

1.
You are the God of wisdom!
You are the God of might!
You are the God of heaven!
You are the God of light!
All praise to Your blest name.
Great God of destiny.
You are Yahweh, the Same
Who made the earth and sky.

2.
You raise up kings and princes;
You change the wheels of time.
You are the God who judges;
The God of peace sublime.
All riches, glory, honour
As crowns must deck Your brow.
We worship and adore
While at Your feet we bow.

Tunes: St. Theodulph, Webb, Wolvercote, St. Edith, Passion Chorale, Greenland, Ahnfelt.

Daniel 2.19-23
Then was the secret revealed unto Daniel in a night vision.
Then Daniel blessed the God of heaven.
Daniel answered and said, Blessed be the name of God for ever and ever:
for wisdom and might are his: and he changeth the times and the
seasons: he removeth kings, and setteth up kings:
he giveth wisdom unto the wise, and knowledge to them that know
understanding: he revealeth the deep and secret things:
he knoweth what is in the darkness, and the light dwelleth with him.
I thank thee, and praise thee, O thou God of my fathers, who hast given
me wisdom and might,
and hast made known unto me now what we desired of thee: for thou
hast now made known unto us the king's matter.

10th December.

CMD.

O Lord, I Know that When I Sleep.

1.
O Lord, I know that when I sleep
You hold me in Your hand;
And when I wake with morning light
I know the day is planned.
You are the Lover of my soul;
My Shield and Hiding Place.
Teach me to trust You day by day
Until I see Your face.

2.
O Lord, I love You for the worth
Which in Yourself I see.
Grant me the grace to be like You
And serve courageously.
You are the Lover of my soul;
My Shield and Hiding Place.
Teach me to trust You day by day
Until I see Your face.

3.
O Lord, tell me of Calv'ry's tree,
And agony You bore.
Tell me of all the torment there
Where wrath Your pure heart tore.
You are the Lover of my soul;
My Shield and Hiding Place.
Teach me to trust You day by day
Until I see Your face.

4.
O Lord, I see an empty tomb,
The place where You once lay;
And now upon the throne of God
I own Your royal sway.
You are the Lover of my soul;
My Shield and Hiding Place.
Teach me to trust You day by day
Until I see Your face.

Tunes: Jesus is God, Bethlehem, No King But Christ, Warrior.

Jeremiah 2.1-2
Moreover the word of the LORD came to me, saying,
Go and cry in the ears of Jerusalem, saying,
Thus saith the LORD;
I remember thee, the kindness of thy youth, the love of thine espousals, when thou wentest after me in the wilderness, in a land that was not sown.

11th December.

66.66D.

Jesus, Mighty in Power.

1.
Jesus, mighty in power,
My Saviour and my Lord;
With compassion You're filled;
By all saints, You're adored!
You are the Redeemer;
Heaven's wonderful Man.
The Lamb that was chosen
Before all time began.

2.
Your love is triumphant!
You rose up from the grave!
All powers You've conquered,
You're mighty now to save!
A Prince in the Glory
You are God's well-loved Son!
Yet, us You'll never leave;
You'll keep us all as one.

3.
As Head of the body,
You nurture and You lead.
As High Priest set on high,
Our weaknesses You plead.
As Advocate keep us
In holiness pure here
That we might approach You
With boldness and cheer.

4.
Your beauty is perfect
In heaven up of above.
O Lord, You are worthy
Of blessing and love.
Your work is completed
And our rest is secured;
Because of the suff'ring
That You have once endured.

Tunes: Invitation (Maker).

Acts 3.13-15
The God of Abraham, and of Isaac, and of Jacob, the God of our fathers, hath glorified his Son Jesus; whom ye delivered up, and denied him in the presence of Pilate, when he was determined to let him go.
But ye denied the Holy One and the Just, and desired a murderer to be granted unto you;
And killed the Prince of life, whom God hath raised from the dead; whereof we are witnesses.

1Corinthians 15.46-47
Howbeit that was not first which is spiritual, but that which is natural; and afterward that which is spiritual.
The first man is of the earth, earthy: the second man is the Lord from heaven.

12th December.

76.76D.

Acts of Kindness, Acts of Grace.

Acts of kindness, acts of grace,
Acts of power we can trace.
Acts of wisdom, acts that heal,
Acts of gentleness we feel.
Acts of joy and acts of love,
Acts of mercy from above.

Acts of wonder through Your name.
Acts of speaking to Your fame.
Acts that humble, acts that shame;
Acts that take away all blame.
Lord, we praise You without fear
Knowing that Your acts are near.

Tunes: Rock of Ages, Toplady, Spanish Hymn, Redhead (Petra).

Psalm 103.6-8
The LORD executeth righteousness and judgment for all that are oppressed. He made known his ways unto Moses, his acts unto the children of Israel. The LORD is merciful and gracious, slow to anger, and plenteous in mercy.

Psalm 106.2
Who can utter the mighty acts of the LORD? who can shew forth all his praise?

Psalm 145.10-12
All thy works shall praise thee, O LORD; and thy saints shall bless thee. They shall speak of the glory of thy kingdom, and talk of thy power; To make known to the sons of men his mighty acts, and the glorious majesty of his kingdom.

Psalm 150.2
Praise him for his mighty acts: praise him according to his excellent greatness.

13th December.

66.66D.

There is a Time of Birth.

1. There is a time of birth,
By Thine own Spirit's pow'r.
There is a time to die -
To enter Glory's hour.
There is a time to plant
The word of life down here.
There is a time to reap
All those with godly fear.

2. There is a time to kill
Thine enemies, O God.
There is a time to heal
All saints 'neath judgment's rod.
There is a time to break
The proud and wilful heart.
There is a time to build
All that once torn apart.

3. There is a time to weep
For this sad, passing world.
Then there's a time to laugh
When love's flag is unfurled.
There is a time to mourn
For souls who know no peace.
Then there's a time to dance
Where praise and thanks increase.

4. There's a time to divide
As evil comes to bear.
There's a time to bind
To show the world we care.
There is a time to hug
To comfort those in need.
There is a time to loose
That Christ alone may lead.

PTO

5. There is a time to get,
To know Thy holy mind
There's a time to lose
Things of a worldly kind.
There is a time to keep
With those who walk Thy way.
There is a time to leave
Those who in sin would stay.

6. There is a time to rend
When love her own would train.
Then there's a time to sew
To bind up souls again.
There is a time to mute
When wisdom has her way.
There is a time to speak
To witness day by day.

7. There is a time to love
That we our Lord might show.
There is a time to hate
That righteousness might flow.
There is a time of war
Against the devil's hordes.
There is a time of peace
The fruit of love's own cords.

8. There is a season formed
For every thing we know.
There is a purpose planned
For us, in time, below.
Then let us praise Thy name,
The God who loves us so.
And in Thy precious will
Show us the way to go.

Tunes: Lausanne, Corbet, Harvington.

Ecclesiastes 3.1…

14th December.

87.87.

Overcome When Sin Invades Thee.

1. Overcome when sin invades thee;
Overcome when death draws nigh;
Overcome through faith in Jesus;
Jesus Christ, the Lord on high.

2. Overcome when foes assail thee;
Overcome the devil's snares;
Overcome through faith in Jesus;
Jesus Christ, the Lord who cares.

3. Overcome the flesh within thee;
Overcome this world of sin;
Overcome through faith in Jesus;
Jesus Christ, the Lord within.

4. Overcome the deepest anguish;
Overcome both grief and shame;
Overcome through faith in Jesus;
Jesus Christ, the Lord the Same.

5. Overcome in pain and weakness;
Overcome when in distress;
Overcome through faith in Jesus;
Jesus Christ, the Lord will bless.

6. Overcome in faithful witness;
Overcome in walk and way;
Overcome through faith in Jesus;
Jesus Christ, our strength and stay.

Tunes: Sussex, St. Andrew (Thorne), Day by Day, Wychbold, Cross of Jesus, Oxford (Stainer), Rathbun.

Romans 12.21
Be not overcome of evil, but overcome evil with good.

15th December.

77.77D.

From a Lowly Cattle Stall.

From a lowly cattle stall
Came the Saviour of us all.
From the cradle to the cross
He has suffered shame and loss.
From the manger to the tree
Jesus went to set us free.
From His birth to the dark grave
Gives Him now the right to save.

Tunes: New St. Andrew, St. Edmund Steggall, St. George's (Windsor), Benevento.

Isaiah 9.6
For unto us a child is born, unto us a son is given: and the government shall be upon his shoulder: and his name shall be called Wonderful, Counsellor, The mighty God, The everlasting Father, The Prince of Peace.

Luke 2.10-11
And the angel said unto them, Fear not: for, behold, I bring you good tidings of great joy, which shall be to all people. For unto you is born this day in the city of David a Saviour, which is Christ the Lord.

Matthew 27.45-46
Now from the sixth hour there was darkness over all the land unto the ninth hour. And about the ninth hour Jesus cried with a loud voice, saying, Eli, Eli, lama sabachthani? that is to say, My God, my God, why hast thou forsaken me?

Isaiah 53.9
And he made his grave with the wicked, and with the rich in his death; because he had done no violence, neither was any deceit in his mouth.

Luke 24.6
He is not here, but is risen: remember how he spake unto you when he was yet in Galilee…

16th December.

10.10.10.10.

Your Love, O Lord, Has Kept Us Day by Day.

1.
Your love, O Lord, has kept us day by day;
It cheers our path and leads us in the way;
It sought and saved us from our every sin;
And sent Your Spirit to give peace within.

2.
Your word, O Lord, has set our souls ablaze;
Revealing You, it lifts our hearts to praise;
It tells Your will and shows the way to go;
It is the bread of life by which we grow.

3.
Your Spirit, Lord, convicts this world of sin;
Righteousness marks Him as lost souls He'd win;
Through judgment, shows You risen from the dead,
Presents You as the Christ - the church's Head.

4.
All praise and glory be to You, O Lord!
May Your blest name for ever be adored!
You are the Father's well belovèd Son!
He loves You more for all the work You've done!

Tunes: Penetentia, Ellers, Eventide, Maori, Woodlands.

John 16.7-11
Nevertheless I tell you the truth; It is expedient for you that I go away:
for if I go not away, the Comforter will not come unto you;
but if I depart, I will send him unto you.
And when he is come,
he will reprove the world of sin, and of righteousness, and of judgment:
of sin, because they believe not on me; of righteousness, because I go to my Father, and ye see me no more;
of judgment, because the prince of this world is judged.

17th December.

75.75D.

Baby of the Virgin Born.

1. Baby of the virgin born,
Thou, the Holy One;
Praise and glory to Thy name
God's belovèd Son.
Refrain:
Hallelujah! Angels say;
Thy praise, shepherds sing!
Wise men offer gifts of love!
We our poor hearts bring!

2. Baby in a manger laid,
Thou art Christ the Lord.
King of righteousness and peace;
Ever be adored.
Refrain:

3. Baby wrapped in swaddling clothes,
Son of God most high;
Jesus, Saviour of the world;
The Man born to die.
Refrain:

4. Baby in a mother's arms
Born of David's seed;
Maker of the universe
Who meets every need.
Refrain:

Tunes: Bruce *(omitting refrain).* Guidance *(including refrain).*

Luke 2.6-7
And so it was, that, while they were there, the days were accomplished that she should be delivered. And she brought forth her firstborn son, and wrapped him in swaddling clothes, and laid him in a manger; because there was no room for them in the inn.

18th December.

CM.

Eternally the Father's Love.

1.
Eternally the Father's love
Rested on His dear Son.
And all God's counsels in Him formed
As He in glory shone.

2.
Angels proclaimed His holy worth
To shepherds cold and worn.
The Father sent His only Son
And Christ, the child, was born.

3.
The Father's will the cross had planned
Where Christ the Lord would hang.
God's curse and judgment on Him fell
The holy Son of Man.

4.
Now seated on the Father's throne
He waits the happy day.
When He, as King of kings, shall reign.
And all shall own His sway.

Tunes: St. Fulbert, Westminster (Turle), Pisgah, St. Agnes, Winchester (Old), Nativity, Beulah, Beatitudo, Belmont,

Proverbs 30.1-4

The words of Agur the son of Jakeh, even the prophecy: the man spake unto Ithiel, even unto Ithiel and Ucal, Surely I am more brutish than any man, and have not the understanding of a man. I neither learned wisdom, nor have the knowledge of the holy. Who hath ascended up into heaven, or descended? who hath gathered the wind in his fists? who hath bound the waters in a garment? who hath established all the ends of the earth? what is his name, and what is his son's name, if thou canst tell?

19th December.

66.66.

You are the light, Dear Lord.

1.
You are the light, dear Lord,
The light of Galilee;
Once promised by the seer
As living near the sea.

2.
Your home was Nazareth,
A town despised indeed.
But in favour You grew,
The Son of David's seed.

3.
You called the fishers there
While mending nets of cord.
Of God's kingdom, You spoke
And on souls blessing poured.

4.
All their disease,You healed,
You took away their pain.
Your gracious words brought joy;
The dead had life again.

5.
Cana's wedding, You blessed;
Made wine from water there.
Resplendent Son of God,
We're praise You for Your care.

Tunes: St. Cecilia (Hayne), Eccles, Ibstone, Quam Dilecta.

Matthew 2. 23
And he came and dwelt in a city called Nazareth: that it might be fulfilled which was spoken by the prophets, He shall be called a Nazarene.

20th December.

77.77.

Kingdoms Here Both Rise and Fall.

1.
Kingdoms here both rise and fall.
They refuse to hear God's call.
In a kingdom yet to come
We shall see God's will is done.

2.
Christ in power shall appear!
Nations then shall quake with fear.
Righteousness shall be His rod
Bringing glory to His God.

3.
God is Sovereign! God is wise,
Ruling well beyond the skies!
See Him reign eternally!
See all nations bow the knee!

4.
Things we do and things we say
Will just fade and pass away.
But if Christ is in them all
They will stand and never fall.

5.
Let us build on Him today.
Let Him lead us in the way.
Then with Him, as kings, we'll be
Praising God eternally.

Tunes: Evelyn (Ashford), Innocents, Buckland, Monkland, St. Bees, St. Prisca, Nottingham.

Hebrews 1. 8
But unto the Son he saith, Thy throne, O God, is for ever and ever: a sceptre of righteousness is the sceptre of thy kingdom.

21st December.

65.65D.

See the Snowflakes Falling.

1.
See the snowflakes falling
From a cold, grey sky.
See the birds and creatures
Quickly passing by.
Hear the mighty thunder
Roar, "The storm is nigh!"
Hear the bubbling water;
Ask the question, "Why?"

2.
See the people suff'ring;
Dying day by day.
See the poor and helpless
Lying in the way.
Hear the constant crying
Of a hungry child.
Hear the boom of battle;
Wonder why we're wild.

3.
See the Saviour dying
On the cursèd tree.
See Him judgment bearing
That we might be free.
Hear His sobs in darkness
When forsaken there!
Hear the cry of triumph!
We need not despair!

4.
God is always Sovereign
In His plans for men.
His Son came to save us –
Give us life again.
Sinner, come to Jesus;
Know love that's divine
Sinner, come to Jesus;
Hear Him say, "You're mine!"

Tunes: 65.65:Armentrout, Eudoxia, North Coates, Quietude, Waken.
11.11.11.11: Ruth (Smith), Evelyns, Happy Faces.

Acts 2.22-24
Ye men of Israel, hear these words; Jesus of Nazareth, a man approved of God among you by miracles and wonders and signs, which God did by him in the midst of you, as ye yourselves also know: him, being delivered by the determinate counsel and foreknowledge of God, ye have taken, and by wicked hands have crucified and slain: whom God hath raised up, having loosed the pains of death: because it was not possible that he should be holden of it.

Acts 20.27
For I have not shunned to declare unto you all the counsel of God.

22nd December.

SM.

Awake, My Soul, and Sing.

1.
Awake, my soul, and sing
Of Him who died for thee!
Of Christ, the Lord in heav'n above;
The Christ of Calvary!

2.
Awake, my soul, and sing!
His suff'ring is complete!
Jesus is risen from the dead!
Our faithful Mercy Seat.

3.
Awake, my soul, and sing
For He shall come once more!
He'll take us to His Father's home
Where we'll praise and adore!

4.
Awake, my soul, and sing
The King o earth shall reign!
Let every nation own His name
And praise without restrain!

Tunes: Carlisle, Cambridge, Bucklands, Boylston.

Romans 13.10-12
Love worketh no ill to his neighbour: therefore love is the fulfilling of the law. And that, knowing the time, that now it is high time to awake out of sleep: for now is our salvation nearer than when we believed. The night is far spent, the day is at hand: let us therefore cast off the works of darkness, and let us put on the armour of light.

Luke 9. 32
But Peter and they that were with him were heavy with sleep: and when they were awake, they saw his glory…

23rd December.

66.66D.

Israel's God is our God.

1.
Israel's God is our God
Our voices now proclaim!
Israel's God is our God
And Yahweh is His name!
He is Saviour and Lord
Who bore our sin and blame!
He is loving and pure
Jesus Christ – the Same!

2.
Israel's God is our God
Our voices now proclaim!
Israel's God is our God
And Yahweh is His name!
His light is shining bright!
His love is shed abroad!
His life fills every thing!
The Father is adored!

3.
Israel's God is our God
Our voices now proclaim!
Israel's God is our God
And Yahweh is His name!
He tells us of judgment
And righteousness displays.
He lives a life that lasts -
The Spirit of God's ways.

4.
Israel's God is our God
Our voices now proclaim!
Israel's God is our God
And Yahweh is His name!
He is our Father God!
He is the blessèd Son!
He is the Holy Ghost!
The mighty Three in One!

Tunes: Corbet, The Blessed Home, Harvington, Denby, Invitation (Maker).

Exodus 3.13-15

And Moses said unto God, Behold, when I come unto the children of Israel, and shall say unto them, The God of your fathers hath sent me unto you; and they shall say to me, What is his name? what shall I say unto them?
And God said unto Moses, I AM THAT I AM: and he said, Thus shalt thou say unto the children of Israel, I AM hath sent me unto you.
And God said moreover unto Moses,
Thus shalt thou say unto the children of Israel, The LORD God of your fathers, the God of Abraham, the God of Isaac, and the God of Jacob, hath sent me unto you: this is my name for ever, and this is my memorial unto all generations.

24th December.

76.76D.

Lord, We Belong Together.

1.
Lord, we belong together
United by Your love.
I am Yours for ever
We'll live in heaven above.
I cannot do without You
You're the object of my life.
Nothing have I outside You
'Cept sin, anger and strife.

2.
I know You'll never leave me
Although I slip and slide.
Your hands will hold - support me,
For I am Your dear bride.
I'm purchased by Your suff'ring
On the accursed tree.
I'm fitted out for glory!
I'll live eternally!

3.
My prayer is oft neglected;
Your word I let slip by.
Your Spirit strives within me;
I sometimes wonder, why?
O Lord, I would be like You
In all I say and do.
And then You will have honour
For I belong to You.

Tunes: Lymington, Thornbury, Ahnfelt, Aurelia, Ewing, Greenland, Passion Chorale, St. Edith.

Proverbs 14.14
The backslider in heart shall be filled with his own ways: and a good man shall be satisfied from himself.

25th December.

88.88D.

The Father's Light, the Father's Love.

1.
The Father's light, the Father's love
Both flood His happy home above.
There grace shall dwell with joy and peace;
There praises swell and never cease.
Oh, 'tis a home most wonderful!
'Tis the most wonderful of all!

2.
Oh, what a home where Jesus dwells;
His lovely face all fear dispels.
The scars in His blest hands and side
Tell us that we're His ransomed bride.
Oh, 'tis a home most wonderful!
'Tis the most wonderful of all!

3.
The Son, the Father's great delight,
Fills the whole scene with glory bright.
With pow'r and love He'll take us there
And in that glory we shall share.
Oh, 'tis a home most wonderful!
'Tis the most wonderful of all!

4.
Oh, 'tis is a home of rest sublime;
It is a home that knows no time.
The Father's will shall take its course;
The Father's heart be our resource.
Oh, 'tis a home most wonderful!
'Tis the most wonderful of all!

Tunes: St. Catherine, Sagina, Melita, St. Petersburgh,

Hebrews 3.6
But Christ as a son over his own house…

26th December.

10.10.10.10D.

Lord, You are Worthy of Worship and Praise!

1.
Lord, You are worthy of worship and praise!
Lord, You are worthy of love that we raise!
Lord, You are worthy, the little Lamb slain!
Lord, You are worthy, in glory to reign!
Worthy of worship! Worthy of praise!
Worthy of love our hearts can raise!
Worthy the Lamb that that once died on a tree!
Worthy the King that has set our song free!

2.
Lord, You are worthy of wisdom and power!
Lord, You are worthy – our Refuge and Tower!
Lord, You are worthy of blessing and might!
Lord, You are worthy – in heavenly Light!
Worthy of wisdom! Worthy of power!
Worthy as our Refuge and Tower!
Worthy of blessing and might evermore!
Worthy the Light that our spirit's adore!

3.
Lord, You are worthy – both faithful and true!
Lord, You are worthy – God's foes to subdue!
Lord, You are worthy His name to reveal!
Lord, You are worthy to tear every seal!
Worthy and pure! Faithful and true!
Worthy as our blest Saviour too
Worthy to show us a Father of love!
Worthy to carry our souls up above!

Tune: Glory Song, Newkirk.

Psalm 18.3
I will call upon the LORD, who is worthy to be praised…

27th December.

CMD.

O Solemn Hour, When Saviour Thou.

1.
O solemn hour, when Saviour Thou,
In weakness and defeat,
Hung high upon Golgotha's tree
With nails in hands and feet.
There, deeper pains than we can know
Did rend Thy heart and mind;
And torments we can never share
Were to Thy soul assigned.

2.
Worthy of death, O God, were we
Thy wrath before us burned;
But Christ, Thy spotless Lamb didst bear
The sin from which we turned.
His soul was made an offering
In love, upon the tree;
And in the anguish of that hour,
From death, He set us free.

3.
O solemn hour, when small and great
Shall stand before Thee, Lord.
And there at Thy white throne above
Be judged with one accord.
Their works in books before Thee spread
And by them justice reigns.
While that of "life", a witness true,
Has blotted out their names.

4.
The sea gives up its dead to Thee
Who in its depths were stored.
Hades and Death, those mighty ports,
Deliver up their horde.
In silence, there, before Thy throne
Their sentence is declared.
A second death keeps them from Thee –
The Hell Thou hast prepared.

Tunes: Land of Rest, Release, Landas, Ishpeming, Bethlehem, Fair Haven, Euphemia, All Saints.

Revelation 20.12
And I saw the dead, small and great, stand before God; and the books were opened: and another book was opened, which is the book of life: and the dead were judged…

28th December.

76.76D.

My Soul is Yours, Lord Jesus.

1. My soul is Yours, Lord Jesus;
I'll magnify Your name.
My spirit too, Lord Jesus,
Rejoices just the same.
My life is Yours, Lord Jesus
Please, use it as You will.
My love is Yours, Lord Jesus,
My heart is Yours to fill.
Refrain:
Another year has ended!
A year of love and grace.
O come, Lord Jesus, come!
Come! Let me see Your face!

2. Your throne lies deep within me;
Your royal law proclaim!
Your seat of mercy beckons;
I pray in Your dear name!
Your grace now rests upon me
In suff'ring and in joy.
It strengthens me in weakness
And grants me sweet employ.
Refrain:

3. You are the One, blest Saviour
Who loved me unto death!
You are my great Redeemer,
My being! Yes, my breath!
You are the Son most holy
Now risen from the dead.
You are my Love, Lord Jesus,
The Christ, my Living Head.
Refrain:

Tune with refrain: Hankey. Omitting refrain: Wolvercote, Lymington, Greenland, St. Theodulph, Ellacombe, Webb, Stand Up.

29th December.

CM.

You Gave Yourself For Us, Dear Lord.

1.
You gave Yourself for us, dear Lord,
All by Your Father's grace.
Now, Son in Heaven glorified;
We long to see Your face.

2.
You gave Your head to bear the crown
Wreathed with the piercing thorn.
You gave Your back to forceful men
Till it was bruised and torn.

3.
You gave Your will up to Your God
In sweet Gethsemane;
There, in the shadow of the cross
Bore deepest agony.

4.
You gave Yourself to sinful men
Who judged You without cause;
You gave Yourself up to the cross
Condemned by foolish laws.

5.
Your feet and hands to nails You gave;
You hung upon the tree.
The Son of God as Son of man,
Was dying there for me.

6.
You gave Your life that we might be
From all sin cleansed by blood.
And in the wonder of that hour
You gave Yourself to God.

7.
Blest Lord, we love You for the cross
You bore so patiently.
We'll love You for Your precious worth;
And that, eternally.

Tunes: Beulah, Hoseley, Pisgah, Sawley, St. Agnes, St. Fulbert.

Galatians 1.3-5
Grace be to you and peace from God the Father, and from our Lord Jesus Christ,
Who gave himself for our sins, that he might deliver us from this present evil world, according to the will of God and our Father:
To whom be glory for ever and ever. Amen.

30th December.

CMD.

I Don't Know Why I Suffer So.

1.
I don't know why I suffer so
With pain and weakness too!
But this I know with all my heart –
My trust is sure in You.
I know the love that brought You down
To suffer in my stead;
Ascended now in glory bright,
You are my Lord and Head.

2.
I don't know why I linger, Lord,
Surely my work is done.
I'd be with You in Heaven's light
Now this short race is run.
O Lord, until the time is right
Please, draw me to Your side;
And when my eyelids close in death,
I shall with You abide.

3.
O wondrous hour, when I shall leave
This "house" of sin and shame;
For I shall fly to You above
And magnify Your name.
'Tis then, O Lord, my soul shall see
My life as wrought by You;
Where every piercing pain I felt
Will prove Your love is true.

Tunes: Bethlehem, Ellacombe, Jesus is God, Land of Rest, Landas, Ishpeming, No King But Christ.

2Timothy 4.6-7
For I am now ready to be offered, and the time of my departure is at hand. I have fought a good fight, I have finished my course …

31st December.

77.77D.

"See!" the Lust of Eyes Would Say.

1. "See!" the lust of eyes would say;
"See!" the things you love today;
"See!" the joys that come your way;
Rather, see Christ – own His sway!
The world seeks to fill your mind;
Seeks to shape you by its kind;
Wants to rule your life through sin
Guard your heart with Christ within!

2. "Feel!" the lusts within you cry;
"Feel!" until the day you die;
"Feel those things that "satisfy!"
Rather, feel the Father's sigh!
The world seeks to fill your mind;
Seeks to shape you by its kind;
Wants to rule your life through sin
Guard your heart with Christ within!

3. "Take!" the pride of life will say;
"Take the glory while it's day!"
"Take the honour, seek the praise!"
Rather, bow to own God's ways!
The world seeks to fill your mind;
Seeks to shape you by its kind;
Wants to rule your life through sin
Guard your heart with Christ within!

Tunes: St. George's (Windsor), St Edmund Steggall, New St. Andrew, Benevento.

Romans 12. 2
And be not conformed to this world:
but be ye transformed by the renewing of your mind,
that ye may prove what is that good, and acceptable,
and perfect, will of God.

The Author.

George Stevens was born in the City of Bath, England. He attended Sunday School and Young Sowers League at Manvers Baptist Church as a junior. It was while learning a poem for a prize-giving that he first realised the reality that Christ had risen from the dead. He attended St. Stephen's Church on Lansdown Rd. during his teenage years. He was a member of the choir - although he would never admit to being a tuneful singer. At the age of about fourteen, he confessed Christ as the Son of God, but had no firm assurance of salvation until he heard the Gospel preached in a small "Gospel Hall" in Hounslow. He was about twenty-four at the time. He has continued meeting with what would be called historically, the Kelly/Glanton assemblies. However, the only label he would boast in is "Christian".

Once assured of salvation and eternal life, one of George's main Bible studies was "Christ in All the Scriptures". He would recommend this study to anyone as it reveals the beauty and consistency of the Word of God and its main subject, the Lord Jesus Christ.

It was about five years ago that he asked His Lord to guide him into writing a hymn each day. By God's grace, he has now written over 1800 hymns.

Extra! Extra! More books by the same author.

"The Adventures of the Red Rubber Ball".
ISBN: 978-0-9557881-0-9
The ordinary life of a young lad called George is changed into one of suspense and adventure when he comes into possession of a red rubber

ball that seems to possess special powers. It's story that grips the imagination! Young primary school children love it!

"The Maiden Voyage of the Falcon".
ISBN: 978-0-9557881-1-6
This is a fictional adventure about a teenager sailing on a nineteenth century clipper ship. It is full of excitement where drunkenness, murder, mutiny and danger are met by the overruling mercy of God. The book bears a Christian bias and is written for children between the ages of eight and twelve years.

"Bah! Humbug!"
ISBN: 978-0-9557881-2-3
This is a play written for children between 9 and 12 years of age. It is an adaptation of "A Christmas Carol" by Charles Dickens. It has been used successfully as a Christmas production in primary schools. It is a "must" for teachers.

"The Pied Piper."
ISBN: 978-0-9557881-3-0
Another play for 9-12 year olds to act out. It's based on the original story of "The Pied Piper of Hamlyn".

"Rumpelstiltskin".
ISBN: 978-0-9557881-4-7
The adaptation of the story by that name into a play form for 9-12 year olds.

"Christ is my Beloved."
ISBN: 976-0-901860-84-2.
A meditation of Christ as depicted in the biblical book called "The Song of Solomon".

"Preparation for Baptism and the Lord's Supper."
ISBN: 978-0-9557881-6-1
This book is set out as a course for Christians who wish to be baptized or to partake in the Lord's Supper. It contains worksheets that may be photocopied for the personal use of the purchaser.